UNCOUNTED

Uncounted

The Crisis of Voter Suppression in the United States

Gilda R. Daniels

NEW YORK UNIVERSITY PRESS

New York

NEW YORK UNIVERSITY PRESS
New York
www.nyupress.org

References to Internet websites (URLs) were accurate at the time of writing. Neither the author nor New York University Press is responsible for URLs that may have expired or changed since the manuscript was prepared.

Library of Congress Cataloging-in-Publication Data
Names: Daniels, Gilda R., author.
Title: Uncounted : The crisis of voter suppression in the United States / Gilda R. Daniels.
Description: New York : New York University Press, [2020] | Identifiers: LCCN 2019012053|
ISBN 9781479862351 (cl.) | ISBN 1479862355 (cl.)
Subjects: LCSH: Suffrage—United States. | Suffrage—United States—History. | Voter registration—Corrupt practices—United States. | Voter registration—Corrupt practices—United States—History. | Elections—Corrupt practices—United States. | Elections—Corrupt practices—United States—History.
Classification: LCC KF4891 .D36 2019 | DDC 324.6/20973—dc23
LC record available at https://lccn.loc.gov/2019012053

New York University Press books are printed on acid-free paper, and their binding materials are chosen for strength and durability. We strive to use environmentally responsible suppliers and materials to the greatest extent possible in publishing our books.

Manufactured in the United States of America

10 9 8 7 6 5 4 3 2 1

Also available as an ebook

CONTENTS

Introduction

Sleeping at a dangerous time!
—Rev. Fluney Jackson

Growing up in rural Louisiana, my grandparents were a treasure trove of advice and sound wisdom that far outpaced their formal education. My grandfather, a sharecropper with a fifth-grade education, taught himself to read. My grandmother worked as a domestic well into her eighties.[1] They raised my mother and aunt, provided a loving family environment for many nonbiological children in the community, and hosted me and my siblings for occasional sleepovers.

On those crisp Saturday mornings when the sun would peek between the cotton curtains with the small faded pattern, my grandpa would allow me to sleep a few extra minutes, but not too much. He would tiptoe into my room off the front porch and say in a stern but loving voice, "Sleeping at a dangerous time!" As a child, I had no idea what that meant. I certainly did not sense any danger after a peaceful night of sleep.

Several decades have passed since my grandfather's morning alarm, and only now can I fully understand it. After being a civil rights attorney for nearly thirty years, the full context and impact of my grandfather's admonition rings like a clarion bell. It is against the backdrop of history aided by the cogency of unobstructed vision and experience that a young woman can understand the words of a wise elder. My grandfather's warning was not about sleeping at all. It was a caution that things were happening while I slept comfortably. I was sleeping at a time when vigilance was needed. I have never forgotten his warning, and I offer it today.

As a country, we have slept through the continuous assault on access to the ballot box in the name of stricter voting requirements, meritless claims of rigged elections, and baseless voter-fraud proclamations. These laws, however, have created a crisis. In the past, these efforts had the primary purpose of eliminating African American voters from the voter rolls. In the new millennium, the enacted laws not only seek to abolish members of a political party but, with the same result, to eliminate voters of color. Obstructionists use race as a political proxy, and substitute party for race by targeting Democratic Party voters and adopting laws that seek to disenfranchise, frustrate, and eliminate minority, poor, and elderly voters. A premeditated strategy composed of laws and deceptive practices has taken root and is eroding the very basis of American democracy—the right to vote! We are, as my grandfather cautioned many years ago, "sleeping at a dangerous time."

The proliferation of election administration legislation on the federal and state level since the 2000 presidential election has amassed legislative measures that affect access to the ballot.[2] The new requirement of government-issued photo IDs as the sole means of voter identification in some states has been criticized as the new poll tax.[3] Additionally, intimidation via threats of incarceration and deportation, vote caging, voter purges, and voter deception tactics have become the new ways to inhibit and dissuade citizens from casting a ballot or showing up at the polls. Moreover, the mid- and late-decade attention to redistricting has become almost daunting in its effort to overly politicize and racialize the right to vote for a representative form of government. Any one of these new-millennium methods standing alone may not cause concern. When taken together, however, the cumulative effect is the disenfranchisement of eligible voters in numbers that, in some instances, silence and, in others, severely frustrate the voices of the masses. These new-millennium laws are akin to, among other things, the disenfranchising poll taxes, literacy tests, grandfather clauses, and other disenfranchisement measures of the past. We are commanded to meet these assaults on the right to vote with battle-tested and proven strategies that can preserve the right to vote from the hands of those who seek to return to the days when only certain Americans could exercise the right to vote without fear.

These are not new attacks on the right to vote. Laws have been proposed and enacted that specifically sought to affect voters of color since the late 1800s and the passage of the Fifteenth Amendment. Moreover, the courts have also been involved in endorsing and restricting these types of laws.

Uncounted examines this phenomenon through the lenses of history, race, law, and the democratic process. It seeks to educate and create power within communities that are severely and regularly disenfranchised. Surely, a way exists that can expand the franchise without sacrificing integrity. What has worked to combat these perennial disenfranchising methods? How do voter ID and other new-millennium methods affect voter participation and confidence? Are these new mechanisms similar in effect to Jim Crow–era laws of the past? Consider this: If you could get rid of voters, eligible voters, without violence and within legal means, would you try it? What if the affected voters were predisposed to vote against you, or so you believed? Would you use or propose laws that had this effect? What role could courts play in endorsing or revoking these laws?

Enfranchisement-minded grassroots organizers, advocacy groups, and determined voters hold the key to unlocking the prize of democracy, the right to vote. *Uncounted* does more than identify new-millennium methods. It explores methods that take away the right to vote, while we sleep. We're "sleeping" comfortably while the right to vote is suffering debilitating blows in the courts and legislative houses across this nation. This book will address the similarities between the more overt and ferocious methods of affecting access to voting with the contemporary ways that we currently endure. Indeed, it will provide the wakeup call that is needed to move beyond the strangulation of voter access versus voter integrity to methods that provide for unencumbered voter participation. It illuminates these deceptive and conniving methods and wakes us to an eye-opening revelation of the power of the vote and the ongoing efforts to take the power away from the people. It provides a framework for understanding voter suppression, its roots in the founding and evolution of our democracy, our contemporaneous struggle to vote, and what must be done to dismantle this suppressive system.

Each chapter will discuss the historical counterpoints to a contemporaneous suppressive tactic, the laws that allow these mechanisms to continue, the impact of the disenfranchising devices with accounts from real voters, and solutions to break the cycle of voter suppression. In chapter 1, I introduce the historical context of disenfranchising legislation and reveal the striking similarities between the pre-civil-rights-era methods of violence and intimidation to specifically disenfranchise black voters and the new-millennium methods of disenfranchisement via legislation and litigation. Using my almost-one-hundred-year-old grandmother as the framework for this discussion, I will illustrate the real impact of voting laws on people of color.

Next, few places have impacted the course of our democratic nation like Selma, Alabama, which served as the pressure point for passage of the 1965 Voting Rights Act (VRA). The VRA has been lauded as the most effective piece of legislation passed in this country's history. For all of its accomplishments, in 2013, the United States Supreme Court found that one of the most important parts of the act had outlived its usefulness. In *Shelby County, Alabama v. Holder*, the Court found part of the act unconstitutional and removed protections from a majority of the South, just as the Hayes-Tilden compromise of 1877 had done in post-Reconstruction. In chapter 2, we walk through the history and need for the VRA, using firsthand accounts of the impact of Jim Crow laws, the liberation that the VRA introduced, and the impact since *Shelby*.

Chapter 3 highlights the hot-button voter ID laws and their impact on voters of color, as well as their historical counterparts, the poll tax and to some extent the grandfather clause. While most scholars have likened voter ID to a poll tax because of the costs in obtaining the underlying documents, such as a birth certificate, other analogies exist that clearly make the case that voter ID is a poorly veiled attempt to disenfranchise certain voters, an attempt that has as its predecessor Jim Crow–era voting measures.

Chapter 4 introduces two types of deception. This chapter could have been subtitled "Why Whites Vote on Tuesday and Blacks Vote on Wednesday," deriving from legendary fliers distributed in neighborhoods of color prior to a presidential election, falsely instructing that Republicans (presumably whites) would vote on Tuesday, the actual Election Day, and Democrats (presumably blacks) would vote on Wednesday, the day after the election. This chapter will explore voter deception, the difficulty in pursuing these types of claims, and its similarities to the voter intimidation tactics of the past. It also offers a framework for political deception, in which elected officials spew false and misleading statements and hide behind the cloak of political speech's seemingly ironclad protection.

Likewise, chapter 5 demonstrates the nexus between voter roll purges and attempts to disenfranchise legitimate voters. Federal law places restrictions on when voter roll purges can occur. With the weakening of federal law through the judicial dismantling of voter protections, however, we have witnessed jurisdictions making questionable purges, particularly near election dates. Moreover, the United States Supreme Court has endorsed this spurious tactic to the detriment of those who are eligible to vote but choose not to vote in every election. Arguably, the purge process in this millennium seems to be on overdrive, with the endorsement of the courts and the federal government's enforcement agency.

In chapter 6, we meet persons affected by felon disenfranchisement and explore policy and legislative measures that have become extremely successful in this new millennium. I compare the three-fifths compromise to modern-day disenfranchisement. The Fourteenth Amendment of the United States Constitution allows states to disenfranchise their citizens who engage in rebellion or other crime. The process of removing persons who previously committed crimes began in earnest shortly after Reconstruction, but not for those who rebelled against the United

States. Felon disenfranchisement became a mechanism designed to disenfranchise African Americans. Almost 150 years after passage of the Fourteenth Amendment, this mechanism continues to disproportionately disenfranchise people of color.

In a chapter filled with contemporaneous examples, chapter 7 highlights efforts to limit the right to vote of the Latinx[4] population and other people of color. Between July 1, 2011, and July 1, 2012, 1.1 million Hispanics were added to the population of the United States. This accounted for almost half of the 2.3 million population increase that occurred during the same time period. This explosion of Latinx population has caused a considerable increase in legislation requiring proof of citizenship and other anti-immigrant laws. With this level of growth, a number of issues arise regarding access to democracy, including changes to how we count persons in the decennial census. These measures are used to disenfranchise people of color and create a hostile environment similar to those witnessed in previous points in our country's history. In chapter 8 of this book, I offer my own observations and insights from other civil rights warriors on where we are in history and how we can confront this crisis of voter suppression.

Finally, this book hopes to inform, inspire, and engage a sleeping populace. *Uncounted* hopes to sound the alarm to the crisis of voter suppression. Democracy is in "dire distress" and "extreme danger."[5] Throughout the text, I advocate varying measures of a simple objective: educate, legislate, and litigate. In these and other efforts to preserve fundamental rights, advocates are equipped with tools that allow us to perform one or all of these measures. If we educate ourselves, our friends, family members, students, colleagues, and constituents, if we run for office or push our elected officials to represent us in meaningful ways or, when that fails, partner with civil rights and advocacy groups to pursue litigation as a means to obtaining equality, then we will realize our power.

As the daughter and granddaughter of Baptist preachers, I have heard a lot of sermons and read quite a few Bible verses. One verse that continues to perplex me is 2 Timothy 3:5: "having a form of godliness, but denying the power thereof." In the voting context, we have a form of democracy, but prevalent and persistent disenfranchising methods have denied it the opportunity to operate in its most powerful form. It is my hope that we will realize our power and exercise the fundamental right to vote freely, without fear and discrimination. Hopefully, this book will provide counterpunches or possibly a knockout blow to end the non-democratic, disenfranchising dynamic that has existed throughout my grandmother's life and from generation to generation with varying degrees of sophistication. The fight to vote continues.

1

History Repeats Itself

[A]ll types of conniving methods are still being used to prevent
Negroes from becoming registered voters. The denial of this
sacred right is a tragic betrayal of the highest mandates of our
democratic traditions and it is democracy turned upside down.
—Dr. Martin Luther King Jr.

In 1957, Dr. Martin Luther King Jr. used the term "conniving" in his
"Give Us the Ballot" speech at the first March on Washington. While he
referenced the *Brown v. Board of Education*[1] Supreme Court decision,
Dr. King especially stressed the need to ensure access to the right to
vote.[2] He argued that nondiscriminatory access to the ballot would alleviate the need "to worry the federal government about our basic rights."[3]
After all, if we could freely exercise the right to vote, then we could
decide for ourselves how best to govern our communities. Almost a
century later, the struggle for free and fair access to the ballot continues.

New-millennium methods, such as restrictive voter identification
laws and voter purges, have the impact of hindering voters of color, the
elderly, the disabled, and others from freely participating in the democratic process. Moreover, changing demographics—that is, the exponential growth of the Latinx and Asian American communities—create new
challenges to the white-black binary and have spawned an expanded
approach to disenfranchisement with proof of citizenship and punitive
immigration laws. Indeed, the conniving methods of the twentieth century that Dr. King cautioned against continue to plague the voting process in the twenty-first century. As such, it is important to recognize the
significance of history as it relates to the continuing and constant efforts
to disenfranchise voters of color.

Efforts to suppress turnout among voters of color have been long-standing and persistent. Scholars can link these suppressive attitudes not only to the twentieth century and the effort to obtain the vote but to the nineteenth century and slavery's impact on political sentiments in the South today. In a 2016 report, entitled *The Political Legacy of American Slavery*, scholars found a correlation between jurisdictions in the South that had extensive slavery in the 1800s and modern-day political attitudes towards African Americans.[4] They were able to show that

> the local prevalence of slavery—an institution that was abolished 150 years ago—has a detectable effect on present-day political attitudes in the American South. Drawing on a sample of more than 40,000 Southern whites and historical census records, we show that whites who currently live in counties that had high concentrations of slaves in 1860 are today on average more conservative and express colder feelings toward African Americans than whites who live elsewhere in the South. That is, the larger the number of slaves per capita in his or her county of residence in 1860, the greater the probability that a white Southerner today will identify as a Republican, oppose affirmative action, and express attitudes indicating some level of "racial resentment."[5]

The efforts to enslave and depress the votes of people of color in the 1800s, 1900s, and 2000s have a strand that connects through the centuries; a consistency of geography and political party. The controlling parties worked incessantly to minimize the power of the democratic process in communities of color. In Dr. King's speech," he considered the efficacy of both predominant political parties, saying, "The Democrats have betrayed it by capitulating to the prejudices and undemocratic practices of the southern Dixiecrats. The Republicans have betrayed it by capitulating to the blatant hypocrisy of right wing, reactionary northerners. These men so often have a high blood pressure of words and an anemia of deeds."[6] Whether Democrat or Republican, keeping the black vote down was a central theme in Dr. King's day and continues to strike a chord in the United States' disenfranchisement soundtrack today. Dr. King's vision and the stark revelation of the report agree that the disenfranchisement of people of color has historical relevance and contemporaneous consequences. When we look back to move forward, we can identify the cycles of voter suppression and develop methods to avoid the disenfranchising methods of the past to enjoy a true demo-cratic existence in the future.

That Was Then, This Is Now

In this new millennium, Republicans have led the wave of suppressive voting and registration measures. Shortly after the 2000 presiden-tial election and the calamitous concerns that it revealed, Republicans developed a contemporaneous conniving method—restrictive voter identification—in an effort to address what it felt was enemy number one: voter fraud.[7] Yet it sought to address fraud using highly restric-tive voter ID requirements primarily. Although restrictive voter ID does not address in-person voter fraud, jurisdictions across the country followed Indiana and Georgia in establishing such restrictions, along with other barriers to the ballot box, such as proof-of-citizenship laws and felon disenfranchisement. Today's voter challenges are not unlike the 1960s courthouse-door challenges of Bull Connor.[8] This century's assault on voter registration is similar to registrars' tactics of former days that established impenetrable demands meant to lock out voters of color from the electoral process.

An instance when historical methods met contemporaneous effects can be seen in one plaintiff's plight in Pennsylvania. In 2011, the state of Pennsylvania passed legislation that required restrictive voter ID. After marching with Dr. Martin Luther King Jr. to obtain the right to vote, ninety-two-year-old Viviette Applewhite found that the new law required her to obtain a birth certificate to vote. Because of this new law, she was forced to fight the battle again to secure her right to vote. The complaint in *Applewhite v. Commonwealth of Pennsylvania* reads as follows:

Petitioner Viviette Applewhite, a registered voter in Pennsylvania, was a 92-year-old African-American woman born in 1919 in Philadelphia. A graduate of Germantown High School, Ms. Applewhite worked as a welder during World War II in the Sun Shipyard in Chester, Pennsylvania. She thereafter worked in hotels in Chicago and Philadelphia. Ms. Applewhite married and raised a daughter who for decades worked for various federal, Pennsylvania, and municipal government agencies. Now a widow, Ms. Applewhite has lived in Philadelphia for much of her life, including the past twenty years, and enjoys five grandchildren, nine great-grandchildren, and four great-great-grandchildren.

Voting is essential to Ms. Applewhite, and she has voted in nearly every election since at least 1960. Ms. Applewhite marched to support civil rights for African-Americans with Dr. Martin Luther King, Jr. in Macon, Georgia and traveled on several occasions to hear him preach in Atlanta's Ebenezer Baptist Church.

Ms. Applewhite has never driven a car and thus has never had a driver's license. Many years ago, her purse, in which she carried her important documents, was stolen. She has attempted on at least three occasions to order a birth certificate from Pennsylvania's Division of Vital Records. Despite paying the fee to obtain a birth certificate, she has never received one. She recently engaged a lawyer, who is trying yet again to get her birth certificate from the Commonwealth of Pennsylvania.[9]

Mrs. Applewhite is a prime example of how conniving methods of the past converge with new-millennium disenfranchisement. We must confront the fact that although she marched with Dr. King to achieve voting rights in the twentieth century, it was in the twenty-first century that Mrs. Applewhite's ability to participate in the electoral process was threatened by potentially disenfranchising methods. Imagine the frustration of voters who, like Mrs. Applewhite, lived through the insidious methods of the past, only to meet the new disqualifying methods that are leaner, more covert, but just as effective. Real people, such as my ninety-eight-year-old grandmother, live in this reality.

My grandmother was in her forties when she voted for the very first time. She recalls that she cast her first ballot in the 1960s, probably after the passage of the Voting Rights Act of 1965—not because she didn't want to vote or perform her civic duty but because, as she says, "black people didn't vote." She was born in 1919 in Natchitoches parish, Louisiana, in an area known as "Cane River." While not as famous as the Mississippi River, Cane River communities are rich in culture and history. My grandmother was born there, was baptized there, was married there, and worked there, and in 2019 we buried her there.

The plantation where her grandparents were slaves is now a national historic site where, when I visited years ago, the tour guides talked more about the architecture than the lives of the people (like my great-great grandparents) who toiled in the hot southern sun in the fields. MaDear (short for "Mother Dear") grew up not far from that plantation and received the equivalent of an eighth-grade education. She married my grandfather and sharecropped in the parish until they realized that it would only lead to permanent servitude, because when they did well, they were lucky to break even. Throughout her adult life, she toiled as a sharecropper's wife, a mother, and a domestic. Through all of this, my MaDear still believes in the United States and the right to vote. In fear, discouragement, and victory, she has seen how the opportunity to participate in the electoral process has allowed for victories in many other areas, such as removing the signs that served as clear demarcations of oppression, gaining access to buildings, water fountains, schools, and so on where, at one point in her productive life, access was denied.

In 1957, when Dr. King gave his "Give Us the Ballot" speech, my grandmother was nearly forty years old and had never cast a ballot due to her race and the many impediments in Louisiana that prevented her and other blacks from voting. In 2018, for health reasons, she moved to Kansas to live with my aunt. MaDear does not have a birth certificate in a state that is fighting to make it harder to vote through the passage of proof of citizenship laws.[10] Without a birth certificate, she cannot prove citizenship. She does not have a passport or other citizenship certification. Thus, in this new millennium, her right to vote could be jeopardized. It is through her almost one hundred years of living that we can chronicle the cyclical route to obtain the right to vote and note the critical stage in which our country currently finds itself embroiled.

The Cycles Begin: Free at Last

> It is for us, the living, rather, to be dedicated here to the unfinished work . . . that this nation, under God, shall have a new birth of freedom—and that, a government of the people, by the people, for the people, shall not perish from the earth.
> —President Abraham Lincoln, Gettysburg Address (1863)

The cycle of voter access and denial has served as an integral part of our country's history from the Founding Fathers to the election of Barack Obama as president of the United States and beyond. Indeed, we can pinpoint as a pivotal part of this cyclical history the passage of the Civil War Amendments in the mid-1860s. In 1863, President Abraham Lincoln's Gettysburg Address admonished listeners that dedicating the cemetery in Gettysburg was not enough to "consecrate" or commemorate the sacrifices that were made to secure the American ideal of one country under God, indivisible.[11] In the midst of a war dividing the country, President Lincoln proclaimed that the ceremony to honor fallen soldiers and declare the land in Gettysburg hallowed would not serve as a sufficient action to complete the business that the soldiers set out to finish, that is, arguably, unifying the country. Neither the ceremony nor the president's eloquent address ended the war. It continued, as did the efforts to emancipate enslaved people and solidify the Union. In an effort to unify the divided states of America, President Lincoln fought to pass the Thirteenth Amendment to the United States Constitution. After his death, the Fourteenth and Fifteenth Amendments, certainly symbols of his unfinished work, provided equal protection under the law and gave former slaves the right to vote.[12]

After the passage of the Civil War Amendments, African Americans who were once slaves met their newfound freedom with an enthusiastic effort to participate in the voting process. They enjoyed electoral success and won seats in local, state, and federal elections in numbers that, in some respects, this nation has yet to see replicated. For example, until 1863 in Louisiana, where my great-great grandparents lived on Cane River, the ability to register and vote was legally limited to white males.[13] Once the state constitution was brought into alignment with the Fifteenth Amendment and former slaves were permitted to vote, Louisiana's African American citizens accounted for almost 45 percent of its registered voters.[14] Between 1870 and 1876 in the South, despite having a majority of black residents, only Mississippi elected two African American United States senators and one member of the House of Representatives. Most southern states, notwithstanding their high African American populations, elected only one African American to federal office. South Carolina was the lone exception with its African American representatives in the majority.[15] The House of Representatives, as well as state and local elected officials, began to thrive once the freedom to vote through the Emancipation Amendments became effective.[16] Although the federal amendments intended to provide security to the former slaves and especially their ability to participate in the franchise, it was not very long before disenfranchising efforts were effectively eliminating these historic political advances.

After the passage of the Fourteenth and Fifteenth Amendments and the end of the Civil War, former slaves got a taste of emancipation. The taste, however, was rather brief. President Lincoln's successor, Andrew Johnson, vetoed the Civil Rights Act of 1866 that declared that "citizens, of every race and color, without regard to any previous condition of slavery or involuntary servitude, . . . shall have the same right, in every State and Territory in the United States, to make and enforce contracts, to sue, be parties, and give evidence, to inherit, purchase, lease, sell, hold, and convey real and personal property, and to full and equal benefit of all laws and proceedings for the security of person and property, as is enjoyed by white citizens."[17] Although Congress overrode President Johnson's veto, the fight for racial equality had only just begun and the assault on equal rights, particularly in voting, commenced. President Johnson's veto embodied the sentiment that enough progress had occurred regarding complete emancipation. Indeed, his actions helped to invigorate efforts to destroy the promise of the Civil War Amendments.

Free at Last, Not So Fast

While President Johnson was vetoing the 1866 Civil Rights Act, groups on the state and local levels were developing a strategy to end the miraculous electoral progress that African Americans enjoyed by establishing codes of conduct for the newly enfranchised citizens, known as the "Black Codes."[18] Some firsthand accounts employed pleas for federal intervention to allow African Americans an equal opportunity to participate in the electoral process:

Calhoun, Georgia, August 25, 1867

General:
We the Colored people of the town of Calhoun and County of Gordon desire to call your attention to the State of Affairs that now exist in our midst.

On the 16th day of the month, the Union Republican Party held a Meeting which the Colored people of the County attended en masse. Since that time we seem to have the particular hatred and spite of that class who were opposed to the principles set forth in that meeting . . . .

There has been houses broken open, windows smashed and doors broken down in the dead hours of the night, men rushing in, cursing and swearing and discharging their Pistols inside the house.

Men have been knocked down and unmercifully beaten, and yet the authorities do not notice it at all. We would open a school here but are almost afraid to do so, not knowing that we have any protection for life or limb.

We wish to do right, obey the Laws and live in peace and quietude but when we are assailed at the midnight hour, our lives threatened and the Laws fail to protect or assist us we can but defend ourselves, let the consequences be what they may. Yet we wish to avoid all such collisions.

We would respectfully ask that a few soldiers be sent here, believing it is the only way we can live in peace until after the Elections this fall. [Twenty-four signatures][19]

Only two years after Congress abolished slavery through the Thirteenth Amendment, African Americans faced threats and violence when trying to live true to the tenets of the United States Constitution and were severely in need of federal protections.[20] Additionally, freedmen were met with poll taxes, literacy tests, grandfather clauses, and secret ballots as mechanisms to thwart the act of voting.

During this time, I can imagine that my great-great-grandparents were caught in quite a quagmire: excited about emancipation and confused about whether equality was genuinely achievable. My grandmother remembers her grandparents talking about life as slaves on the Oakland Plantation and, afterward, recalling only that "life was hard." African Americans were experiencing the pain and horror of discrimination and disenfranchisement. The United States Supreme Court participated in eviscerating the African American vote when it used its power to remove the semblance of order and protection that the presence of federal troops brought to the hearts and minds of those who were once enslaved. In less than twenty years, the protective measures that Congress passed to remedy the dark days and inequities of slavery through the Civil War Amendments and other means were whittled away and rendered impotent to stop the flood of state laws that prevented former slaves from exercising the franchise.

In 1883, the Supreme Court found the Civil Rights Act of 1875 unconstitutional in the *Civil Rights Cases* seeking equality in public accommodations.[21] The Court held that the Fourteenth and Fifteenth Amendments did not apply to private individuals and organizations, greatly assisting state and local governments in establishing disenfranchising laws. In 1898, Louisiana legislators adopted the Grandfather Clause, which limited voting to those persons whose fathers or grandfathers were registered voters before January 1867, that is, before the passage of the Fifteenth Amendment. While my great-great-grandfather may well have voted during the twenty years after the Fifteenth Amendment, that experience came to a screeching halt, and it was only just the beginning of the many tactics that southerners would use to make sure that African Americans did not vote. The emancipation business would remain unfinished for almost a century.

Twentieth-Century Jim Crow

At the turn of the twentieth century, without federal protection to complete the unfinished work, southern segregationists sharpened the tools of voter suppression. In 1897, the last African American Reconstruction-era congressman from the South was elected, and he left Congress in 1901.[22] At the dawn of the twentieth century, segregationists employed the country's most violent measures to ensure white political supremacy. In 1900, Senator "Pitchfork" Ben Tillman of South Carolina, who led that state's push for segregation, stated, "We have done our level best. . . . We have scratched our heads to find out how we could eliminate the last one of them. We stuffed ballot boxes. We shot them. . . . We are not ashamed of it."[23]

Southern whites, who were outnumbered by former slaves, realized that to allow African Americans to vote would permit the full-scale integration of former slaves into society and could eliminate the ability of whites to control elected bodies. This would provide an opportunity for African Americans to dictate political outcomes, which made segregationists uncomfortable and led to the enactment of various disenfranchising laws.[24]

Segregationists began to "turn back the clock on the broadly progressive franchise provisions that had been etched into state constitutions."[25] The South enacted measures such as poll taxes, literacy tests, and all-white primaries that would limit the effect of the new and populous electorate.[26] In early 1900s Louisiana, where now my great-grandfather Felix Helaire lived and toiled, the state not only utilized a grandfather clause but also imposed "educational and property qualifications for registration. These requirements combined to reduce black voter registration from approximately 135,000 in 1896 to less than 1,000 in 1907."[27] Likewise, in 1901, Alabamans adopted a state constitution that included a number of subjugating devices, including poll taxes, literacy tests, and grandfather clauses.[28] These measures enabled drastic reductions in voter registration among newly enfranchised African Americans. In Alabama in 1890, 140,000 black men were registered to vote, but in 1906, only 46 black persons were registered to vote in the state.[29]

The efforts to remove voters of color from the voter rolls were fueled by southern whites' fear of the potential voting power of newly enfranchised citizens. This process morphed into Redemption for the South, a devious strategy that involved violence, intimidation, and death for those former slaves who dared live as freed persons and, God forbid, as equals. Firsthand accounts of this period provide harrowing details of fear, violence, intimidation, and man's inhumanity to man:

> From the onset of Redemption, Democrats in the eleven states of the former confederacy aggressively cultivated a culture in which voting Democratic equated race loyalty for whites. As Senator Tillman put it, "We organized the Democratic [P]arty with one plank, and only one plank, namely, that 'this is a white man's country and white men must govern

it."' The white supremacy strategy was a direct response to the bi-racial coalitions of Reconstruction. . . .

So, it was the elite white regimes in the South who were directly threat-ened by the potential power of an alliance of poor black and white farmers. The National Farmers Alliance developed "the world's first large-scale working class cooperative." . . . In the end, any possibilities for a sustained, interracial political alliance were defeated by exploiting whites' fear of being dominated by Negroes.[30]

Indeed, southern segregationists rallied against the party of Lincoln and its efforts to provide an egalitarian government. Although the party affiliation has changed through the years, the efforts to depress the votes of people of color remain as a standard strategy of southern separatists and segregationists.

Real People, Real Voters

Throughout the twentieth century, African American citizens endured the pain of discrimination and feared the sting of death in many juris-dictions for attempting to vote. After the Supreme Court outlawed Louisiana's grandfather clause in 1915,[31] the state turned to new, insidi-ous strategies, including an understanding clause, which was akin to a literacy test, poll taxes, all-white Democratic primaries, and voter roll purges. In 1920, a year after my grandmother was born, less than 1 per-cent of eligible African Americans were registered to vote in the state, proving the effectiveness of these disenfranchising tactics.[32]

The level of violence and laws that were used to destroy these ad-vances tremendously affected African Americans' ability to get elected and participate in the electoral process for almost a century. Congress again attempted to solidify Lincoln's promise with the Civil Rights Act of 1957 and other congressional actions to address African American dis-enfranchisement and denigration of the African American. Nearly one hundred years after the passage of President Lincoln's unfinished work and many attempts to complete the promise of the Civil War Amendments, Congress finally realized that a comprehensive response to the brutality and widespread disenfranchisement was warranted.

Despite the passage of the Nineteenth Amendment to the United States Constitution, which gave women the right to vote in 1920, African American women, like my grandmother living in the South, could not register or vote because of their race. While my grandmother was age eligible to vote in 1940, the constant barrage of disenfranchising efforts required her to wait more than twenty additional years before casting her first ballot. In 1940, 3 percent of African American men and women were registered to vote in the South.[33] Around that time in Orleans Parish, Robert Perry attempted to register in the Orleans Parish registrar's office and was told that he could not register because he was African American. He worked for the Boy Scouts and went to the white supervisor, who told him to put on his Boy Scouts uniform and go back to the registrar. The white supervisor then called the registrar's office and "vouched" for Mr. Perry. The supervisor told the registrar that he was "sending a negro down there and you are going to register him."[34] Mr. Perry was allowed to register. However, it would take Herculean efforts to advance the cause of voting equality and make it a reality for him and other African Americans in the South.

Voter registration in Montgomery, Alabama, during the late 1950s was unpredictable and discretionary. Myrtle Pless Jones moved to Montgomery in 1955, after she married an Alabama native, Robert F. Jones. Before relocating to Alabama, Mrs. Jones earned a bachelor's degree from South Carolina State College and a master's degree from Michigan State University. As a new resident of Alabama, Myrtle Jones felt it was her civic duty to register to vote. She and her husband were members of the Dexter Avenue Baptist Church. Pastored by Dr. Martin Luther King Jr., Dexter's congregants were civically and socially engaged and supported Dr. King's efforts to galvanize blacks to assert their democratic rights and privileges.

Mrs. Jones described her initial voting registration experience as one of intimidation. Alabama imposed a so-called literacy test, which election officials ostensibly designed to ensure that voters were able to read and write. Aware of the stereotypes about African Americans, she dressed professionally to go to the voter registration office. As a stay-at-home mother of two preschool-age daughters, Mrs. Jones did not have to take off work or risk being fired. At that time, Alabama required potential voters to read a passage of the Alabama Constitution out loud. After she read without error, the voting official then verbally asked, "How many bubbles are in a bar of soap?" Her answer, "over 100," resulted in failing the Alabama voter literacy test that day. The second time she took the literacy test, no oral question was asked, and Myrtle Pless Jones became a registered voter.[35]

Additionally, my father-in-law, Rufus Daniels,[36] graduated from high school in Dozier, Alabama, on the day that the United States Supreme Court announced *Brown v. Board of Education*.[37] He attended segregated schools, like my parents and most African Americans of that era, particularly in the South. After graduating from high school, he studied at the historically black college Alabama State University in 1954. While attending Alabama State, he worshipped at Dexter Avenue Baptist Church, where a young Dr. Martin Luther King Jr. was the pastor, and participated in the Montgomery Bus Boycott. In 1958, he graduated from Alabama State and registered to vote in Montgomery, Alabama. He characterized his registration process as "a part of [his] settling down and becoming a real citizen."[38] He recollected being questioned but did not consider it rigorous. The registration office was downtown near what was colloquially called the "white house of the Confederacy,"[39] the state capitol, which was approximately a block from Dexter Avenue Baptist Church. The proximity of these two institutions, one that stood for justice and freedom and the other for the permanence of racism, was not lost on my father-in-law. Dad Daniels recalls that his "registration to vote was between two pillars that were in absolute poles of each other."[40]

VOTER SUPPRESSION TOOLS

Historical	Contemporary
Poll taxes	Voter ID
Literacy tests	Voter deception
Intimidation	Voter intimidation
Vouchers	Voter purge
Felon disenfranchisement	Felon disenfranchisement
Grandfather clauses	Racial purges

The disenfranchising mechanism may change in name or have various nuances. However, the impact remains the same, that is, the disenfranchisement of voters of color. These voters are disproportionately impacted when voter suppression schemes are introduced into the electoral process.

Lift Every Vote

In the 1960s, the country was ripe for voting reform legislation and seemingly had reached the boiling point. The violence and discriminatory practices and procedures used to abolish the African American vote were extremely effective. Louisiana was exemplary of the types of measures that segregationists used to ensure that barriers to participation existed. The brutality in the South had received considerable attention; the plight of African Americans regarding public accommodations, freedom of assembly, and voting had seemingly come full circle.

Supreme Court

The landmark Supreme Court case *Gomillion v. Lightfoot*[41] demonstrates the extent to which segregationists would go to disenfranchise African Americans. To yet again thwart democratic advances, the Alabama legislature used the redistricting process to eliminate African Americans from the districts to severely dilute their voting strength. According to attorney Fred Gray, who represented Dr. Martin Luther King Jr. and the Southern Christian Leadership Conference throughout most of the civil rights movement, Macon County, Alabama, which is the county that includes the city of Tuskegee and the famed Tuskegee Institute,[42] had long served as a site to challenge Jim Crow laws.[43] Dr. C. G. Gomillion helped form the Tuskegee Civic Association, which mounted challenges, among other things, against segregated education,[44] farm subsidies,[45] and jury selection.[46] He also served as lead plaintiff in *Gomillion v. Lightfoot*, which addressed a 1957 redistricting that notoriously changed the shape of the legislative district in Tuskegee, Alabama, from a square to a twenty-eight-sided figure and deliberately carved out all but approximately four black citizens from the predominantly black city.[47]

The Supreme Court case *Gomillion v. Lightfoot*[48] demonstrated the extremes that southern lawmakers who were determined to disenfranchise African American voters would endeavor. An exchange between the Supreme Court justices and attorney Fred Gray helps to illustrate the experiences of African American citizens before the passage of the VRA:

> MR. FRED D. GRAY: [A]s a result of changing all of these boundaries not one white person as well as we've been able to ascertain has been excluded . . . (*Inaudible*). This action must be considered, we submit, in the light of the racial composition of Macon County and the history of Macon County. For example, Macon—the residence of Negroes in Macon County has had substantial difficulty in getting registered. Approximately, 78% of the persons in Macon County are Negroes, leaving only 18% white. A constitutional amendment to the Alabama Constitution now gives the Legislature the authority to abolish Macon County and divide its territory into the adjoining counties if the need arises. The complaint further alleges that Act 140 is another device in a continuing attempt on the part of the State of Alabama to disenfranchise Negro residents of Macon County of which Tuskegee is the county seat. The complaint further alleges that the admitted purpose of the Act was to assure continued white

control of Tuskegee City election. Macon County had no [voter registrar] to qualify applicants for more than 18 months at the time this complaint was filed. And since that time, a registrar has been appointed in Macon County, but only three Negroes has been qualified, which means that over a period of some four years, only three Negroes has been able to become registered voters in Macon County.

JUSTICE: Is that at all affected? Is that result influenced by or affected by this redistricting?

MR. FRED D. GRAY: No more, Your Honor, than the few Negroes who still remained in Tuskegee who are not registered will have difficulty getting registered as—is illustrated by the difficulty that they've had over 30 years to get registered.[49]

Gomillion helped to shine a spotlight on redistricting and other tactics used to ensure white domination in the electoral process, such as the coordinated and concerted effort not to register black voters through the use of literacy tests and other devices. The courts began to consider issues of racial discrimination in redistricting cases and not shy away from them in the name of politics. Additionally, repeated pleas from enforcement agencies, especially the US Civil Rights Commission[50] and the United States Attorney General, implored Congress for a mechanism that could assist it in the effort to achieve unfettered access to the ballot for African Americans.

Almost ninety years after passage of the Fifteenth Amendment, Congress passed a civil rights bill that included some voting protections, including making voter intimidation a federal crime.[51] Congress passed additional legislation in 1960 and 1964 that included voting rights provisions, but it used a jurisdiction-by-jurisdiction approach that was costly, time-consuming, and ineffective.[52] Notwithstanding congressional intentions and the hard work of Department of Justice (DOJ) officials, the previous acts were admittedly widely ineffective in combating voter discrimination. This vacuum of meaningful voting rights legislation impacted real people like my great-grandfather Felix Helaire, whose picture is now prominently displayed in a slave-era house on the Oakland Plantation on Cane River in Bermuda, Louisiana. He and other courageous souls sought the ability to live freely and equally in the deep South, despite the dangers that were apparent. In 1963, he joined the National Association for the Advancement of Colored People (NAACP), a brave act, akin to joining the Black Lives Matter movement today. Most African Americans, despite being otherwise eligible, were not permitted to vote. The frustration and efforts of organizations like the Southern Christian Leadership Conference, led by Dr. Martin Luther King Jr., the National Association for the Advancement of Colored People (NAACP), the Congress of Racial Equality (CORE), and Voters' League Associations, which were popular in Louisiana and other parts of the South, prompted a groundswell of opposition to the disenfranchisement of African Americans.

These organizations and the will of the disenfranchised typified United States Attorney General Nicholas Katzenbach's petitions to Congress and President Lyndon B. Johnson to grant the DOJ more authority to combat the racial disparities in voter registration and the ghastly means used to intimidate black voters. In addition, while violence continued in the South, civil rights marchers were thwarted in their attempts to begin a march from Selma to Montgomery, Alabama, to bring awareness to the problems associated with the right to vote. In President Johnson's speech on March 15, 1965, one week after the thwarted Selma march across the Edmund Pettus Bridge, designated as "Bloody Sunday," he stated,

> There is no cause for pride in what has happened in Selma. There is no cause for self-satisfaction in the long denial of equal rights of millions of Americans. . . . But about this there can and should be no argument: every American citizen must have an equal right to vote. There is no reason which can excuse the denial of that right. There is no duty which weighs more heavily on us than the duty we have to ensure that right. Yet the harsh fact is that in many places these countrymen and women are kept from voting simply because they are Negroes. For the fact is that the only

way to pass these barriers is to show a white skin. We have all sworn an oath before God to support and to defend that Constitution. We must now act in obedience to that oath.[53]

The horrors of Bloody Sunday prompted President Johnson and Congress to give the federal government the tools it needed to combat the conniving methods of the South. One powerful weapon was the Voting Rights Act (VRA), proposed soon after the events in Selma.

In the VRA legislation, Congress wanted to preserve the progress of the past and hopefully "achieve full participation for all Americans in our democracy [that] will continue in the future."[54] President Lyndon B. Johnson declared that the VRA was a "triumph for freedom as huge as any ever won on any battlefield. . . . The act has attacked the shameful blight of voter discrimination."[55]

The VRA opened the gates for free and fair access to the polls. The Voting Rights Act of 1965 is considered one of the most important and effective pieces of congressional legislation in United States history.[56] It addressed the devious actions that legislators employed against the United States' "unwanted voters." The VRA outlawed practices such as literacy tests, empowered federal registrars to register citizens to vote, and gave the attorney general the power to bring extensive litigation instead of the piecemeal approach of the past. Congress gave the attorney general the authority to investigate and prosecute voting discrimination throughout the United States and its territories, conduct administrative review of changes in voting practices and procedures in certain jurisdictions, and monitor elections in various parts of the country. The act prohibits discrimination based on race, color, national origin, or language-minority status. Its impact was extensive, and the ability to provide federal registrars and observers in places like Louisiana, Mississippi, and Alabama helped to eliminate wide gaps between black and white voter registrations.

After enactment of the Voting Rights Act of 1965, much like after the passage of the Civil War Amendments, African American voter registration[57] and the number of African American elected officials began to rise.[58] In March 1965 in Alabama, 19.3 percent of blacks were registered, compared with 69.2 percent of whites, an almost 50 percent gap in registration. Likewise, other southern states also had substantial deficits in registration: Georgia, −35.2 percent; Louisiana, −48.9 percent; North Carolina, −50 percent; South Carolina, −38.4 percent, Virginia, −22.8 percent. The most egregious state was Mississippi, at −63.2 percent. In Mississippi, only 6.7 percent of the state's eligible black voting-age population was registered.[59] Passage of the Voting Rights Act of 1965, however, helped to dismantle traditional barriers and led to a sharp increase in black voter registration. Nearly 250,000 African Americans registered to vote from the time of the passage of the act in August 1965 and the end of that year.[60] Additionally, there were only four states in the South that had less than 50 percent of voting-aged African Americans registered to vote at the end of 1966.[61] By 1968, even Mississippi had registered more than 50 percent of its voting-age African Americans.[62] Further, before the passage of the Voting Rights Act, only 19.39 percent of African Americans were registered to vote in Alabama, and in 2005, 79 percent of voting-age African Americans were registered.[63]

Black Like Me

The rise in voter registration also assisted in the election of African American officials. As a result, in approximately thirty years, wide disparities between blacks and whites in voter registration narrowed considerably throughout the South, and the number of African American elected officials increased exponentially.[64] In 1965, the same year as the passage of the Voting Rights Act, there were only six African Americans in the House of Representatives and none in the Senate.[65] Additionally, in 1965 there were only three African Americans in state legislatures in the states that were part of the old Confederacy, and in 1985 there were 176 African Americans in the state legislatures of those states.[66]

From 1970 to 2000, the number of African American elected officials increased from 1,469 to 9,040.[67] One of those persons was my father, who ran for office after the passage of the Voting Rights Act and the parish's first districting plan. In the mid-1970s, he ran to become a member of the Winn Parish Police Jury and was faced with the opportunity to help govern the parish.[68] After winning and becoming the first African American elected to that position, he was met with hostility from his fellow jurors. He recalls "resentment from [white] police jurors": "They tell you what you thought you could do and couldn't do. . . . They didn't mind speaking their minds either, . . . [saying], 'We ain't never had no problems with nothing like that. And you come up here with that stuff.' And they understood where I stood, and that's what I went on. And that's the way it was, and we did that all the way through. People resented me as a police juryman, but that didn't matter; as long they kept their hands to themselves, everything was fine."[69] He never had any death threats or violence, but there were many nights when I lay in bed awake until he got home after hearing him discuss particularly contentious meetings. I inevitably knew that what he was doing was courageous and that it was not welcome in our segregated town. It is plausible that the resentment that he endured was shared among other newly elected officials of color.

Between 1973 and 2004, Latinx officeholders increased by 279 percent, from 1,280 in six states to 4,853.[70] In fact, from my grandmother's first vote in the 1960s to my father's election as the first African American member of our parish's Police Jury took less than twenty years, a feat that would not have been possible without effective voting rights legislation that eliminated barriers to equal participation.

On the federal level, in 1999, African Americans held thirty-seven seats in the United States House of Representatives, constituting 9 percent of the seats in the House. Only one African American governor, however, and two African American United States senators were elected in the twentieth century. At the end of the century, African Americans constituted only 2 percent of elected officials nationwide.[71] In the 2005–7

Congress, there were forty-two African Americans in the House of Representatives and one in the Senate.[72]

Even with this success, elected officials of color still constituted a tiny percentage of total elected officials, as new restrictive devices were being erected. As President Johnson cautioned, merely removing the barriers did not eliminate the need for remedies. President Johnson could have easily referenced the battle of Gettysburg and the unfinished business of the Thirteenth Amendment. Although it took almost a century for such powerful legislation to become law, the Voting Rights Act was passed to remedy the large-scale disenfranchisement of people of color, particularly in the South and Southwest. President Lincoln's "unfinished business" moniker is appropriately used to refer to the unfinished nature of the Voting Rights Act, which is grounded in the authority of the Fourteenth and Fifteenth Amendments and passed to ensure that the unfinished business of the Civil War was nearing completion. Even with this new progress, like that achieved after the Civil War Amendments, more was needed to nullify continued efforts to disenfranchise voters of color in the next one hundred years.

The Fire This Time

In 2000, my grandmother turned eighty-one years old. After living through Jim Crow laws, school segregation, sharecropping, and the civil rights movement, she witnessed the rapid decline of the electoral process evinced in the first presidential election of the twenty-first century. We all watched as election officials in Florida counted ballots after presidential candidates demanded recounts in a too-close-to-call contentious election. The Florida and United States Supreme Court proceedings and the daily ballot counts changed the way the United States approached the process of electing the president. The aftermath of the presidential election also significantly changed the way we access the right to vote.[73]

Since the 2000 presidential election, state and federal legislators have attempted to address the complicated task of correcting the many problems that were exposed, such as outdated voting machines, inaccurate voter removal (purges), and voter discontent. America watched as the courts, both state and federal, determined who would be president. While much attention was placed on Florida, voting irregularities, such as long lines and broken machines, occurred in states across the country and in more significant proportions. The stark realization that the 2000 election problems were not confined to Florida, but were symptomatic of issues across the nation prompted many legislators to act.[74] On both the state and federal levels, legislators sought to remedy the myriad election administration dilemmas.

This newfound attention to voting rights had some unintended consequences. In some instances, instead of enlarging the right to vote, exercising the franchise became more cumbersome and restrictive. The proliferation of election administration legislation on the federal and state level since the 2000 presidential election resulted in thousands of legislative measures that, unfortunately, were often based on anecdote, innuendo, and rumor instead of empirical data.[75]

The Civil Rights Commission held hearings and collected data after the 2000 election calamity. It found that "[s]tatewide, based upon county-level statistical estimates, black voters were nearly 10 times more likely than nonblack voters to have their ballots rejected."[76] Additionally, it estimated that 14.4 percent of black voters in Florida had their ballots rejected, compared to 1.6 percent of nonblack voters in the state. Finally, black voters constituted 11 percent of voters in the state, but in the election, African Americans astonishingly cast more than half of the spoiled ballots, according to the precinct data in several counties.[77]

On the federal level, Congress sought to address the 2000 presidential election by implementing comprehensive changes to the United States' election administration process. While admirable, some of the reforms had inadvertent consequences. In 2002, in response to the 2000 election catastrophe, Congress used its Elections Clause authority and passed the Help America Vote Act (HAVA),[78] with the stated purpose of "establish[ing] a program Election Assistance Commission (EAC) to assist in the administration of federal elections and to otherwise provide assistance with the administration of certain federal election laws and programs, to establish minimum election administration standards for States and units of local government with responsibility for the administration of federal elections, and for other purposes."[79]

After HAVA, legislators began to adopt laws that were supposed to make voting easier and provide voters with the assurance that their vote would be counted. Unfortunately, in the decade that followed, many laws were passed that made voters even more suspicious about the accuracy and authenticity of the election process. Politicized secretaries of state, adoption and failure of electronic voting machines, and the emergence of a concerted effort to suppress votes, veiled as an attempt to destroy the invisible foe of voter fraud, caused many voters to revisit the lack of confidence that they had experienced in the aftermath of 2000. The adoption of voter fraud measures led to widespread acceptance of restrictive voting laws that made it harder for certain voters to participate in the process. Many of these voters faced obstacles that were less violent and obvious than the Jim Crow, Bull Connor, and Bloody Sunday eras, but were just as real.

Because of the 2000 presidential election debacle, many voters of color questioned the legitimacy and accuracy of the electoral system. The increased security and identity measures instituted after the 2000 election and September 11, 2001, terrorist attacks caused many Americans to become concerned about security and some reform methods. Just as other laws were meant to correct for widespread discrimination in voting and to open the gates to suffrage, new laws were passed to close those gates once again. Many states instituted voter ID laws, and in 2005, the state of Indiana passed the most restrictive law in the country, allowing only government-issued identification. The law was challenged, and the Supreme Court, in the spring before a historic presidential election, gave voter ID its blessing. *Crawford v. Marion* served as a watershed moment for voter suppression and efforts to make it harder to vote.[80] After getting the green light from the Supreme Court, states began to pass more restrictive voting laws; much like after the Supreme Court ruling in 1883, the Court's implied imprimatur shaped the wave of restrictive laws that were soon to come.

The Supreme Court Strikes Again

The Voting Rights Act has endured many blows and challenges to its constitutionality, the first coming shortly after its passage and then for reauthorizations thereafter.[81] A huge swing came in *Shelby County, Alabama v. Holder,*[82] a challenge to the constitutionality of Section 5 of the VRA, one of the critical provisions of the act. Section 5 required certain "covered jurisdictions" to submit voting changes to the federal government for approval. Section 4 provided the coverage formula for Section 5 of the act. In *Shelby,* the Supreme Court held that the coverage formula was unconstitutional, which essentially meant that jurisdictions no longer must submit voting changes to the federal government for approval. Consequently, until Congress prescribes a new formula, those jurisdictions may implement any voting change without federal oversight. A world without Section 4 is effectively a world without Section 5, which has served as a valuable tool in achieving equality in voting. Similar to the Supreme Court's action in the *Civil Rights Cases* in 1875, here its *Shelby* decision reinforced the state's ability to impose disenfranchising devices. Additionally, since the *Shelby* decision, more than half of the formerly covered jurisdictions had new statewide voting restrictions in 2016, and more than 850,000 Latinx voters endured new stricter voter ID requirements in that election. Moreover, just one change in Fayette County, Georgia, threatened to impact more than 100,000 people.[83]

The South Shall Rise Again

One of the major arguments for finding Section 4 unconstitutional was that limiting Section 5 to only certain jurisdictions stigmatized the South and violated the "equal sovereignty of the states."[84] This argument is akin to those forwarded post-Reconstruction and during the height of the civil rights movement when opponents to integration argued that any federal intervention in voting infringed on states' rights, that is, the right of the state to impose any laws that it deemed necessary. It is ironic that the state of Alabama's Bloody Sunday served as the impetus for the Voting Rights Act and that Shelby County, Alabama, would serve as the force to severely limit it. Moreover, Alabama has remained at the epicenter for disenfranchisement and has maintained that status with help from the federal courts and Congress.

The movement and Supreme Court action to eliminate safeguards that protect voter access to the ballot and the overturning of Congress's authority to adopt legislation under the Fourteenth and Fifteenth Amendments to the United States Constitution is part of a political strategy to dismantle the gains of the past—indeed, gains that provided increases in people-of-color participation and representation. These actions are connected to Jim Crow and post-Reconstruction measures meant to make it more difficult for voters of color to participate in the electoral process. The suggested rationales—state sovereignty and postracialism—are very similar in scope to those of a previous era. While my grandmother has little interest in or knowledge of the names of actual Supreme Court cases, she recognizes that erosion of rights and freedoms is occurring in our country. In her mind, it appears that we are going backward, that is, moving away from doing better as a society and instead getting worse.

The United States has seen a world without federal oversight in the area of voting, the first coming shortly after Reconstruction, when Supreme Court decisions and congressional action removed the troops that protected the former slaves from violence and other shenanigans at the voting booth.[85] At a time when minimal margins decide elections, placing more burdens on voters will adversely impact voter participation. The "conniving methods" of the new-millennium tools continue to affect voters of color disproportionately. If we don't pay attention to the many connections to past injustices, we may well regress to a painful time less than a century ago, when laws that promoted exclusion were the rule. In the oral argument of a Supreme Court case involving the 2006 challenge to the Voting Rights Act's constitutionality, Justice Anthony Kennedy voiced this possibility based on progress and the states' rights to govern, two popular rationales:

> JUSTICE KENNEDY: Well, the overall historical record, Katzenbach said there had been unremitting and ingenious defiance, and that was certainly true as of the time of the Voting Rights Act. Democracy was a shambles in those—that's not true anymore, and to say that the States are willing to yield their sovereign authority and their sovereign responsibilities to govern themselves doesn't work. We've said in Clinton's New York that Congress can't surrender its powers to the President, and the same is true with reference to the States. Wouldn't you agree?
>
> MR. KATYAL: That is correct. And here this Court has repeatedly said this isn't any sort of surrendering of power. It was justified because of the record of discrimination. South Carolina v. Katzenbach, Justice Kennedy, I don't quite think said that defiance was the precondition; rather it found that the onerous amount of case-by-case litigation itself wasn't enough. And I would caution this Court because this Court had examples before in which the historical record looked good at a narrow moment in time. If we think back 100 years to Reconstruction, 95 percent of African-Americans in the franchise, 600 black members in the State legislatures, 8 black members of Congress, 8 black justice[s] in the South Carolina Supreme Court. Things looked good, and that led this Court in the civil rights cases over Justice Harlan's lone dissent to say the era of special protection was over.[86]

Despite these warnings, the United States Supreme Court opted to eliminate protective measures rather than empower, once again. This constriction of power, unfortunately, is very familiar to those who have lived through periods of progress and regress. Accordingly, my grand-mother has seen this kind of disenfranchisement before and is horrified that ghosts of Jim Crow have yet to be laid to rest. The unfinished business of protecting the integrity of elections and the free and fair access of all voters remains. The original Constitutional Convention was met with an effort to address the need to lessen the effect of having black bodies on southern soil and prohibiting their ability to have a voice in society through the three-fifths compromise. Importantly, the fall of Reconstruction and with it the demise of the great achievement of freedom abruptly ended the grand experiment. Indeed, President Lincoln's work remains unfinished.

2

The Voting Rights Act

Shelby, Lord, Shelby

In 1965, when the Voting Rights Act was passed, that gave us a great deal of hope. We began to come into the halls of the legislature, city councils, the mayor's races, all of these things happened. Had it not been for the Voting Rights Act, you would not see some of us sitting here today. Now you're putting back what many of us fought our lives for and gave our lives for. . . . Forget all of the gains of the 20th century. That's what you're doing with this bill you are trying to pass tonight. I would ask you to take these 57 pages of abomination and confine it to the streets of hell for the rest of eternity.
—North Carolina Representative Henry McKinley "Mickey" Michaux (2013)

On August 6, 1965, President Lyndon Johnson signed the Voting Rights Act of 1965 (VRA) into law. Among other things, the VRA abolished literacy tests and poll taxes and provided voter registrars in recalcitrant jurisdictions throughout the South. While the cycle of progressive electoral engagement ebbed and flowed during the approximately fifty years after its passage, the VRA was heralded as an overwhelming success. Arguably, it was because of this success that the VRA experienced continual assaults on its ability to provide protection for access to the ballot.

Representative Michaux understood what happens in the minds of some elected officials when voters of color make too much progress at a speed that makes those in power uncomfortable. Indeed, North Carolina has a history of adopting disenfranchising mechanisms. One of the bloodiest massacres occurred in 1898 in Wilmington, North Carolina. The Wilmington Riot occurred, in part, because the whites in power, who at that time were Democrats, refused to peacefully relinquish the local government to the newly elected Republicans. A massacre occurred that led to approximately one hundred African Americans losing their lives and countless others losing their land and livelihood. Many African Americans fled the city and the state seeking a safe harbor. It has been noted that "black political participation has alarmed racist white North Carolinians for far longer. Though it prompts ID laws, early voting restrictions, and roll purges today, 120 years ago, this fear sparked the deadliest race riot in state history. 'The ultimate goal [of the 1898 Wilmington Riot] was the resurgence of white rule,' historian LeRae Umfleet wrote in 2005. . . . Efforts to suppress black political power may have been bloodier before, but they are not new."[1]

As a witness to history, Mr. Michaux watched as North Carolina involved itself in the cyclical and sickening swing from political progress to regress. From the 1898 Wilmington Riot to the 1990s, when Jesse Helms's "White Hands" advertisement appealed to the fears of whites and, most pundits believed, led to Helms's reelection against the civil rights pioneer and Charlotte mayor Harvey Gantt,[2] to the first African American presidential candidate winning the state of North Carolina in 2008 and near parity in the voter registration and turnout rates of African Americans, to the omnibus voting legislation that sought to wipe all of those gains away. In the case challenging these measures, the court found that the North Carolina legislators were acting to preempt African American voting strength. In fact, the court found,

> Before enacting that law, the legislature requested data on the use, by race, of a number of voting practices. Upon receipt of the race data, the General Assembly enacted legislation that restricted voting and registration in five different ways, all of which disproportionately affected African Americans.

In response to claims that intentional racial discrimination animated its action, the State offered only meager justifications. Although the new provisions target African Americans with almost surgical precision, they constitute inapt remedies for the problems assertedly justifying them and, in fact, impose cures for problems that did not exist. Thus, the asserted justifications cannot and do not conceal the State's true motivation. "In essence, the State took away [minority voters'] opportunity because [they] were about to exercise it."[3]

This legislation served as a reminder to Mr. Michaux and others who had unfortunately experienced firsthand North Carolina's appetite for destroying civil rights gains. In a spring 2017 interview with the *Durham Voice*, Mr. Michaux recalled, "I wrote a majority of the voting laws, like the first law opening up voter registration. Before, you had to get a registrar at the Board of Elections to register to vote. These registrars were mostly white people who didn't want to register black people to vote. The bill I wrote opened up registration, so all they had to do was fill out a form and send it into the Board of Elections to verify."[4] He recounted in a 2016 interview, "It didn't come easily and it didn't come quickly. . . . But slowly, too slowly if you ask me, we made some progress."[5]

Understandably, Mr. Michaux reacted to his state's response to reverse the gains he and others had fought diligently to obtain, calling his state's legislation an "abomination" and damning it to hell. Notwithstanding his powerful attack, the Republican-led legislature pushed through the legislation that imposed strict voter ID regulations, cut early voting hours, eliminated same-day registration, and eliminated out-of-precinct voting and preregistration for sixteen- and seventeen-year-olds.[6] The horrific legislation that served as a poor but not surprising response to the democratic gains of African Americans in the state was, in fact, a direct response to a crippling blow to voting rights protections. Representative Michaux understood that he could not look to the federal government for help due to the United States Supreme Court decision in *Shelby County v. Holder*.[7] The Supreme Court's decision removed the federal government's authority contained in Section 5 of the VRA as a preemptive prophylactic against the discriminatory voting legislation.

When the Constitution Is Not Enough

In passing the VRA, Congress relied on its authority in the Civil War Amendments that opened the door for previously enslaved persons to enjoy the benefits of citizenship. The Thirteenth Amendment "freed" the slaves. It reads, "Neither slavery nor involuntary servitude, except as a punishment for crime of which the party shall have been duly convicted, shall exist within the United States, or any place subject to their jurisdiction." The Fourteenth Amendment ensured that all citizens would enjoy, among other things, equal protection under the law. Here the text says, "All persons born or naturalized in the United States, and subject to the jurisdiction thereof, are citizens of the United States and of the state wherein they reside." Additionally, the Fifteenth Amendment to the United States Constitution granted the right to vote. The language reads, "The right of citizens of the United States to vote shall not be denied or abridged by the United States or by any state on account of race, color, or previous condition of servitude."

However, these Civil War Amendments lacked potency in their ability to secure the right to vote. Indeed, the hard-fought effort to pass the Civil War Amendments to ensure the right to vote and fundamental personhood for former slaves was a significant milestone in this country's history. Unfortunately, the promise of freedom was short-lived. During Reconstruction, the last African American congressperson was elected in 1897 and left in 1901. It took sixty-eight (or "nearly seventy") years before African Americans from former slave states, William Clay Sr. from Missouri[8] and Parren Mitchell from Maryland,[9] would serve in the Congress of the United States of America.

Jim Crow laws and Black Codes were adopted at the beginning of the twentieth century and blocked access to the ballot. For nearly a century, these laws erased the hard-fought electoral gains made after the passage of the amendments. African Americans faced seemingly insurmountable challenges in the quest for freedom.

In that dark century of US history between ratification of the Civil War Amendments and passage of the Voting Rights Act, African Americans were subjected to violence, loss of employment, humiliation, threats, and death for attempting to register and/or to vote. The time period was stained with blood. It was clear that the Fifteenth Amendment was not enough, and it would take a civil rights movement and televised violence, primarily the events in Selma, Alabama, to secure the right to vote. In fact, it would take approximately one hundred years from the adoption of the Civil War Amendments to pass legislation that would enable African Americans to access the ballot. The law was needed to give the Civil War Amendments the power to effectuate real change. The onslaught of disenfranchising mechanisms was brutal in the evisceration of the right to vote. Thus, Congress had to provide an extraordinary measure to ensure that the path to the voting booth was barrier-free.

The Need for the Voting Rights Act

Almost a century after passage of the Fifteenth Amendment, Congress passed what is considered the most effective piece of legislation in the United States' history, the Voting Rights Act of 1965. Congress passed the VRA after the historic march across the Edmund Pettus Bridge, marked forever in history as Bloody Sunday.[10] On that day, marchers, led by John Lewis and Hosea Williams, were met with horses, tear gas, and billy clubs for attempting to march from Selma to Montgomery, Alabama, to demonstrate the atrocities to democracy that existed in Selma, Alabama, and throughout the South.

Civil rights advocates were pressuring the federal government to acknowledge the issues facing African American citizens and their efforts to acquire the right to vote. This pressure was not persuasive; the vote was worth the battle. Disenfranchising devices like the poll tax, grandfather clauses, and literacy tests achieved their desired objectives, that is, denying the right to vote on the basis of race. President Lyndon B. Johnson's preference was to wait for the right time to propose omnibus legislation. However, Bloody Sunday catapulted voting rights to the top of the legislative agenda.

Before passage of the VRA, African Americans faced seemingly insurmountable obstacles to obtaining the right to vote. Previous legislative solutions were found lacking in enforcement. For example, states and locales would merely reimplement any disenfranchising devices after the government or some other entity would bring a challenge. As disenfranchising devices became more prevalent and pernicious, the need for stopgap legislation was obvious. What was less obvious was the political will to proffer the legislation. The civil rights movement and its leaders provided the constant force and voice that ultimately convinced the leaders of the free world to relent and pass legislation. Derrick Bell has argued that it was less the civil rights icons and more how the United States looked to the rest of the world, particularly after Bloody Sunday, that genuinely informed and enabled passage of the VRA.[11] The right to vote was cemented into US history in Selma, Alabama. After the VRA's enactment, the yoke of disenfranchisement seemed to ease ever so slightly. Federal agents registered voters where local registrars refused, and descendants of former slaves were free at last to vote.

Congress passed the Voting Rights Act of 1965 to put an end to discrimination in voting. The act included two primary provisions: Section 2[12] and Section 5[13]. As with any legislation, compromises were needed for passage, and one such compromise was the inclusion of temporary provisions that required periodic congressional reauthorization.[14] For example, Section 5 of the VRA required certain jurisdictions, primarily but not exclusively in the South, that had low voter registration or used a disenfranchising device like a literacy test or poll tax to get permission from either the United States attorney general or a federal court in Washington, DC, before implementing law that affected the right to vote.[15]

Section 5 of the VRA

The temporary provisions, such as Section 5, required periodic reauthorizations. These provisions were extended in 1970, 1975, 1982, and 2006.[16] Congress, when determining whether to pass the 1982 amendments, discussed the importance of the VRA[17] and wanted to make sure that "the hard won progress of the past [was] preserved and that the effort to achieve full participation for all Americans in our democracy [would] continue in the future."[18] Consequently, at that time, Congress amended Section 2,[19] extended the language-assistance provisions,[20] and added a section governing assistance to voters who are blind, disabled, or illiterate.[21] Likewise, in the 2006 reauthorization, Congress once again extended the temporary provisions of the act.[22] In doing so, it renewed several essential provisions, provided for language assistance and Election Day monitors, and continued the requirement for Justice Department preapproval of voting changes.[23] In 2006, the committee discussed the importance of the VRA and its protections:

> The right to vote is the most fundamental right in our democratic system of government because its effective exercise is preservative of all others. Prior to the enactment of the VRA, parts of the United States condoned the unequal treatment of voters of color, including denying the most fundamental right of citizenship—the right to vote. The vestiges of such discrimination continue today. In enacting the VRA in 1965, Congress sought to protect the Nation's most vulnerable citizens' right to vote. In renewing and extending the VRA, Congress sought to ensure that even higher numbers of our citizens were protected, including citizens whose primary language is not English, and to ensure that all aspects of the right to vote are protected, including the right to cast a meaningful ballot.[24]

During the deliberations, the House Judiciary Committee found that "without the continuation of the Voting Rights Act of 1965 protections, racial and language minority citizens will be deprived of the opportunity to exercise their right to vote, or will have their votes diluted, undermining the significant gains made by minorities in the last forty years."[25] Congress unequivocally found that considerable progress had been made but also stressed that the work of Section 5 and the VRA was unfinished, stating, "Substantial progress has been made over the last 40 years. Racial and language minority citizens register to vote, cast ballots, and elect candidates of their choice at levels that well exceed those in 1965 and 1982. The success of the VRA is also reflected in the diversity of our Nation's local, State, and Federal Governments. These successes are the direct result of the extraordinary steps that Congress took in 1965 to enact the VRA and in reauthorizing the temporary provisions in 1970, 1975, 1982, and 1992."[26] Congress's desire and authority to renew the temporary provisions were clear.[27] It unmistakably sought to protect and continue the federal protections contained in Section 5 of the VRA. Notwithstanding this clear determination to extend the temporary provisions of the VRA and its impressive success in expanding the electorate, the VRA faced constant challenges to its existence.

SELECT SUPREME COURT CASES AFFECTING SECTION 5 OF THE VRA

South Carolina v. Katzenbach (1966)
This case challenged the constitutionality of Section 5.
    The Court found that Congress appropriately gathered evidence of racial discrimination in voting and that its coverage formula "evolved to describe these areas [and] was relevant to the problem of voting discrimination, and Congress was therefore entitled to infer a significant danger of the evil"[28] in the covered jurisdictions.

NAMUDNO v. Holder (2009)
This case again challenged the constitutionality of Section 5; the United States Supreme Court had concerns about the Act. Nonetheless, it merely cautioned Congress, and expanded bailout provisions.

The Supreme Court expanded the ability to seek release from Section 5's requirements through the use of the bailout provision. Since 1967, more than fifty jurisdictions have successfully "bailed out" of Section 5.

Shelby County, Alabama v. Holder (2013)

This case challenged the constitutionality of Section 4 of the act, which contained the formula that determined whether a jurisdiction had to comply with the requirements of Section 5; the United States Supreme Court admonished Congress and found Section 4 unconstitutional. This decision effectively ended Section 5 of the act and the requirement for jurisdictions to submit voting changes to the federal government.

The question presented in Shelby County was "[w]hether Congress' decision in 2006 to reauthorize Section 5 of the Voting Rights Act under the pre-existing coverage formula of Section 4(b) of the Voting Rights Act exceeded its authority under the Fourteenth and Fifteenth Amendments and thus violated the Tenth Amendment and Article IV of the United States Constitution."[29]

Shelby County, Alabama

If Selma, Alabama, serves as the birthplace of the VRA, Shelby County, Alabama, could certainly serve as its resting place. Shelby County, Alabama, is located in central Alabama near Birmingham. In 2010, its population was less than 200,000 persons. The African American community constituted approximately 12 percent, while the Hispanic population made up less than 6 percent of its residents. The county ranks fifth in population among Alabama counties. While small in stature, Shelby County has made a profound impact on the lives of all Americans. In 2013, the county challenged the United States' ability to require jurisdictions to receive permission or preclearance before enacting voting changes. This was profound, not because it challenged the federal government's authority, but serendipitously because the United States Supreme Court was primed to rescind and reverse centuries of progress in the area of voting. The *Shelby County v. Holder* decision gave the green light to jurisdictions that had as their mantra to turn back the hands of time on the right to vote.

In 2013, the Court held in *Shelby* that the coverage formula contained in Section 4 of the Voting Rights Act of 1965 was outdated and constitutionally invalid. As such, the Court also immobilized Section 5 of the VRA, which required "covered jurisdictions" to obtain approval of any and all voting changes before implementation. Without Section 5, the attorney general and communities in previously covered jurisdictions lacked the power to prevent the application of discriminatory devices, receive notice of proposed and passed legislation, and send federal observers to jurisdictions within Section 5 coverage.

After numerous challenges to Section 5's protections, the Court in Shelby found a way to destroy the VRA's ability to preempt discriminatory voting changes in its holding that the coverage formula in Section 4 of the act was unconstitutional. For the majority, the progress made under the VRA demonstrated that the extraordinary measure of requiring some states to seek approval for voting changes was no longer needed. The majority ruled that the formula that determines which states must submit voting changes was outdated and stated that Congress must develop "another formula based on current conditions."[30] The Court spent a considerable amount of time stressing that requiring some states to submit changes and not others was a "dramatic departure from the principle that all States enjoy equal sovereignty." The Court also stressed that the conditions that existed at the time the formula was devised were a thing of the past, stating, "There is no denying, however, that the conditions that originally justified these measures no longer characterize voting in the covered jurisdictions."[31]

The Formula

The "outdated" formula contained in Section 4 of the VRA determined which states or other jurisdictions were "covered" under Section 5. Section 5 preclearance requirements applied to states and political subdivisions that maintained a "test or device" or had less than 50 percent voter registration or turnout in the 1964 presidential election.[32] Congress had previously altered the formula through amendments, and the DOJ's enforcement of Section 4's bailout provision has allowed previously covered jurisdictions to remove themselves from the purview of Section 5.[33] This view is consistent with Supreme Court precedent, as the formula continued to adapt to contemporary circumstances and ensured that the right to vote is not denied based on race, ethnicity, or English literacy.[34]

The Decision

According to Chief Justice John Roberts, "voting discrimination still exists, and no one doubts that."[35] Yet he and four other United States Supreme Court justices dismantled the protections contained in Section 5 of the Voting Rights Act. After numerous challenges to Section 5's constitutionality, the Court in *Shelby* struck down Section 4 of the act, which provided the coverage formula through which Section 5 was implemented. Without Section 4, there is no Section 5.

The Court spent a considerable amount of time stressing that requiring some states to submit changes and not others was a "dramatic departure from the principle that all States enjoy equal sovereignty." The Court also stressed that the conditions that existed at the time the formula was devised were a thing of the past, stating, "There is no denying, however, that the conditions that initially justified these measures no longer characterize voting in the covered jurisdictions."

Incredibly, the Court opined that "[n]early 50 years later, things have changed dramatically. . . . [B]latant[ly] discriminatory evasions of federal decrees are rare. And minority candidates hold office at unprecedented levels."[36] In fact, the decision in *Shelby* was a direct reaction to the 2008 presidential election, in which the United States elected the first African American president.

Just as in other eras of US history, the courts became complicit in condemning voters of color to second-class citizenship. Indeed, the Court's actions in *Shelby* turned the hands of time backward on voting rights. Nationally, voter turnout had plummeted to the lowest level since 1942. In Texas and across the country, the electorate was older, whiter, and more conservative than in 2008 and 2012.[37]

Kareem Crayton,[38] an elections law scholar and executive director of the Southern Coalition for Social Justice, a civil rights organization that specializes in voting rights litigation, believes that the Court's decision in *Shelby* meant more than the loss of federal oversight. He maintains,

> One of the main benefits of having Section 5 was that minority communities could get leverage and the development of power . . . related to voting, without having to sue to do it—and all of the harm that comes with that, sending a lot of paper, wasting a lot of time, and not really being able to fundamentally change a structure but instead go piece by piece for policy-level improvements. I think the impact of Section 5 has always been the additional leverage that minority communities had no experience with, before Section 5, [particularly in areas] that had a very established record of denying and limiting political opportunity—and, more to the point, not just political opportunity but governance, in communities of color that have had a long experience of being excluded from power. Those are the spaces in which a genuinely changed system allows for partnerships to emerge, alliances to be built. And Section 5 was a tool to help that happen. It [represented] . . . the difference between having zero influence and some influence.[39]

From Zero to Negative Fifty

Without Section 5, jurisdictions are free to implement changes without federal approval. In a typical year, the United States attorney general would receive approximately 5,000 Section 5 submissions that included between 14,000 and 20,000 voting changes.[40] The gutting of Section 5 meant that those 20,000 changes will occur without the benefit of federal scrutiny to determine if the changes will have a discriminatory effect on voters of color. In fact, hours after the *Shelby* decision, former Section 5 jurisdictions announced that they would implement changes that in some instances had previously been found intentionally discriminatory.

Shortly after *Shelby*, United States Attorney General Eric Holder announced that the Justice Department was suing to block Texas's redistricting maps, which had been found intentionally discriminatory under Section 5. This was the department's first action to protect voting rights following the *Shelby* decision.[41] Prior to *Shelby*, the VRA would have mandated that covered states like Texas, Georgia, North Carolina, Louisiana, and South Carolina obtain approval for each voting change before they could implement the change. After *Shelby*, citizens lack notice of harmful changes until often too late. The need to have voting changes approved by the federal government was lost with the Supreme Court's decision in *Shelby County v. Holder*. This decision has been compared to *Plessy v. Ferguson*[42] in its potentially far-reaching implications for the ability of people of color to exercise their freedom. Like *Plessy*'s denial that inequalities existed that the law was obligated to recognize, *Shelby* also ignored the realities of the right to vote and the efforts to strip the power of the vote from voters of color.

In many instances, courts have found these measures intentionally discriminatory and unconstitutional, under the Fourteenth and Fifteenth Amendments of the United States Constitution and Section 2 of the Voting Rights Act of 1965.[43] These victories took years to attain. Importantly, after several appeals, states continue to argue that courts should allow them to implement these discriminatory measures, primarily under a theory of states' rights or preventing voter fraud. Neither theory has required a serious investigation into the impact of the proposed change. While statewide changes have received an inordinate amount of coverage, other changes such as limiting polling places or decreasing the number of voting machines in predominantly black jurisdictions have become regular disenfranchising tactics post-*Shelby*. In Randolph County, Georgia, election officials sought to close a majority of the polling places, blaming costs and American Disability Act compliance as neutral, nondiscriminatory rationales. A retired Randolph County school superintendent remarked "I think it was an effort to suppress the vote. . . . This is one typical strategy in the Republican playbooks."[44]

Section 2 of the VRA

While the effects of the loss of Section 5 were apparent in the lack of notice and immediacy of the implementation of voting changes, the section's evisceration also lessened the ability to effectively and efficiently challenge those changes. Without Section 5, we are only left with Section 2's nationwide prohibition against discrimination in voting. The *Shelby* decision left advocates with fewer tools to combat the onslaught of legislation and litigation proffered with the intent to weaken the democratic process and quash access to the ballot. As mentioned, Section 5 of the VRA served as a temporary provision to protect the right to access the franchise. A valuable tool that remains is the VRA's Section 2,[45] which provides a national prohibition against discrimination in voting. Opponents of Section 5 often point to this provision of the VRA as evidence that the need for Section 5 protections was overblown. Although Section 2 serves as a nationwide prohibition, it has limitations in enforcement. Moreover, the biggest impediment regarding Section 2, in contrast to Section 5, concerns its retroactive approach, as opposed to the proactive, preemptive approach included in Section 5. While Section 2 does apply nationwide, its cost and time to challenge legislation is retrospective and has little deterrent effect. The average cost for Section 2 litigation is approximately $1 million.[46]

Section 2 litigation takes years to conduct, as compared to Section 5 review, which generally received a sixty-day review process to determine whether the submission should receive federal approval. As Dr. Crayton explains, "It is harder, more expensive, and takes a lot longer to get anything that looks like a remedy to what may be even a blatant problem. And so, in some ways, it's a perverse incentive. It gives more encouragement to people who would like to use political power to weed out minority communities, to give it a shot. Because even if they're wrong, it takes so long to get to a court order that says, 'Okay it's unconstitutional, don't do it again.' But you get all the benefit of it."[47]

Section 2 continues to survive as a valuable tool. However, from my years as a voting rights litigator, it is apparent that the lack of another primary tool, such as Section 5, impacts the ability to adequately address voting rights discrimination. The cost and time needed to investigate, file, and litigate Section 2 of the VRA violations are cost-prohibitive for many communities. Also, Section 2 does not have the same capacity as Section 5 in that Section 2 is reactive, that is, after the legislation has been enacted, whereas Section 5 was preemptive, freezing legislation until the federal government could preclear the proposed and, in many cases, legislatively passed changes. Section 5 could determine whether the practice or procedure would ever get implemented, whereas Section 2 can only attempt to stop the practice or procedure after it has become the law of the land. It is much harder to stop a moving train. It is much easier to hold the train at the station until you know that the path and tracks are clear, which was the genius and preventative nature of Section 5.

Many jurisdictions pass laws without federal approval, and advocacy groups engage in years trying to undo the legislation, while the legislature enjoys the spoils of its bounty. Justice Anthony Kennedy suggested that Section 2 was enough of a viable tool to combat racial discrimination in voting. However, as Crayton states, "Years later [after *Shelby*], you've got communities that have used a ton of energy and resources to arrive at an answer that basically sets you up for another opportunity to do the next crazy thing that [election officials or legislative bodies envision]." Further, he states, "What we see now is a plethora of litigation projects that have emerged in the South, but not a lot of undoing of many of these, I think, retrograde policies that make it more difficult for minority voters to participate. Frankly, what you've seen is a slight decline in certain cases."[48] Since *Shelby*, advocacy groups have attempted to combat disenfranchisement, but history has already demonstrated the need for more tools to ensure that the right to vote is not once again considered a fallacy for people of color.

The Impact of *Shelby*

While voting rights proponents have continued to fight nefarious voting changes that did not or would not have received Section 5 preclearance, the election in 2016 marked the first without the full protections of the Voting Rights Act. Many of the previously covered jurisdictions instituted new voting restrictions, such as closing polling places and midterm redistricting without a sweeping and thorough review to determine whether the change violated federal state voting laws. Regarding impact, new voter ID laws were imposed on more than 850,000 Latinx voters,[49] and Fayette County, Georgia, sought to affect more than 100,000 of its voters with a proposed discriminatory change.[50] Also, in Sparta, Georgia, officials "systematically" questioned the eligibility of 20 percent of its African American citizens, which affected turnout and led to white candidates winning municipal elections. Before *Shelby*, Section 5 would have required the covered jurisdictions to submit the change and receive approval.[51]

Case Study: North Carolina

The Supreme Court's *Shelby* decision allowed states and municipalities—which for decades were required to request permission from the United States attorney general—to execute changes without federal approval or preclearance. North Carolina was once one of those jurisdictions covered by Section 5. Without this requirement, state legislatures were able to provide a nail in the coffin to the ability to vote free from discrimination and political imaginations.

North Carolina became the case study for what a post–Section 5 world would look like, a striking refutation of Chief Justice Roberts's belief that voting discrimination was mainly a thing of the past and that Section 5 was no longer needed. Perhaps no jurisdiction was as explicit in its attempts to disenfranchise post-*Shelby* as the state of North Carolina. A week after the *Shelby* decision, hundreds of people packed into the Christian Faith Baptist Church. It was another week of the Moral Monday protests, as they came to be known.[52]

The Moral Monday movement started in the same place where the 1960s civil rights movement began—in Greensboro, on the campus of North Carolina A&T University. Almost fifty years prior, four freshmen at A&T sat down at the lunch counter at Woolworth's and refused to leave until they were served. The sit-ins spread throughout the state to Winston-Salem, Durham, Raleigh, and Charlotte. Two months later, the Student Nonviolent Coordinating Committee was founded at Shaw University in Raleigh. That was then; this time, the Moral Mondays started when Republicans in North Carolina, who controlled the legislature and the governorship in 2013, introduced the most stringent voting restrictions in the country.[53] Much to Representative Michaux's dismay, the Republican legislature was hell-bent on ensuring that the progress made in the previous election would be wholly undone for years to come.

North Carolina's voting changes included, among other things, strict voter ID, cutting early voting, eliminating same-day registration during the early voting period, ending the $2,000 child dependency tax deduction for parents whose college-student child votes where he or she attends school, and rescinding the automatic restoration of voting rights for ex-felons. North Carolina, where forty counties had previously been subject to Section 5, no longer had to have its voting changes approved by the federal government.

North Carolina Republicans used the same rhetoric to argue for those sweeping changes as their comrades in Texas and other jurisdctions, with claims of evidence of voter fraud and the ever present yet rarely detected potential risk of fraud.[54] Those who defended North Carolina's new laws also argued that the state was under no obligation to present specific evidence of voter fraud because of the United States Supreme Court's *Crawford v. Marion County Election Board* voter ID decision.[55] A states'-rights-focused reading of *Crawford* argues that before a state enacts a voter ID or any other type of voting procedure, if the interest that the state is trying to achieve is combating fraud, then it does not have to provide evidence that such fraud has been committed in the state.[56]

Unlike Texas, which ranked forty-eighth in voter turnout in 2012, North Carolina had the most progressive election laws in the South. The state had not always had this distinction. In 1996, North Carolina ranked forty-third in voter turnout. However, to expand voter participation, the state adopted electoral reforms, such as early voting in 2000, out-of-precinct ballots counting as regular ballots in 2005, and same-day registration during the early voting period in 2007. As a result, North Carolina skyrocketed from thirty-seventh in voter turnout in 2000 to eleventh by 2012. These reforms had a particularly beneficial impact on African American voters. Rev. William Barber II, the leader of the Moral Monday protests, stated, "North Carolina has the best election laws in the country. . . . We've had elections for 237 years without voter ID. And only after the massive turnout of African Americans, Latinos, progressive whites, students, and the elderly fundamentally changed the electorate in the South did false witness and distortion about fraud begin."[57]

Indeed, three weeks after *Shelby*, the North Carolina Senate significantly toughened the House's voter ID bill (HB 589), eliminating student

IDs from public universities, out-of-state driver's licenses, and county, municipal, and public employee IDs from the list of acceptable voter IDs. The bill was stricter than the Texas voter ID law that was blocked by the courts in 2012 under Section 5.[58] A report comparing data in 2014 and 2016 found that "black voters constituted 11.4 percent of those voting in Texas in 2016 with ID but 16.1 percent of those voting without ID, which shows clear evidence of a disparate racial impact. Likewise, Latino voters made up 19.8 percent of those voting with an ID but 20.7 percent of those voters without an ID. So even if voter ID laws haven't swung election outcomes, they can deny thousands of people their right to vote—denials that fall disproportionately on black and Latino citizens."[59] Likewise, millions of North Carolina citizens would be affected by the new restrictions. More than 2.5 million of them voted early in 2012, nearly 100,000 used same-day registration, 50,000 registered in high schools through preregistration in their civics classes, and 300,000 registered voters did not have government-issued IDs.

Congressional Inaction

In *Shelby*, the Supreme Court challenged Congress to act, and it has refused to do so. Thus far, Congress has made two feeble attempts to restore the protections lost in the Supreme Court decision. The Voting Rights Amendment and Advancement Acts, or VRAA, bills have not received hearings or a vote in the House of Representatives or Senate, despite bipartisan support.

In early January 2014, a day after Dr. Martin Luther King Jr.'s eighty-fifth birthday, Congressmen Jim Sensenbrenner and John Lewis introduced the Voting Rights Amendment Act of 2014 to restore Section 5 of the VRA. It was a modest bill, offering a new coverage formula, but it represented a promising start for a post-*Shelby* legislative fix.[60]

The Voting Rights Amendment Act evoked as its purpose, "To amend the Voting Right Acts of 1965 to revise the criteria for determining which States and political subdivisions are subject to section 4 of the Act, and for other purposes."[61] The key components included a new coverage formula in which a state would be subject to Section 5 preclearance if, among other things, it committed five voting violations in fifteen years. This new coverage formula, however, would cover only Georgia, Louisiana, Mississippi, and Texas.[62] A political subdivision, like a county, parish, or city within a state, would be covered if it had three violations within a fifteen-year period or one violation and "persistent and extremely low minority voting turnout."[63] The bipartisan bill, which also included a process for jurisdictions to "bail in" under Section 3(c), provided limited notice and transparency and restored election observer coverage.[64] While this attempt was significant, it did not go far enough. Unfortunately, the new coverage formula did not provide coverage for long-standing wrongdoers like North Carolina and Alabama.

Congress made another attempt a few months later with the Voting Rights Advancement Act. This bill updated the coverage formula to include more states as "covered jurisdictions," such as Alabama, Arizona, Arkansas, California, Florida, Georgia, Louisiana, Mississippi, New York, North Carolina, South Carolina, and Virginia. It provided an expiration of federal approval or preclearance after ten years for states and local jurisdictions without violations. It also included a notice and transparency provision in requiring public notice of voting changes that occurred 180 days before an election, expanded a court's ability to order preclearance as a remedy, and restored the federal observer program to its full capacity.

Voting Rights Amendment Act

Bipartisan bill introduced in House and Senate

Purpose

"To amend the Voting Right Act of 1965 to revise the criteria for determining which States and political subdivisions are subject to section 4 of the Act, and for other purposes."

Key Components

Coverage formula:

- A state would be subject to Section 5 preclearance
  1. if it commits five voting violations in fifteen years; and
  2. at least one of the violations is undertaken by the state itself.
- A political subdivision within a state would be covered if it has three violations within a fifteen-year period or one violation and "persistent and extremely low minority voting turnout."
- Bail-in under Section 3(c).
- Includes notice and transparency components.

VOTING RIGHTS ADVANCEMENT ACT

Purpose

"To amend the Voting Right Act of 1965 to revise the criteria for determining which States and political subdivisions are subject to section 4 of the Act, and for other purposes."

Key Components

Updates the coverage formula:

- Includes Alabama, Arizona, Arkansas, California, Florida, Georgia, Louisiana, Mississippi, New York, North Carolina South Carolina, and Virginia. Preclearance would expire after ten years for states and local jurisdictions without violations.
- Requires public notice of voting changes that occur 180 days before an election.
- Expands a court's ability to order preclearance as a remedy.
- Restores the federal observer program.

Neither of these measures is sufficient, nor can they replace Section 5 of the VRA. They do not address modern-day disenfranchisement while also limiting the reach of federal oversight. What is needed is a more expansive and imaginative approach that requires any voting legislation to undergo extreme vetting to determine the impact on the ability to vote.[65] Moreover, the *Shelby* decision allows jurisdictions to combat voter participation from every angle, for example, registration, residency, access to the ballot, IDs, and early voting. Since *Shelby*, voting measures are not subject to federal review unless the jurisdiction is under a separate court order. Otherwise, in most cases, it can move forward without anything other than an anecdotal accusation.

Efforts to return to a time of federal oversight have been highly unsuccessful. However, this is not cause to abandon the attempt to eliminate racial inequalities in the area of voting. Crayton says,

> I don't think this means that we abandon the project of dealing with racial equality. Because I don't think that's been a completed project, as the court seems to believe is the case, but it doesn't necessarily also mean that tools that we've used to correct this problem, i.e., Section 5, is the only tool that is equal to addressing [it]. Maybe it's time to think creatively about a tool that takes race equity seriously in the political sphere, that doesn't necessarily utilize the very same tools, to push the court to tell us what they really mean. If we need to have a new statute that addresses it, and perhaps even in a more ambitious way, let's do it.[66]

The Way Forward

Derrick Johnson, president and CEO of the National Association for the Advancement of Colored People (NAACP), advocates for a more imaginative approach to restoring the protections of Section 5. He is concerned with "our overreliance on the Voting Rights Act." He also encourages us to develop new strategies to protect the right to vote. He reiterates that we should not "give up on the Voting Rights Act. . . . But the reality is it's under attack, and if the Supreme Court goes the way that [he] believes it's going, . . . Section 2 will be the next thing on the chopping block. So we would have this shell of an act without the two most important sections in the act."[67]

Just as at other points in our history, the deterioration of democracy requires a more aggressive and creative approach to maintain and advance racial equality. Although these times have some similarities to the past, what is different from the Jim Crow indignities that my grandmother experienced is that we now have more tools at our disposal concerning education and position. We are starting at different points than before. We are not mere years from slavery or the end of segregation. We recently experienced feats that my grandmother never thought that she would witness, for example, the election of an African American to the presidency of the United States.

Our quest for equality is difficult and full of obstacles such as the dismantling of Section 5 of the Voting Rights Act. Nonetheless, the forecast is brighter and more sure than past generations. My grandmother does not follow the Supreme Court, nor does she have any interest in reading its decisions. She does, however, feel that these days are feeling unfortunately familiar to a former time when violence, hate speech, and vulgarity ran rampant. Unfortunately, we will continue this cycle of progress to regress and liberation to oppression, if we do not imagine measures that advance the ability for all people to register and vote without regard to racial or ethnic identification.

While Congress attempted to return us to a modified version of Section 4, Chief Justice Roberts's words suggested that the original formula did not go far enough. With rampant discrimination, the courts and legislatures should expand federal oversight to include all states and all changes affecting the right to vote. On previous occasions, I have advocated for a type of nationwide Section 5 that would require jurisdictions to provide a period of notice before making voting changes and for federal oversight to assess the impact of the change. It would determine and inform decisions, as well as communities, on the type of change and whether the change conformed with federal voting laws, while also evaluating the impact on voters and communities of color.

Years ago, I suggested that Congress adopt a new way to require jurisdictions to make sure that their laws were free of discrimination, through the use of Voter Impact Statement (VIS). Under what was previously Section 5 of the Voting Rights Act, the submitting jurisdiction was required to provide to the attorney general of the United States information regarding the nature of the change (i.e., the statutory or judicial authority for the change, copies of the previous ordinance or change, a statement explaining the reason for the change, and an explanation of the anticipated effect on racial or language minorities in the jurisdiction).[68] Accordingly, on the statewide level, legislators hoping to offer legislation affecting the right to vote would have to first receive an opinion from either the attorney general's or the secretary of state's office finding that the proposed legislation does not abridge the right to vote. The state officials' statement would include the following: the former election practice, the proposed change, any alternatives considered, and any evidence of public involvement, including comments from disabled people, communities of color, and other underserved groups. The state or local official would have to certify that the proposed legislation does not run afoul of federal voting rights statutes. Moreover, the VIS would serve as a type of nationwide Section 5, requiring states to verify that voting changes would not unnecessarily make it harder to vote or discriminate against their citizens.

Congress has the power to regulate elections under the Elections Clause, Article I, § 4, of the United States Constitution, which reads, "the Congress may at any time by law make or alter . . . regulations."[69] Under the Elections Clause, Congress has broad authority to regulate all aspects of elections, and it should use this power to implement prophylactic measures like VIS. Congress accessed its Elections Clause powers in passing the Help America Vote Act (HAVA). Accordingly, Congress could use this power to alter HAVA to require jurisdictions to adhere to VIS requirements for all election-related changes. It is easy to argue that as a democratic society, we should want the assurance that any and all changes that affect the right to vote do not do so in a way that discriminates. Courts have rightly held that Congress has the authority to regulate the election process, arguably from voter registration to ensuring that ballots cast are accurately counted consistent with the apparent wishes of the voter. In 1879, the Supreme Court found that Congress's power to regulate congressional elections "may be exercised as and when Congress sees fit to exercise it," and "when exercised, the action of Congress, so far as it extends and conflicts with the regulations of the State necessarily supersedes them."[70] In *Smiley v. Holm*, the Court wrote, "It cannot be doubted that these comprehensive words embrace authority to provide a complete code for congressional elections, not only as to times and places, but in relation to notices, registration, supervision of voting, protection of voters, prevention of fraud and corrupt practices, counting of votes, duties of inspectors and canvassers, and making and publication of election returns; in short, to enact the numerous requirements as to procedure and safeguards which experience shows are necessary in order to enforce the fundamental right involved."[71]

In addition to the Elections Clause, Congress has also used its Spending Clause power to ensure that voter access is not impeded. In enacting the National Voter Registration Act and HAVA, Congress attached its allocation of funds to the requirement for providing voter registration opportunities under the NVRA and upgrading election equipment under the HAVA. Certainly, Congress could require jurisdictions to provide a detailed VIS that would include comments from affected communities in order to receive HAVA or other funding. This level of oversight is needed to ensure that states and local jurisdictions cannot adopt measures that discriminate or disparately impact their eligible voters' ability to cast a ballot or otherwise participate in the electoral process.

A mechanism such as the VIS would require states to explain the purpose and need[72] for the proposed action. It would change the current practice of basing legislation on anecdote or unfounded assertions of voter fraud or threats to national security. The need for heightened scrutiny for laws that affect voting serves as a constant refrain from those who are affected by the devious efforts to keep people of color from the polls. Unfortunately, Congress does not appear, however, to have the political will in ensuring that the right to vote is free from discrimination.

Moving On

After *Shelby*, the fight to vote continues. Despite advocates' best efforts, the battle to vote continues. The courts no longer serve as a beacon of light in the darkness of discrimination. Instead of voting rights, it is essentially voting fights. We are fighting much more as opposed to arriving at consensus decisions in a nonlitigative posture that allows previously disenfranchised groups to influence policy. This post-*Shelby* process also involves courts much more than they claimed they wanted to be involved in resolving many of these conflicts.

Whereas embattled groups could once use the federal court system to expose hidden antidemocratic practices, no refuge exists anymore in the Supreme Court or in Congress. After *Shelby*, the hard-fought gains for voter equality are quickly eroding, but the battle continues. Efforts such as Moral Mondays and Representative Michaux's brave work and statements should encourage the people to respond with an even louder voice. While we may not currently hold power to damn the disenfranchising legislation to hell, we can fight to remove these types of measures from consideration and provide political consequences for those who support them. As Representative Michaux knows well, the "arc of the moral universe is long, but it bends toward justice."[73] It is the bending process that mandates the hard work of thinking and acting creatively, in spite of the measures meant to stop people of color from participating fully in the political process.

3

Voter Identification

I want to see my vote counted. Let me be there. I wanna be
there. I want to see that.
—Alberta Currie

Instead of "Can you hear me now?," taken from an early-millennium
Verizon advertising campaign and the exasperated cries from numerous cell phone users with dropped or hard-to-hear calls in remote and
suburban areas, in the voting rights spectrum, voter ID laws tend to ask,
"Can you see me now?" Just like the immeasurable dropped calls, many
voters, like Ms. Currie in the epigraph, find themselves dropped from
the opportunity to participate in the election process.

In jurisdictions across the country, longtime voters like Alberta Currie, an African American who endured literacy tests in order to cast a
ballot, found that sweeping voting changes would deny the ability to
stand in a polling place and cast a ballot, as they desired.[1] For many
African American voters, who historically were shut out of the voting booth or who for decades were forced to enter places of business
through the back door or not at all, this new-millennium requirement of
identification in order to vote seemed strikingly similar to past measures
affecting their right to vote and, as such, insulting to their democratic
sensibilities. As my father explained, blacks could not enter through the
front door in white-owned establishments, like restaurants, department
stores, or the main floor of the movie theater. Further, in many places,
they were invisible to whites. My grandmother describes this experience as "no 'count," which is short for "no account," meaning worthless.
Because African Americans were relegated to second-class citizens on
many levels, the right to vote held special pride, and many regarded vot-

ing day as a special occasion. Men and women would wear their Sunday best to the polls: men in jackets and ties and women wearing hats and carrying their pocketbooks. Once we received the right to vote, with the passage of the VRA, as we had during Reconstruction, we "grabbed hold" of the process and participated at high levels.

Traditionally, voters of color are less likely to take advantage of absentee voting or other measures that do not require in-person ballots—not for nefarious reasons but because they remember when access to the vote was prohibited by law. For my grandmother, getting dressed up to go vote meant that we were full citizens and equal to whites in the most important ways. It was very important for African American voters to show up at the polls and vote in person. Currently, some states, like Oregon and Washington, conduct their elections via mail. Reportedly, this process costs less and enjoys high turnout rates. However, some people cite as a disadvantage that it does not allow for the communal aspect of voting in person. While voting by mail can serve as a more convenient option, in southern states, in recent years, forces have attempted to make voting, generally, less convenient and harder. These legislators, not only in the South but throughout the country, have instituted restrictive voter ID laws that would require registered voters to bring a government-issued form of identification, such as a driver's license, passport, or military ID, in order to cast an in-person ballot.

Voter ID Laws

Voter ID laws require voters to provide some form of identification prior to casting a ballot. These laws come in various forms and with various requirements. At the beginning of this century, only eleven states required all voters to show identification.[2] In most states, the primary form of identification was signature verification, which allowed voters to sign the voter rolls instead of presenting ID.[3]

Subsequently, the Help America Vote Act (HAVA) of 2003 required states to mandate identification from first-time voters who registered via mail and did not verify their identity when they registered.[4] HAVA does, however, allow photo and nonphoto forms of identification, such as a utility bill or government-issued document with the voter's name and address.[5] In an effort to comply with HAVA's voter ID requirements for first-time mail registrants, many states adopted laws that changed the voter ID requirements to comply with federal law. Consequently, some states changed their voter ID requirements, not just for first-time mail registrants but for all voters. Some states that lacked an identification requirement were compelled to include one to comply with HAVA's identification for first-time voters who registered through mail. Instead of limiting identification to this small group of voters, some states implemented voter ID requirements for all voters regardless of the type of registration, that is, in person or through the mail.

While some states still allow signature verification as the primary requirement for voting, after the 2010 midyear elections, an onslaught of state legislatures sought to require government-issued photo ID as the only acceptable form of identification. In fact, in 2011, a majority of states, thirty-four, had legislators introduce voter ID bills; of those states, fourteen had existing laws that required voters to show some form of identification, yet the bills sought to make it tougher by restricting the acceptable forms of identification to a few options. Indeed, the Lawyers' Committee for Civil Rights Under Law created the "Map of Shame" to demonstrate the magnitude of the legislation and the sweeping changes across the country.[6] In 2018, thirty-four states required some form of identification to vote. We have seen a dramatic increase from the fourteen states that requested some form of ID to vote prior to HAVA. These fourteen jurisdictions, while requiring identification, did not turn people away if they lacked identification and would allow them to cast a regular ballot.[7]

A Brief History of Modern-Day Voter ID

States require various forms of identification in order to vote.[8] Most require some form of photo identification; others find a signature or a phone bill, bank statement, or some other form of address verification acceptable to allow a person to access the franchise. The debate surrounding voter ID has centered around restrictive voter ID laws that severely limit the types of affordable identification that a voter can present in order to cast a ballot. Advocates oppose voter ID laws that are restrictive because they intentionally limit the number of voters to a particular subset of citizens and place an undue burden on the right to vote. Moreover, restrictive photo ID prohibits people like Ms. Currie from meeting the requirements and relegates them to no longer having the choice to vote in person.

To be clear, requiring some form of identification to vote is not in itself discriminatory. What has evolved is that many states have taken the HAVA requirement for first-time registrants and unnecessarily expanded it to all voters. Some states have merely added a photo ID, such as a driver's license, to the long list of acceptable forms of identification. Others have reduced the acceptable forms to only government-issued forms of identification, instead of more readily available forms of identification, such as a utility bill or other mail with a person's address. Those states that limit the forms of acceptable ID to only government-issued ones, such as driver's licenses, passports, or military IDs, are considered overly restrictive and limit access to the ballot.

Approximately two-thirds of all states require some form of identification. Half of those states require some form of photo ID. Seven of those states only allow for governmental-issued photo ID, such as driver's license or passport. At the beginning of 2011, there were just two states—Georgia and Indiana—with strict photo ID laws. In 2015, the number had grown to seven with the addition of Kansas, Tennessee, Mississippi, Virginia, and Wisconsin.[9] For clarity, we can categorize what states do, using the level of restrictiveness, as follows:

Preventive ID
Restrictive/narrow: states allow for very few acceptable forms of photo
    identification.

- Voters must show a government-issued photo ID in order to vote.
- Voters who are unable to show photo ID at the polls are permitted to vote a provisional ballot, which is counted only if the voter returns to election officials within several days after the election to show a photo ID.

Verified ID

Limited: a photo ID is required, but states will allow voters to vote on a regular ballot if they can meet other criteria.

- Voters are asked to show a photo ID in order to vote, but the lists of acceptable forms of identification expand beyond government-issued photo IDs.
- Voters who are unable to show photo ID are still allowed to vote if they can meet certain other criteria, such as signing an affidavit attesting to their identity or allowing a poll worker or other registered voter to verify their identity.
- Approximately eight states, including Connecticut, Missouri, and Arkansas, require a picture identification but also provide safeguard methods to ensure that a person can vote through another form of verification.

Flexible

Inclusive: a wide array of forms of identification are accepted, not exclusive to photo ID.

- The list of acceptable IDs is varied and includes nonphoto options, such as a utility bill or bank statement with the voter's name and address.
- These states—West Virginia, Pennsylvania, California, and Nevada—provide a wide array of acceptable ways to access the right to vote, including signature verification.

Accordingly, the types of voter ID vary widely. While presidential commissions have reviewed the existence and increase in voter ID laws, no federal standard exists. However, voter ID laws cannot violate the United States Constitution or federal statutes like the VRA, NVRA, or HAVA.

The Devil Ain't Got No New Tricks

The passage of voter ID laws is not a new phenomenon but an attempt to affect the ability of "certain" voters to freely participate in the act of voting. To that end, voter ID has been called the poll tax of the new millennium. The poll tax was introduced after newly freed slaves enjoyed widespread electoral success in the states where they once were subjugated to working in chains and denied the rights of citizenship. This new-millennium device has some similarities to the poll tax, a Jim Crow method instituted to limit the number of persons who could access the right to vote by use of a tax that was payable at one point in the year and whose documentation was needed to access the franchise. The first poll taxes were implemented in 1873 in Delaware and in Georgia, which added residency and registration requirements that substantially reduced black voter turnout.[10]

The poll tax has deep roots in the disenfranchisement of people of color. It is no secret that one of the primary purposes of the poll tax was to disenfranchise black voters. In 1890, during the Mississippi Constitutional Convention, it was described as "the most effective instrumentality of Negro disfranchisement."[11] Nonetheless, some scholars argue that the poll tax was not implemented to disenfranchise the black population but to further the aims of a political party. In Louisiana, the 1896 Constitutional Convention called for a suffrage amendment that required, among other things, literacy and property qualifications, as well as a poll tax. In Louisiana, the purpose seemed to be the disenfranchisement of blacks, while in South Carolina, party preservation served as the primary motivation.[12]

The Texas poll tax statute read as follows:

> Every person subject to none of the foregoing disqualifications (Art. 5.01, Election Code) who shall have attained the age of twenty-one (21) years and who shall be a citizen of the United States, and who shall have resided in this State one (1) year next preceding an election, and the last

six (6) months within the county in which he or she offers to vote, shall be deemed a qualified elector, provided that any voter who is subject to pay a poll tax under the laws of this State, shall have paid said tax before offering to vote at any election in this State and holds a receipt showing that said poll tax was paid before the first day of February next preceding such election.[13]

Thus, this statute included a residency requirement and a poll tax requirement.

An argument for voter ID analogizes payment for ID to other uses of photo ID, such as to cash a check, to go to the movies, and so on. Moreover, the necessity of paying to vote has deep roots in our democratic system. In the early days of the republic, only property owners, that is, those who were able to pay, regardless of citizenship, were allowed to cast a ballot. However, in 1966, the Supreme Court addressed this argument, and it found that voting is different:

It is argued that a State may exact fees from citizens for many different kinds of licenses; that if it can demand from all an equal fee for a driver's license, it can demand from all an equal poll tax for voting. But we must remember that the interest of the State, when it comes to voting, is limited to the power to fix qualifications. Wealth like race, creed, or color, is not germane to one's ability to participate intelligently in the electoral process. Lines drawn on the basis of wealth or property, like those of race, are traditionally disfavored.[14]

At the time of the Supreme Court order, the poll tax only amounted to $1.50, which in 2014 would equal approximately $11.35, a sum that seems paltry to some people today. However, the United States Supreme Court deemed it sufficient to serve as an unconstitutional barrier to the franchise. Similar to the poll tax, with voter ID, the power lies in the ability to pay, particularly to purchase underlying documents. Today, as in previous years, the inability to pay serves as an impediment to participation. It is the cost of the underlying documents needed, such as a stamped/sealed birth certificate, that precludes many citizens from obtaining the necessary ID to participate in the electoral process.

In many jurisdictions, the cost of underlying documents often starts at $15, and a driver's license costs between $20 and $100. Additionally, the costs of states' providing "free ID" has served as a rude awakening for many jurisdictions. The National Conference of State Legislatures estimates that states spend between $2 million and $3 million annually on implementing voter ID requirements. In fact, in three years from 2007 to 2010, Indiana, the first state to implement a preventive ID, spent more than $10 million on free IDs.[15]

How do we account today for the funds needed to purchase a birth certificate that is required to obtain even a free voter ID, not to mention the cost of a driver's license? The cost of a driver's license may seem minimal, unless, like 25 percent of African Americans in Georgia, you do not own a car. Additionally, arguments that Americans use identification to board an airplane or that everyone can get a free acceptable form of identification serve as modern-day myths. It is a myth that anyone and everyone can get a free ID. In fact, the ID is not free: the voter must pay for the underlying costs of birth and marriage certificates. Indeed, compare the costs of these documents to the former $1.50 poll tax and its unconstitutional end. Another myth is that voter ID laws are needed to address and thwart voter fraud. It is widely recognized that voter ID laws would only preclude voter impersonation. However, studies have found that this type of fraud occurs as often as someone getting struck by lightning. Notwithstanding these realities, legislatures continue to pass laws that require fewer and more restrictive acceptable forms of identification.

Impact of Voter ID Laws

Similar to 1896, today's voter ID laws can serve many purposes, such as disenfranchising people of color and advancing political agendas.[16]

While poll taxes were meant to disenfranchise black voters, they also captured poor whites. Likewise, voter ID not only disproportionately impacts voters of color; it also impacts the elderly, young voters, and those from lower socioeconomic levels. Today, proponents of restrictive voter ID argue that it is needed to prevent voter fraud and that it is not meant to disenfranchise voters of color. Nonetheless, it is well established that voter ID does not prevent in-person voter fraud and that actual voter fraud in many jurisdictions is statistically nonexistent. One comprehensive report found "31 credible instances of voter impersonation out of more than 1 billion votes cast between 2000 and 2014."[17]

That said, the impact of these laws on a particular party is well documented. Undeniably, Indiana's restrictive voter ID law hit Democratic voters the hardest. It also was not lost on the court that those Democratic voters happened to be African American. Surprisingly, Judge Richard Posner, the author of the 2007 *Crawford* majority opinion in the United States Seventh Circuit Court of Appeals that was appealed to the United States Supreme Court, dissented in a subsequent voter ID case in the Seventh Circuit Court of Appeals, *Frank v. Walker*.[18] Judge Posner illustrated the partisan divide and impetus for the passage of restrictive voter ID laws, noting that Republican legislatures tend to impose restrictive voter ID requirements.[19] He argued the following:

> The data imply that a number of conservative states try to make it difficult for people who are outside the mainstream, whether because of poverty or race or problems with the English language, or who are unlikely to have a driver's license or feel comfortable dealing with officialdom, to vote, and that liberal states try to make it easy for such people to vote because if they do vote they are likely to vote for Democratic candidates. Were matters as simple as this there would be no compelling reason for judicial intervention; it would be politics as usual. But actually, there's an asymmetry. There is evidence both that voter-impersonation fraud is extremely rare and that photo ID requirements for voting, especially of the strict variety found in Wisconsin, are likely to discourage voting.

This implies that the net effect of such requirements is to impede voting by people easily discouraged from voting, most of whom probably lean Democratic.[20]

Advocates have repeatedly argued, just as with the poll tax, that the law has been used for partisan gain, with disparate adverse impact on voters by race, language ability, and age. The overwhelming impact on racial and ethnic minorities is undeniable. Just as with the poll tax, regardless of whether the purpose of the law is to advantage a particular political party, the effect remains the same. In 2012, a Brennan Center report found that approximately 11 percent of citizens in the country lacked the requisite voter identification.[21] In Texas, a federal court found that more than 600,000 persons lacked the requisite voter ID, many of them people of color. These numbers demonstrate that a large percentage of persons lack birth certificates or access to the documents required for voter ID.

North Carolina Reveals Its Soul

In 2013, shortly after the Supreme Court's *Shelby* decision, North Carolina passed a restrictive voter ID law. In October 2013, Don Yelton, a Buncombe County Republican captain and a member of the Republican Party Executive Committee, gave an interview to *The Daily Show with Jon Stewart*, where he discussed the reason for the law, stating, "If it hurts the whites, so be it. If it hurts a bunch of lazy blacks that want the government to give them everything, so be it."[22] Yelton also testified before the North Carolina House Rules Committee, saying, "The photo ID requirement would 'disenfranchise some of [Democrats'] special voting blocks [*sic*],' and that 'that within itself is the reason for the photo voter ID, period, end of discussion.'"[23]

Three years later, during the litigation around the law, the United States Fourth Circuit Court of Appeals cited Yelton's statements as evidence of intent. The court noted, "These statements do not prove that any member of the General Assembly necessarily acted with discriminatory intent. But the sheer outrageousness of these public statements by a party leader does provide some evidence of the racial and partisan political environment in which the General Assembly enacted the law."[24] Accordingly, this exclusion of voters references an earlier time. Whether it is called a poll tax or voter ID, racial and ethnic minorities, "who lean Democratic," are adversely impacted by such restrictions.

The Impact on Real Voters

Voting in person has become more difficult for many Americans with the passage of restrictive voter ID laws. This excerpt from *One Wisconsin Inst., Inc. v. Thomsen* depicts the plight of elderly Americans in states with restrictive voter ID:

> Mrs. Smith has lived in Milwaukee since 2003. She was born at home, in Missouri, in 1916. In her long life she has survived two husbands, and she has left many of the typical traces of her life in public records. But, like many older African Americans born in the South, she does not have a birth certificate or other documents that would definitively prove her date and place of birth. After Wisconsin's voter ID law took effect, she needed a photo ID to vote. So she entered the ID Petition Process (IDPP) at the Wisconsin Department of Motor Vehicles (DMV) to get a Wisconsin ID. DMV employees were able to find Mrs. Smith's record in the 1930 census, but despite their sustained efforts, they could not link Mrs. Smith to a Missouri birth record, so they did not issue her a Wisconsin ID. She is unquestionably a qualified Wisconsin elector, and yet she could not vote in 2016. Because she was born in the South, barely 50 years after slavery, her story is particularly compelling. But it is not unique: Mrs. Smith is one of about 100 qualified electors who tried to but could not obtain a Wisconsin ID for the April 2016 primary.[25]

Importantly, the cyclical effect of progress to regress is apparent in the fight over voter ID requirements. These laws, like other suppressive measures, have real-world impact on the ability to access the ballot. Some courts have recognized the burden that these new-age poll taxes cause voters. In *Frank v. Walker*, the district court outlined a number of difficulties that voters who lack a driver's license would have in getting a free ID, including determining the requirements for getting a free ID card and the time it takes to obtain the ID, including the trip to the Department of Motor Vehicles office, which typically closes at 5:00 p.m.[26] Notably, people who lack a driver's license probably do not have a vehicle; thus, they need to arrange for transportation and, if they work, take the time from work to obtain the "free" ID. Additionally, these voters will need to arrive at the DMV with the requisite underlying documentation. If they lack it, they will need to go to yet another appropriate government agency and spend the time and effort to gather the documents and pay the appropriate fees. These voters will need to do these and other feats in time to vote in the next election. The affidavit of Mrs. Bettye Jones, described in the following subsection, illustrates that the massive effort to obtain the required documents often falls short of Election Day.

Bettye Jones

In Wisconsin, Mrs. Bettye Jones described her ordeal of obtaining a voter ID. In her affidavit, she explained that she was a seventy-seven-year-old African American woman and registered voter who lived in Brookfield, Wisconsin. Mrs. Jones was born at home in Tennessee in 1935. A doctor assisted in her birth, but because there was no hospital nearby serving African Americans, no official birth certificate was ever issued or filed on her behalf. Mrs. Jones moved to Cleveland, Ohio, in 1949 and registered to vote there when she was twenty-one years old. Mrs. Jones lived through the time when African Americans had to fight for their right to vote and has voted in every election since 1956. She has always been politically active. Her family was active in desegregating schools and neighborhoods, and Mrs. Jones has always worked to break down barriers to political and social participation for people of color. She organized events in her home to support the passage of the Voting Rights Act of 1965 and other civil rights initiatives. In the 1970s, Mrs. Jones was even more politically active, working to get Carl and Louis Stokes elected to political office. Mrs. Jones resided in Cleveland until her husband passed away in 2011. Shortly thereafter, in November 2011, she moved to Brookfield to live with her daughter.

The Wisconsin legislature passed a restrictive photo ID law that required Mrs. Jones to obtain a birth certificate in order to obtain the requisite photo ID. Despite the fact that Mrs. Jones possessed several forms of valid ID, including a current Ohio driver's license, which had been renewed the previous year, she realized she would need to get a Wisconsin ID if she wanted to vote. There were numerous trips to the Department of Motor Vehicles in Wisconsin, where she was told that she did not have sufficient ID and that she would need to provide a certified birth certificate in order to prove her identity and legal presence. She tried presenting her Social Security card, but to no avail. After being told that her existing ID was insufficient, Mrs. Jones and her daughter embarked on what Mrs. Jones termed a "wild goose chase" to obtain a certified Tennessee birth certificate to enable her to get a Wisconsin photo ID to vote under Act 23. For Mrs. Jones, it was the beginning of a harrowing, expensive, and multimonth ordeal. She first wrote to the Tennessee Office of Vital Records, which responded that it had no record of her birth. Mrs. Jones then paid a fee for the office to conduct an additional records search, but it was still unable to find anything. Because Tennessee could not find any original birth certificate for Mrs. Jones, she began a long process of requesting a delayed, postdated birth certificate from the state of Tennessee to use to prove her identity so that she could obtain the ID she needed to vote in Wisconsin. The process required her to present her parents' records and documentary proof of her place and date of birth. Mrs. Jones experienced major difficulty in tracking down these records. Mrs. Jones made multiple requests to the Tennessee Office of Vital Records for a delayed birth certificate, which were denied. Mrs.

Jones kept reapplying and providing additional information, fees, and notarized documents as she received them.

Ultimately, after four months and more than $100 in fees and approximately fifty hours of time making and following up on document requests, Mrs. Jones finally obtained a delayed, postdated birth certificate from the state of Tennessee in April 2012. Days before she received it, Mrs. Jones and her daughter decided to go to a different DMV from the one to which they originally applied, to see if her application might be more favorably received. They took bags with copies of all of Mrs. Jones's documentation, including all existing records about her, and explained her ordeal. Mrs. Jones provided that DMV with her Social Security card, her valid Ohio license, the birth certificates of her children, and the official letter from the Tennessee Office of Vital Records documenting that no record of her birth existed. Mrs. Jones's daughter also had to provide her valid Wisconsin identification and attest that she lived with Mrs. Jones. Ultimately, without Mrs. Jones having a birth certificate proving her identity and legal presence, and after an appeal to and meeting with the supervisor of the DMV office, Mrs. Jones was finally issued a Wisconsin state ID, for which she had to pay $35. Though she obtained a Wisconsin photo ID, she did not have one during the primary elections. Fortunately, shortly before the elections, a judge issued an injunction barring implementation of the Wisconsin photo ID law. If that injunction had not been in place, Mrs. Jones would not have been able to cast her ballot in that election—for the first time since 1956.

Mrs. Jones found the entire ordeal very disturbing and expressed concerned about the many others like her who probably do not have the help, time, and resources that she had in order to obtain a Wisconsin photo ID. She is concerned for all of the people born in the South, at home like her, because no hospital would take them, and therefore would have no official record of their birth.[27]

Unfortunately, Mrs. Jones passed away before she could vote in the November 2012 election. She spent a considerable part of her last days trying to regain her right to vote. Mrs. Jones, however, refused to get trapped in the web of voter ID. For example, women who need a voter ID must use their birth certificate to obtain one. Yet when they pay for the birth certificate and take it to get a driver's license, they are told that the birth certificate does not match their present name. Thus, these voters also need to provide a marriage certificate.

Latasha

During the early voting period, Latasha learned that she did not have any of the acceptable forms of identification. She learned about the option to obtain a free ID but lacked the necessary copy of her birth certificate. She embarked on a quest to get her birth certificate that took many turns throughout the day, including several visits to numerous county offices to obtain the proper documentation to enable her to vote. She was required to pay for her birth certificate, despite the state's claim that citizens can request a fee waiver. Nonetheless, after visiting two different Department of Public Safety offices, returning to her home to gather her voter registration card, birth certificate, student ID, divorce decree, and lease, and after waiting additional hours, she was allowed to cast a ballot.[28] Her journey, nonetheless, involved considerable time and funds, including taking time away from her job to gather all of the documents and wait to complete the process. Also consider the extraordinary measures that voters must take in order to make sure that their votes are counted.

Trish B.

Trish B., who had regularly voted from the age of eighteen, was refused the opportunity to cast a ballot by officials because her birth certificate and marriage certificate did not match. "She reported that a DPS [Department of Public Safety] employee told her that she would need an ID, a birth certificate, and a marriage license to receive a Texas EIC [Election Identification Certificate]. She had all of those items but was told that the birth certificate was unacceptable because it was not sealed or a recent copy. She then returned with her Social Security card and her voter registration card and was again refused an EIC. Trish reported that the DPS employee referred her first to the Department of Vital Records in Del Rio, Texas and then to an official at the Texas Secretary of State office. An official at the Texas Secretary of State office instructed Trish to travel 70 miles to another Texas office to get a certified copy of her birth certificate, which she did."[29]

Clifford G.

Veterans are not exempt from the burden of voter ID. A veteran voting since 1960, Clifford G. no longer has a driver's license because of a car accident; thus, he lacked an acceptable form of ID in his home state of Tennessee. His Veterans Administration card is not an approved form for identity purposes. He is an Air Force veteran, but his VA card is not one of the approved forms of photo ID in Tennessee.[30]

Marge C.

Another Wisconsinite, sixty-two-year-old Marge C., was denied the opportunity to vote in a presidential primary despite being recognized by the poll workers due to her voting in the same precinct for approximately forty years. Although the poll workers could find her name in the poll book, she did not have the newly required photo ID. Although poll workers recognized her, the lack of a photo ID precluded her from voting.[31]

Elizabeth G.

Elizabeth G. was born in rural southwestern Louisiana in 1938, in the small town of Jennings, the county seat of Jefferson Davis Parish. After growing up in the Jim Crow South, she always felt that voting was important. In 2013, after retiring as a school cook, she moved to Texas to live with her daughter in Austin. She had a driver's license and birth certificate from Louisiana but ran into problems when she tried to get a driver's license in Texas, which she needed to vote. She was told that the name on her birth certificate, which had been incorrectly filled out by the midwife who had delivered her at home and listed her mother's maiden name, had to match her current name. She returned to a Department of Public Safety office to apply for a voting-only ID but was once again told that her documentation needed to match the birth certificate. She then hired a lawyer in Louisiana to get her an amended birth certificate. She did not know when or if that would happen and could not vote in her new home state in the meantime. She called the cost and time of getting a new birth certificate another form of a poll tax.[32]

Floyd Carrier

During the state's municipal elections in November 2013, Floyd Carrier, an eighty-three-year-old who had been an army paratrooper in the Korean War, brought his expired driver's license, VA card, and voter registration card to the polls in China, Texas, where he has lived and voted for sixty years. The poll workers immediately recognized Carrier but would not let him vote because, they said, he did not have a valid voter ID. "I felt terrible because all I did for the country and they turn me down, so I just felt like I wasn't a citizen anymore."[33]

* * *

A litany of compelling accounts demonstrates the level of hardship that restrictive voter ID causes many voters in order to cast an in-person ballot on Election Day. In most states, these voters would have been allowed to cast an absentee ballot, but most voters of color are not aware nor are they inclined to vote absentee. They want to vote in person; they want to be seen.

The Courts Are Coming

Despite the overwhelming evidence of how restrictive voter ID laws discriminate against voters, states continue to pass these laws because they are effective, not at eliminating voter fraud but at eliminating eligible voters who tend to vote Democratic. As mentioned, the stated rationale for adopting restrictive voter ID was to prevent voter fraud. In most cases, restrictive voter ID legislation only applied to in-person voting. Persons utilizing absentee voting procedures were not susceptible to voter ID requirements. This, however, created quite the quagmire; more instances of voter fraud occur using absentee ballots than using in-person voting procedures. Although legislators needed little to no evidence of voter fraud to enact legislation, the courts have given high deference to legislative propensities.

In *Crawford v. Marion County*, the Seventh Circuit Court of Appeals acknowledged that Indiana had an "absence of prosecutions" for fraud but placed the burden on voters to prove the severity of the harm from the state's voter ID law, instead of asking the legislature to prove the need for the legislation and then weigh any potential harm to the voters. The court stated, "How many impersonations there are we do not know, but the plaintiffs have not shown that there are fewer impersonations than there are eligible voters whom the new law will prevent from voting,"[34] thus shifting the burden from the legislature to the voters. Circuit Judge Terence T. Evans, a dissenter in *Crawford*, characterized the Indiana voter ID law as "a not-too-thinly-veiled attempt to discourage election-day turnout by certain folks believed to skew Democratic."[35]

In Wisconsin, "[t]he [state] could not point to a single instance of known voter impersonation occurring in Wisconsin at any time in the recent past."[36] According to the state's own evidence, it is a rare occasion when a poll worker has even a slight suspicion—not actual instance—of fraud. An expert witness who studied Wisconsin elections that took place in 2004, 2008, 2010, and 2012 found zero cases of in-person voter-impersonation fraud.[37] In the Wisconsin case, Judge Posner found that "[s]ome of the 'evidence' of voter-impersonation fraud [was] downright goofy, if not paranoid."[38] Yet this "goofy" evidence has led to laws that have found acceptance in the courts, adversely affecting voters' ability to cast a ballot.

In the years after *Crawford*, the onslaught of laws has been ongoing, despite evidence of hundreds of thousands of voters lacking the ability to obtain the underlying documents needed to obtain the requisite form of ID. Apparently, the unsubstantiated claims of voter fraud are considered more credible than the disenfranchisement of eligible citizens.

In North Carolina, a federal court found that the state acted with "surgical precision" to eliminate voters of color. In Texas, federal courts found that the state's voter ID law was "intentionally discriminatory" and would disenfranchise hundreds of thousands of voters of color. Yet the efforts continue without apology to destroy certain voters' opportunity to participate in the democratic process.

An egregious example of how courts have allowed burdensome laws to remain in spite of findings of discrimination can be found in Texas. For a 2014 Texas election, early voting began on October 20. On October 11, the district court in *Veasey v. Perry* entered a final order striking down Texas's voter identification laws. The district court also ordered that Texas implement laws that were in place prior to the enactment of Senate Bill 14 (SB 14) in May 2011. While the district court found the voter ID law discriminatory, the appeals court reasoned that the timing of the decision would create logistical problems for the state. It decided that it would be extremely difficult, if not impossible, to train the 25,000 poll workers at the 8,000 poll locations about the changes that resulted from the injunction in time for early voting or Election Day. Moreover, it reasoned that there would be an inconsistent treatment of voters, because the state would have to rely on word of mouth to notify the poll workers about the changes. Thus, some voters would be disenfranchised because of some poll workers' noncompliance with SB 14. With this decision, it is clear that courts value preserving the status quo much more than they value preserving the franchise for all voters. The court decided that the state's interest in having an orderly election outweighed the burden of voters to obtain the requisite voter ID. On appeal, the United States Supreme Court agreed with the appeals court and allowed the discriminatory mechanism to remain.[39]

Justice Ruth Bader Ginsburg argued in her dissent that more weight should have been given to the federal district court opinion due in large part to the extensive trial that took place. The district court found a violation of Section 2 of the Voting Rights Act because the law was enacted with a discriminatory purpose and would yield a discriminatory result. Moreover, the law significantly weighed on minority voters and advantaged the Texas legislature and governor because it gave them the partisan advantage. Furthermore, the district court found that the law acts as an unconstitutional poll tax. Justice Ginsburg argued that these decisions should have been given more consideration and that the existence of discrimination, not the state's interest in an orderly election, should have been the primary factors in the court's decision. Instead, the United States Supreme Court allowed a discriminatory voting method to go forward.

Consequently, Texas serves as a primary example of procedural law and the preservation of the electoral status quo trumping substantive justice. The voting rights of citizens should have superseded the state's implementation of a discriminatory law. It was well documented that a Texas voter ID law placed a fiscal burden on voters and caused them to travel enormous distances between cities to obtain a voter ID from the Department of Transportation, and no exemptions were in place for voters who could not obtain alternative methods of identification. Texas certainly had numerous alternatives to its voter ID law that would have made it less restrictive,[40] but one has to wonder if it achieved its unstated yet obvious goal of thwarting voters who "skew Democratic."

Impact on the Democratic System

Despite the courts' blind spot toward all things labeled preventive of voter fraud, the impact on voters cannot be denied. Nicole Austin-Hillery, the Brennan Center's inaugural chair of its District of Columbia office who presently serves as Human Rights Watch's US Program executive director, has warned that with the wave of voter ID laws in 2016, we will experience

> the full force of how these laws are going to actually impact voters. . . . [W]e have a lot of anecdotal evidence from voters who have said, "I stayed away from the polls because I was fearful of how this might impact me." And then there were other voters who said, "I got to the polls, and there were issues with my ID and I didn't get to vote. But right now, that evidence is primarily anecdotal. . . . In 2016, . . . that will be the first time where we're really going to be able to measure the impact of those laws.[41]

Austin-Hillery's statement regarding having a clear picture on the impact of voter ID was part prophetic, part predictable. In fact, the University of Houston's Hobby School of Public Affairs conducted a survey to determine the impact of the Texas voter ID on the 2016 election in Harris County and Congressional District 23. The study found that the photo ID requirements had an impact on who voted and who won the elections in those jurisdictions. The study found, "Among this sub-set of non-voters whose nonparticipation was attributed at least in part to the photo ID requirements, approximately two-thirds of those with a preference would have voted for the Democratic candidates in the Harris County District Attorney and Sheriff races and in the CD-23 race. This suggests that had these individuals participated, the Democratic candidates in the former two contests would have enjoyed even larger margins of victory and the Democratic candidate in CD-23, Pete Gallego, would have defeated his Republican rival, Will Hurd, instead of losing to Hurd by 1.3% of the vote."[42]

Accordingly, scholars do believe that the voter ID laws and other restrictive measures have some impact on voter turnout.[43] In the 2014 midterm elections, voter turnout was exceptionally low, the lowest in seventy-two years. However, many variables exist that can affect turnout, such as weather, quality of candidates, and work schedules. Regarding close elections, however, voter ID and other laws may have contributed to suppressing turnout. In Texas, Democratic officials believe that the voter ID laws were part of the reason that the state had some of the lowest voter turnout in the county. A study by the Government Accountability Office found that voter ID laws contributed to lower voter turnout among minorities, young people, and poor people in the 2012 elections in Kansas and Tennessee.

Republicans dispute these claims by pointing to races such as the 2014 landslide victory of the former Texas attorney general Greg Abbott, a Republican candidate who won a gubernatorial race. However, Abbott's election and his landslide victory are false equivalencies when compared to the impact of voter ID laws. Texas maintains a voter turnout percentage of its voting-age population of less than 50 percent. In years when gubernatorial races are held, the voting-age population turnout has been consistently less than 30 percent.[44] In Colorado, where lawmakers expanded the franchise by allowing all voters to mail in ballots, turnout was the fourth highest in the country, at 53 percent.

Furthermore, voter ID and other restrictions could be a major factor in close elections. For example, in Kansas, Governor Sam Brownback beat challenger Paul Davis by a margin of 2.8 percent (or less than 33,000 votes). There were strict voter ID laws in place at the time, including a new requirement for documentary proof of citizenship in order to register to vote. The Kansas secretary of state noted that more than 24,000 Kansans attempted to register but had their registrations held in "suspense" because they failed to produce documentary proof of citizenship. Moreover, in Virginia, Senator Mark Warner beat challenger

Ed Gillespie by only 0.6 percent of the vote (or just over 12,000 votes). Although no studies have analyzed the impact of the voter ID laws in Virginia, it was noted that generally such laws tend to reduce turnout by about 2.4 percent. If this figure were applied to Virginia in the previous election cycle, it would amount to a reduction in voter turnout by more than 52,000 voters, which exceeds the margin of victory in the previously mentioned race.

Strategies are needed that not only provide access but information, accountability, and opportunity. Barriers such as voter ID, especially preventive ID, preclude many persons from casting ballots. In a country with an abysmal voter turnout rate—during the 2014 midterm election, less than 35 percent of eligible persons actually voted—creating user-friendly, comprehensive methods of exercising the right to vote is extremely important. Less restrictive voter ID is a viable alternative to the current system. Voters in Texas, Georgia, Florida, and North Carolina who lack the financial means to obtain underlying documents, such as a birth certificate or passport, can potentially lose the right to vote.

Nicole Austin-Hillery believes that we need "to figure out how to expand the franchise without getting bogged down by some of the old issues." Further, she believes that "we have spent so much time, energy, and resources trying to fight against voter ID and other measures—all of these issues that we would call efforts to close opportunities to minority voters. And now I'm not saying those things aren't important, but I think we have to be on the offensive."[45] She maintains that if we used our resources to advocate for modernization of the voting process with mechanisms such as automatic and online registration, we could ultimately render the "old issues" like voter ID moot.

Modernization of the voting process certainly serves as an area where policy arguments could possibly lead to real change in the voting process. After the 2000 federal election, we witnessed how antiquated our voting systems were, and Congress adopted HAVA to attempt to address those problems. Nonetheless, the election system is still operating in the twentieth century, not the twenty-first. The onset of social media, the internet, and the ability to synthesize information quickly argues for a system that utilizes twenty-first-century tools to make voting easier and less burdensome for voters.

Litigation has served to thwart some efforts to impose a national voter ID. Litigation, however, is lengthy and expensive. Also, the litigation option occurs only after the legislation has already been voted into reality. Challenges under state constitutions have been somewhat successful. Recent challenges using Section 2 of the Voting Rights Act have also reaped a small level of success. For voter ID, it is hard to put the genie back into the bottle. Courts recognized this phenomenon in Texas and other jurisdictions, where after several lower courts found voter ID intentionally discriminatory, the United States Supreme Court utilized the *Purcell* principle, which prohibited it from issuing an opinion shortly before an election.[46] In a lower court opinion in the Texas case, Judge Nelva Gonzales Ramos held that "[t]he Court holds that SB 14 creates an unconstitutional burden on the right to vote, has an impermissible discriminatory effect against Hispanics and African-Americans, and was imposed with an unconstitutional discriminatory purpose . . . [and] holds that SB 14 constitutes an unconstitutional poll tax."[47] But the victory was short-lived. The United States Court of Appeals for the Fifth Circuit, one of the most conservative courts in the country, overruled *Ramos* five days later, reinstating Texas's voter ID law for the 2014 election. The Supreme Court reaffirmed the appeals court ruling on October 18, 2014, less than three weeks before the midterm election. It was the first time since 1982 that the Court had approved a voting law that had been deemed intentionally discriminatory by a trial court.[48]

In this way, the Court ignored the fundamental right to vote and the impact on communities of color, to the advantage of states that have historically been known to implement voting changes that disadvantaged voters.

As I have previously maintained, what is needed are Voter Impact Statements that would adopt some of the strengths of Section 5, such as providing notice to citizens regarding voting changes, requiring a period of review and comment, and placing the burden on the jurisdiction to demonstrate that it engaged in a thorough review of how the change would impact its constituency, including racial, economic, and geographic studies. With a Voter Impact Statement approach, prior to implementing a new voter ID law, the jurisdiction would have to establish the extent of fraud underlying the proposal and how the legislation would combat fraud without impinging on voters' rights or access to the polls. Under this approach, legislators would be forced to consider the disparities in the number of persons with driver's licenses and other government-issued IDs and the costs involved. This squarely places the burden on the state and local jurisdictions, not on the voters. These measures compel lawmakers to substantiate spurious claims of voter fraud, requiring a thorough analysis of the impact of such laws on the electorate.[49]

Indeed, unfounded claims are made from the highest position in the country. In campaign speeches and tweets, Donald Trump, without any evidence or justification, suggested that the election process was "rigged" and warned that people would vote multiple times.[50] What Mr. Trump neglected to share is that courts, scholars, and studies have found that while voter fraud occurs, it is virtually nonexistent.[51] Indeed, the noted scholar and expert Lorraine C. Minnite found,

> There is a long history in America of elites using voter fraud allegations to restrict and shape the electorate. In the late nineteenth century when newly freed black Americans were swept into electoral politics, and where blacks were the majority of the electorate, it was the Democrats who were threatened by a loss of power, and it was the Democratic party that erected new rules said to be necessary to respond to alleged fraud by black voters. Today, the success of voter registration drives among minorities and low income people in recent years threatens to expand the base of the Democratic party and tip the balance of power away from the

Republicans. Consequently, the use of baseless voter fraud allegations for partisan advantage has become the exclusive domain of Republican party activists.[52]

Moreover, comments that fraud or rigging exists create an environment of distrust. The rigging happens with the number of laws passed, like voter ID, that make voting harder and the inability to combat suppressive measures on the federal and state levels. The recent decisions demonstrate the need for federal intervention and oversight in the area of voting to protect against discrimination.

KEY VOTER ID STATS

11 percent of Americans, approximately twenty-one million people, lack a government-issued photo ID, that is, a driver's license, passport, or military ID, including

- 25 percent of African Americans;
- 16 percent of Latinxs; and
- 8 percent of white voters.

States with restrictive ID laws include Alabama, Indiana, Kansas, Mississippi, New Hampshire, North Carolina, North Dakota, Rhode Island, South Carolina, Tennessee, and Virginia.

Courts struck down the voter ID laws in Texas and Wisconsin:

- The United States Fifth Circuit Court of Appeals found Texas's voter ID law intentionally discriminatory; more than 600,000 registered voters, predominantly African American and Latinx voters, did not have a government-issued identification.
- Wisconsin's voter ID law had the potential to block more than 300,000 persons from casting ballots; the court granted a preliminary injunction and would allow voters to present an affidavit instead of a photo ID.
- In another Wisconsin voter ID case, *One Wisconsin Institute v. Thomsen* (198 F.Supp. 3d 896, 903 (W.D. Wis. 2016)), the court stated, "The

evidence in this case casts doubt on the notion that voter ID laws fos-
ter integrity and confidence. The Wisconsin experience demonstrates
that a preoccupation with mostly phantom election fraud leads to
real incidents of disenfranchisement, which undermine rather than
enhance confidence in elections, particularly in minority communities. To put it bluntly, Wisconsin's strict version of voter ID law is a
cure worse than the disease."

- The United States Fourth Circuit Court of Appeals ruled that North
Carolina's restrictive voter ID and elimination of same-day registration and early voting was done with the intent to disenfranchise
minority voters.

Voter ID Myths

Myth 1: Voter ID Laws Do Not Affect Turnout

In 2012, the Government Accountability Office found that voter ID laws
contributed to lower voter turnout among minorities, young people,
and poor people in the 2012 elections in Kansas and Tennessee. Fourteen states had higher turnout compared with the 2010 midterms. All
featured highly competitive governor's races or figured in the battle for
Senate control, which brought a deluge of outside spending on TV ads
and intense news coverage. The states included Louisiana, Wisconsin,
Kentucky, North Carolina, Florida, and Kansas.[53]

Myth 2: Voter ID Is Necessary to Prevent Voter Fraud

In North Carolina, according to the State Board of Elections data, over
the past ten years, in-person voter impersonation has accounted for fewer
than one in 100,000 votes cast. An expert in *NAACP v. McCrory* found,

> Between 2000 and 2014, the North Carolina State Board of Elections re-
> ferred just two cases of voter impersonation to county district attorneys

for prosecution. Over the same period, there were no federal indictments for voter impersonation in North Carolina. More than 35 million votes (35,134,262) were cast in the 16 primary and federal elections alone between 2000 and 2014 in North Carolina. If we count the two referrals as cases of voter impersonation, the rate of voter impersonation fraud in these elections is .000005692449. . . . Given the lack of evidence substantiating a problem of voter fraud, stringent photo identification requirements, including those in North Carolina, are not justified to reduce or prevent voter impersonation and other forms of voter fraud.[54]

News21, a student journalism project at Arizona State University, analyzed fraud cases from 2000 to 2012 and found that "while fraud has occurred, the rate is infinitesimal, and in-person voter impersonation on Election Day, which prompted 37 state legislatures to enact or consider tough voter ID laws, is virtually non-existent."[55]

Cycles of Change

We play the game. They write the rules. We win the game. They change the rules.
—Thomas N. Todd

While attending a required program as a student at Grambling State University, I heard attorney Thomas N. Todd (TNT) make this profound statement. He encouraged us to strive for greatness but cautioned that we were playing a game where we had to be nimble, smart, and strategic, because inevitably as we became better at winning, the rules would change. What is needed is the power to write the rules.

What should the person who is concerned about the proliferation of voter ID laws do in order to participate in dismantling the rabid rule changes? It is imperative that citizens concerned about voter ID continue to educate themselves on the changing voting laws. They must also join and communicate with advocacy groups that are engaged in protecting the right to vote. Citizens cannot impact the right to vote if they are not registered or if they do not reach out to friends and family who may be discouraged from voting. It is important to educate and organize around voter ID and other issues, but an action plan must be in place. Because of the rapid rule changes, we must stay alert and aware of proposed changes. Section 5 of the Voting Rights Act made this fairly easy with the requirement that jurisdictions alert the DOJ with any potential changes that affected the right to vote. However, this type of notification was only present in covered jurisdictions that were primarily in the South. With the elimination of this extremely helpful device, vigilance is necessary. Regular appearances at legislative hearings, checking the docket, and communicating with elected officials all work to replace what is missing from VRA.

The accounts from Ms. Currie and others serve as warnings about the rapid rule changes affecting voter ID. Voters have a level of confusion as to whether and what they are required to provide in order to cast ballots. The voter ID battle is not over, as we have seen in states like Texas, where a court can strike down the law but another higher court can allow it to go forward in the name of legislative and administrative efficiency.

My grandmother drove until she was ninety-six years old. She, however, does not have a birth certificate. She was not born on the land that was the plantation where her grandparents were slaves and her parents were essentially indentured servants and then sharecroppers. No record of her birth exists. Can you imagine if, after only being allowed to vote for the first time in her forties, she would be denied the opportunity to vote because of a lack of a birth certificate or driver's license? For many Americans, the reality is that the right to vote has been taken away from them because they lack a driver's license and/or the requisite documentation, like a birth certificate, to obtain a photo ID.

The voter ID laws that the courts have found intentionally discriminatory reminds my grandmother of a time when the path to the voting booth was blocked with laws and practices meant to stop blacks from voting. It reminds her of the grandfather clause and poll taxes of yesteryear. You could register, but if you did not have the piece of paper or the right answer or someone to vouch for you, then you would not get to vote. Today, in some states, if you do not have the right kind of ID, you do not get to vote. My grandmother moved to Kansas to live with relatives. In Kansas, without proof of citizenship or a birth certificate, she is not able to register and vote. Because my grandmother does not have a birth certificate, her fifty years of voting may have just come to an end.

Although we have seemingly reconciled ourselves as a country to the notion that voter ID is here to stay, the impact on citizens' ability to access the franchise cannot be discounted. This new-millennium device is just a new iteration of past tactics, and like its predecessors, it can take on different forms but have the same effect. As a country, we must ask if the constant rule changes benefit a functioning democratic system. If after we achieve some minor levels of success in expanding the franchise, the rules are inevitably changed to thwart that success, is that democracy? Without question, the 2008 election of Barack Obama prompted the 2010 Republican sweep and the restrictive voting laws that came with it.

At one symposium, lawyers spoke about how the fight was on the state level. Many lauded the success in the Pennsylvania voter ID case, as well as the advances won through advocacy and policy change instead of the courts. But it was as though many had resigned themselves to the existence of voter ID in some form throughout the country. Still shaken from the shock of the *Shelby* decision and the lack of a congressional response, most advocates resigned themselves to working without the federal protection and oversight that Section 5 of the Voting Rights Act afforded. In doing so, they seemed to surrender to the partisan and punitive plans of a distinct few, instead of allowing the majority the freedoms that they deserve. Nonetheless, many organizations continue to challenge the existence of restrictive voter ID and are working to change it. Success will certainly require a multilayered approach. Citizens, organizations, attorneys, legislatures, and courts must all participate in thwarting the rise of voter ID and other disenfranchising mechanisms.

Different century, same result. Needless to say, my grandmother has seen periods of great progress and regress. She has witnessed laws that impacted her ability to vote, much like today's strict voter ID laws. We win the challenge to voter ID laws, and the legislature has the ability to change the law once again, to something seemingly more heinous than before; or it can choose to develop laws that conform to the United States federal and state constitutions. It is important for voters of color to have opportunities to vote in person, without fear. With much diligence, advocates have won long, hard-fought battles in a few states. Nevertheless, they are battles; the war continues.

4

Voter Deception

I have always told you some version of the truth.
—*Something's Gotta Give*

Jefferson Riley, a metro Atlanta mayor, posted on his personal Face-book account, "Remember the voting days: Republicans vote on Tuesday, 11/8 and Democrats vote on Wednesday 11/9."[1] At Michigan State University, students found fliers "falsely claiming that students could vote for Democratic presidential candidate Hillary Clinton by posting 'Hillary' on Facebook and Twitter and hashtagging it '#PresidentialElection.'"[2] After winning the presidential election, Donald J. Trump announced to Republican lawmakers that millions of "illegals" cast ballots in the 2016 election, causing him to lose the popular vote.[3] These three statements are examples of the level of deception present in our democratic process. These kinds of statements are regularly ignored or minimized to the degree that many election officials consider it harmless banter. However, it is not. Indeed, these words and others like them cause voters to second-guess participating in the electoral process and ensure a loss of confidence in the very system that serves as the foundation of our republic.

This is voter deception, and it is worsening and placing our governmental system in jeopardy. The level of deception in the election process has evolved in a few short years, such that it now occurs at our nation's highest level. Moreover, we now find ourselves ensnared in targeted misinformation that causes voters to remove themselves from the electoral process.

Defining Deception

Merriam-Webster dictionary defines deception as "the act of causing someone to accept as true or valid what is false or invalid; something that deceives."[4] Voter deception involves the distribution of false information regarding the time, place, and manner of elections as well as voter eligibility.[5] Voter deception has accelerated in the age of the internet. The connection between deception and voting, however, has existed for centuries.

Today, we are faced with the enormous task of ensuring not only that the public exercises the appropriate level of civility and accuracy in the election process but also that public officials do. Traditionally, it has been what I call public deception that has manifested itself in false calls or fliers making false claims of noncitizens voting or threatening prosecution for unpaid child-support payments or traffic tickets. However, we now see political deception, that is, elected officials filling the atmosphere with untruths with a blatant disregard for the truth. This chapter examines traditional levels of deception and the new iterations of chicanery that allow falsehoods that threaten eligible voters' exercise of the franchise without consequence. Whether it is a flier that encourages Democrats (blacks) to vote on Wednesday when the actual election is held on Tuesday or a president who espouses the false notion that millions of persons voted illegally, it is all deception and has its roots in the worst type of political gamesmanship, which causes fear in those who should trust the electoral process. My mother used to say that a lie outruns the truth, meaning that it is harder to track down the source of a lie or to provide a correction to a lie. Moreover, a lie spreads so quickly that it is utterly impossible for the truth to stand. Notwithstanding the difficulty, the need remains and is even more pronounced to identify instances of verifiable voter deception and to chase down the lies in the hope that the truth may, in fact, overtake it.

A History of Lies and Violence

From emancipation to the election of the first African American president, the right to vote has been challenged, and deceivers continue to use misinformation and threats to control the electorate. In post-Reconstruction, former slaves were targeted, and Jim Crow laws were introduced and required voters to demonstrate extraordinary endurance to cast a ballot. Voter intimidation, which has a similar purpose as voter deception, became a primary tool in denying the franchise, serving as a surrogate for poll taxes, grandfather clauses, and literacy tests.

Too Afraid to Vote

In the post-Reconstruction era, violence was the tool of choice to ensure that newly enfranchised voters would fear participating in the political process.[6] A lesser-known event that framed the ability of the new citizens to participate in the democratic process occurred on Easter Sunday in 1873 in Colfax, Louisiana. This small city became the symbol for white supremacy and aggression. Colfax, like other small enclaves in the South after the passage of the Civil War Amendments, had more people of color than whites. The Union troops were in place in certain places throughout the South to protect newly freed persons from white terrorist organizations like the White Leagues and the Ku Klux Klan. With regard to Colfax,

> The election of 1872 produced rival claimants for the governorship, a situation paralleled in localities throughout the state. In Grant Parish, freedmen who feared Democrats would seize the government cordoned off the county seat of Colfax and began drilling and digging trenches under the command of black veterans and militia officers. They held the tiny town for three weeks; on Easter Sunday, whites armed with rifles and a small cannon overpowered the defenders, and an indiscriminant slaughter followed, including the massacre of some fifty blacks who laid down their

arms under a white flag of surrender. Two whites also died. The Colfax Massacre was the bloodiest single instance of racial carnage in the Reconstruction era.[7]

The number of victims of the massacre varies from two to three whites and 60 to 150 African Americans.[8]

The author Charles Lane has described the Colfax Massacre as "the day that freedom died."[9] He provides a thorough investigation into the many injustices that occurred before, during, and after the massacre. He writes that in August 1874, Louisiana Governor William Pitt Kellogg believed that the subsequent acquittals of the violent perpetrators "establish[ed] the principle that hereafter no white man could be punished for killing a negro." At that time, there were only 130 United States troops in Louisiana. Kellogg warned that unless the army came back soon, his government could fall. "'If Louisiana goes,' Kellogg wrote, 'Mississippi will inevitably follow and that end attained, all the results of the war so far as the colored people are concerned will be neutralized, all the reconstruction acts of Congress will be of no more value than so much waste paper and the colored people, though free in name, will practically be remitted back to servitude.'"[10] Unfortunately, Governor Kellogg was right.

A marker on the grounds of the former Colfax Courthouse reads,

Colfax Riot
On this site occurred the Colfax Riot in which three white men and 150 negroes were slain. This event on April 13, 1873, marked the end of carpet bag misrule in the South.[11]

Colfax, Louisiana, is located less than fifty miles from the Oakland Plantation where my maternal great-great-grandparents were enslaved, freed, and remained. The proximity of this atrocity was not limited to Grant Parish, where Colfax is located. White vigilante groups wreaked havoc on Republican elected officials and sympathizers. "After a siege by white vigilantes, the Republican government of Natchitoches Parish, which is next door to Grant Parish, resigned en masse on July 27. Five Negroes were lynched that same day in the town of Lafayette."[12]

Other Violence Related to Voting

Similarly, in 1898, in Wilmington, North Carolina, a multiracial, democratically elected government was overthrown. "White supremacists carefully planned the overthrow of a popularly elected government, banished prominent blacks and whites from the city, and killed scores of black citizens. At the state level, the Democrats broke up the interracial Populist-Republican alliance with an aggressive campaign of white supremacy and violent deployment of 'Red Shirts' that kept blacks away from the polls."[13] The "Red Shirts" and other terrorist organizations wielded a violent brand of white supremacy that took over the North Carolina state government and denied newly freed people the right to vote. The multiracial coalition that had formed after Reconstruction was dismantled, and the tyranny of terror reigned for almost a century in North Carolina and throughout the Southern states.

Not surprisingly, extremely violent events like those of Wilmington, North Carolina, Rosewood, Florida, and Oklahoma City, Oklahoma, along with the decades-long practice of lynching, convinced many, if not most, southern blacks to accept their banishment from the political sphere. Because of the strong force of white-supremacy politics, the interracial cooperation of late-nineteenth-century Wilmington, North Carolina, would not be seen again in the South for at least six decades.

WHITE SUPREMACIST GROUPS: RECONSTRUCTION PERIOD

Rifle Clubs: The clubs began years before joining the violent Red Shirt campaigns of 1876–77 and were focused on attempting to intimidate black voters.

Red Shirts: A paramilitary group that arose in 1875 in Mississippi and the Carolinas and operated as a "military arm of the Democratic Party" to restore white supremacy.

Ku Klux Klan: Organized in 1867, the Klan terrorized blacks and whites who supported "corrupt" Republicans. In 1870, North Carolina Governor William Holden called out the militia to stop the Klan and began what came to be known as the "Kirk-Holden War."

An explosion of violence accompanied the campaign for Mississippi's 1875 election, in which Red Shirts and Democratic rifle clubs, operating in the open and without disguise, threatened or shot enough Republicans to decide the election for the Democrats. Republican Governor Adelbert Ames asked President Ulysses S. Grant for federal troops to fight back; Grant initially refused, saying public opinion was "tired out" of the perpetual troubles in the South. Ames fled the state as the Democrats took over Mississippi. Moreover, the objects of the Klan were to banish the so-called carpetbaggers from the state, to restore the freed people to positions of servanthood under their former masters, and to regain control of the state government. The band of vigilantes carried weapons of war and used them to torture those who were known or believed to vote against white domination.

Near the site of the Colfax Massacre, my great-great-grandparents continued to toil on land where their parents were slaves. I can imagine that news of the terrorist acts that occurred in Colfax and in other areas in Louisiana and throughout the South led them to engage in self-preservation and to do as my grandmother mentioned—not attempt to vote—for fear that they could lose their lives. As they had only recently gained freedom, navigating the treacherous road to the right to vote was overwhelming, when living as a free person had just begun and with the authentic reality that your life could end if you cast a ballot. I can imagine that the terror that was allowed to reign in the state of Louisiana and throughout the South weighed heavily on them and other newly freed persons. The slight taste of freedom that they had and the resistance to change that they witnessed forced them to make a choice. Having escaped the horrors of slavery and only experiencing liberty for a short period of time, they would have been led by the white retaliation and violent measures to make decisions to determine how to live or to resist the tyranny and terror and participate in the political process. It was clear that the Colfax Massacre's message was that blacks would not be allowed to vote for reconstructive measures or Republicans. The threats of bodily harm intimidated black voters to the extent that my grandmother recalls that for the first half of the twentieth century, most blacks did not vote.

These horrid acts of intimidation thus caused voters to question and fear whether casting a ballot was worth losing one's life. The impact of the massacre, the threats of violence, and widespread lynchings sent explicit messages that it was not. These acts of violence persuaded voters of color that the right to vote, while contained in the Fifteenth Amendment, was not meant for the African Americans in the unjust Jim Crow era. Accordingly, the nexus between intimidation and the right to vote is related to deception. These kissing cousins have offspring that has as its mission to keep people of color from exercising the full levels of freedom provided in the United States Constitution. Fear of retaliation, incarceration, violence, and the end of life can all serve as viable and real impediments to the voting process—so much so that the lack of protection makes the act of voting unattainable.

Supreme Truth

In this age, everyone speaks his or her own truth. The United States Constitution sets the parameters for acceptable speech. The Supreme Court defines core speech protected under the First Amendment as "both the expression of a desire for political change and a discussion of the merits of the proposed change."[14] In limiting political speech, the legislative body "must . . . be prepared . . . to articulate and support its argument with a reasoned and substantial basis demonstrating the link between the regulation and the asserted governmental interest."[15] In fact, the Founders included the right to free speech to allow "the free discussion of governmental affairs."[16] The Supreme Court views free speech as "the essence of self-government."[17] The First Amendment of the United States Constitution protects political speech as the highest form of speech.[18] It has deemed money as speech, limiting the legislature's ability to regulate campaign contributions.[19] It has also found that corporations have First Amendment protections to give money to candidates as a form of protected speech.[20] The hope is that the free expression of ideas will allow the truth to prevail. The protection that the Court envisioned was a protection for the citizenry to speak truth to power. It was not envisioned as a protection for the powerful.[21] The Supreme Court accepts restrictions on political speech only if they "are content-neutral, are narrowly tailored to serve a significant government interest, and leave open ample alternative channels of communication."[22]

Likewise, the Supreme Court upholds actions involving political speech, including the right to criticize political officials, signage, signatures for petitions, campaign finance, and the ability to assemble peaceably.[23] Not all speech is protected, including some political speech, for example, false commercial speech,[24] electioneering within a certain distance of an entrance to a polling place on Election Day,[25] and destroying Selective Service certificates.[26] The Supreme Court has clearly stated, "That speech is used as a tool for political ends does not automatically bring it under the protective mantle of the Constitution. For the use of the known lie as a tool is at once at odds with the premises of democratic government and with the orderly manner in which economic, social, or political change is to be affected."[27] It has further stated that "the knowingly false statement and the false statement made with reckless disregard of the truth, do not enjoy constitutional protection."[28]

The difference between public deception and political deception is power. When the government uses its power to intimidate, threaten, or confuse citizens to impact their ability to participate in the electoral process, the result should subject political officials to particular consequences. If we genuinely believe that the right to vote is fundamental, then we should hold attempts to lessen its power as actionable, especially when those who are speaking have the power to block eligible voters' access to the ballot box.

Acts of Deception

During the civil rights movement, the need to discourage voters heightened. Deceivers focused their attention on voter registration and preventing black citizens from getting to the polls. Dr. King explained that all kinds of "conniving methods" were used to deceive and deny black voters. From the civil rights movement to this new millennium, deceivers continue to employ measures that they hope will limit the right to vote for voters of color and other vulnerable groups. Instead of death threats, more subtle devices are used to block voters' exercise of their right to vote.

Intimidating efforts were organized around registering voters and providing access to the electoral process. Although historical accounts of voter intimidation are often full of death threats and fear, today's intimidation and deception tend to exist in a less fatal form but continue to target communities of color. Threats of incarceration or deportation instead of death often accompany voter intimidation and deception efforts. For example, in 2006, in certain counties in Virginia with considerable minority populations, voters received automated calls misinforming them that they would be arrested if they tried to vote on Election Day and falsely reported that their polling places had changed. In the 2008 presidential election, the country also saw the proliferation of the use of the internet, in both political campaigns,[29] to advance political misinformation.[30] The government's inability to prosecute offenders for printed fliers or other traditional methods of conducting deceptive practices maximizes the possibility of propagating misinformation via the internet.[31] The resulting blow to public confidence discourages citizens from participating in the electoral process. Indeed, the 2016 election exploded with false election information. Without any federal oversight of social media, the practices of disseminating false information regarding the election process caused considerable damage to the confidence of the electoral bodies across the country.

While the political tool of deceiving voters has been used for centuries, surprisingly little has been done to defeat the onslaught of deceptive electioneering and propagandizing. The internet and social media are the primary tools for misinformation meant to convince targeted groups not to exercise the right to vote. The most harmful examples, such as incorrect information about voting days or voting methods, are trends that demonstrate the need for federal oversight and criminal accountability.

Other examples of deception follow.

Maryland 2010

On Election Day in 2010, while the voting polls remained open, more than 100,000 registered Democratic households in Maryland received robocalls stating, "Hello. I'm calling to let everyone know that Governor O'Malley and President Obama have been successful. Our goals have been met. The polls were correct, and we took it back. We're okay. Relax. Everything's fine. The only thing left is to watch it on TV tonight. Congratulations, and thank you."[32] The robocalls were authorized by Paul E. Schurick, the campaign manager for former governor Robert Ehrlich, and they were made to voters in the state's two largest African American–majority jurisdictions.

In one of the very few cases of a trial for deceptive practices, Schurick was prosecuted under Maryland election law, which prohibits a person from willfully and knowingly influencing or attempting to influence, through the use of fraud, a voter's decisions whether to go to the polls to cast a vote. A jury found Schurick guilty of trying to control elections through fraud and failing to identify the source of the call as required by law, and also found him guilty on two counts of conspiracy to commit those crimes. One court document that was admitted into evidence suggests that the robocalls were explicitly intended to "promote confusion, emotionalism, and frustration among

African American Democrats, focused in precincts where high concentrations of African Americans vote."[33]

Mississippi 2011

In 2011, a church pastor in Mississippi posted false information on his Facebook page that he "just heard a public service announcement" concerning a vote on a contested state constitutional amendment on personhood and conception. The message instructed those who intended to vote yes to vote on Tuesday (Election Day) and those who intended to vote no to vote on Wednesday.[34]

Wisconsin 2012

In June 2012, Wisconsin voted on the recall of its governor. Wisconsin voters received robocalls saying, "If you signed the recall petition, your job is done and you don't need to vote on Tuesday."[35] Governor Scott Walker's campaign denied any involvement with the calls. The source of the calls remains unknown.[36]

Maine 2016

Fliers with the headline "Bates Election Legal Advisory" were found at Bates College in Lewiston, Maine. The flier said, "If you choose to register and vote in Lewiston you MUST pay to change your driver's license to Lewiston, Maine within 30 days, pay to re-register any vehicle you have in Lewiston. This includes a Maine state vehicle inspection requirement. Usually hundreds of dollars in total."[37] Governor Paul LePage issued a statement regarding residency and voting on the day before the election that read, "Democrats for decades have encouraged college students from out of state to vote in Maine, even though there is no way to determine whether these college students also voted in their home states. Casting ballots in two different states is voter fraud, which is why Maine law requires anyone voting here to establish residency here. We welcome college students establishing residency in our great state, as long as they follow all laws that regulate voting, motor vehicles, and taxes. We cannot tolerate voter fraud in our state."[38]

Voters of color and students are the regular targets of voter deception and intimidation. These serve as examples of the more traditional type of deception that includes the dissemination of false information. When this misinformation comes from elected officials and has clear partisan implications, it quickly moves into the area of political deception. The threats included in the governor's response and the false statements contained in the initial flier undoubtedly raise voter deception and intimidation concerns. Yet these actions were not prosecuted. Unfortunately, federal laws do not consider deceptive statements as injurious to our democratic system and do not consider them worthy of federal prosecution.

Deception Protections

While voter intimidation began in earnest after Reconstruction, Congress did not pass any laws that penalized it until 1939, when it passed the Hatch Act.[39] Consequently, two federal statutes, 42 U.S.C. § 1971(b) and Section 11(b) of the VRA,[40] served as the primary means to combat voter intimidation. Congress also included some protections in the National Voter Registration Act but neglected to include criminal penalties. Neither of these provisions includes a private right of action. Moreover, the federal government has been reluctant to utilize the statutes, and when it has opted to use them, the results have been less than stellar.

Surprisingly, the United States does not have a federal law that punishes voter deception. It lacks a universal definition for voter deception. In the past, Congress attempted to define deceptive election practices in numerous pieces of legislation. The House of Representatives considered legislation regarding voter deception and intimidation in 2005, 2012, and 2018.[41] The 2012 version of the bill, entitled "Deceptive Practices and

Voter Intimidation Prevention Act," identified deceptive acts as when a person "knowingly deceive[s] another person regarding the time, place, or manner of an election . . . or the qualifications for or restrictions on voter eligibility for any such election, with the intent to prevent such person from exercising the right to vote in such election."[42] The 2018 version of the Act under the same name likewise included a knowledge and intent requirement.[43] Congress notes that deceptive and intimidating tactics deny the right to vote, are "designed to prevent members of racial, ethnic, and language minorities from exercising that right, [and] are an outgrowth of discriminatory history, including slavery."[44] The proposed language does include a private right to sue for deception that without this legislation does not exist in the federal courts. The nexus between race and the denial of a constitutional right endures through multiple generations.

The Senate, during this time, also considered its own legislation on deceptive practices in elections.[45] These proposed bills defined deception as "knowingly deceiv[ing] another person," which would only capture those persons who intended and actually deceived another person.[46] However, it would not capture those who attempted to mislead a voter. I think this is a critical distinction, particularly with the rise of deceptive practices using email or social media. For example, a blast email is sent to students at a university, and the mail appears to be from the dean of the school. The email falsely informs students that the elections have been postponed to Wednesday instead of Tuesday. Furthermore, the bill's language would make it cumbersome on law enforcement to identify persons who were actually deceived by the communication.

In addition, this language would only capture those persons making the communication and not the persons behind the overall strategy to provide deceptive information. Any person knowingly involved with communicating the false statements should be held to the same standard as the actual person conveying the information. Finally, these definitions only include an intent to prevent a person from exercising his or her right to vote. The descriptions should be expanded to include an intent to interfere with or impede a person's right to vote and not merely to prevent it. Otherwise, misleading communications that instruct voters to do something that creates obstacles to their ability to vote may not be included in this definition.

The Senate measures include far more prescriptive definitions of deceptive practices. However, what is lacking in these bills is a concise, broad definition of deceptive practices. Any description of deceptive election practices should include a broad definition of dissemination, false information, and an intention to prevent or the actual prevention of a person from voting.[47] With these parameters in mind, we can define voter deception as producing, communicating, or disseminating materially false information, or causing to disseminate such information, concerning the time, place, or manner of voting with the intent to mislead voters or to prevent or discourage voters from exercising their right to vote. In this millennium, Congress has presented perennial legislation on deceptive practices with very little to show for it. For the most part, these bills were introduced but were never seriously debated or considered to have a real chance to become law. Without legislation, the country continues to underestimate the need to thwart deceptive practices. Moreover, with the distinct possibility that Congress will not address voter deception and strengthen intimidation laws, we are left with state and federal laws that are underutilized and undervalued.

Federal Protections from Deception

When I served in the Department of Justice, it was understood that we served as the nation's litigator. We proudly represented and enforced the laws of the United States. In the past, the Department of Justice has served as the primary protector of the right to vote. However, the Department of Justice possesses a paltry number of tools in its arsenal to prevent voter deception and intimidation, such as 42 U.S.C. § 1971(b)[48] and Section 11(b) of the Voting Rights Act. The statutes' language provides the potential to prosecute against persons who interfere with the right to vote.[49] The NVRA includes a provision, 42 U.S.C. § 1972gg-10(1),[50] that prohibits the fraudulent and intimidating acts surrounding the voter registration process and includes imprisonment and monetary fines as punishment. These laws do not, however, include a private right of action for intimidation.

Threats of prosecution and deportation for committing the act of voting illustrate the types of intimidating actions that currently encompass voter intimidation. Often without a known perpetrator, the anonymity and ease with which persons can create false or misinformation are commonplace in the age of the internet and fast computers. The lack of tools to address this behavior demonstrates the United States' entrenched position that these acts are harmless. They are not.

It is not particularly necessary to create a distinction between deception and intimidation. However, deception is more focused on misinformation,[51] while intimidation is characterized by more aggressive actions. A broad definition of voter suppression is inclusive of voter intimidation and deceptive practices. The federal government agency responsible for enforcing voter intimidation defines voter suppression, generally, as seeking to decrease the number of eligible voters and, usually, to take the electoral power away from individuals or groups.[52] Unfortunately, no federal statute exists that provides criminal penalties for voter suppression. Likewise, few state laws exist that provide criminal penalties for voter suppression.[53]

The prevalence of public deception has unfortunately not led to investigations or prosecutions. The Department of Justice has prosecuted only a few voter intimidation cases. The most famous were brought against black voters, not on behalf of them, despite the widespread intimidation and deception that is targeted toward voters of color. However, the new category of deception that is promulgated by elected officials should receive attention, investigations, and charges that will silence the dispensation of information that is false and intimidating. When public officials issue threats regarding criminal penalties or deportations or musings regarding election results, democracy should have a filter to prohibit the harmful activity.

Some people might argue that the level of deception in which the Trump administration engages should receive protection for political speech. However, the Trump administration's political chicanery is undeserving of political speech protections. Ideally, the electorate would determine the veracity of the statements made in the process of running for election or during the political process. The infiltration of social media and bots disseminating false information that could sway an election is deserving of an investigation. Moreover, a political candidate or official who not only espouses falsehoods but has the power to execute the acts of incarceration or deportation indeed raises voter deception to another level. It cannot be the case that politicians are all-powerful in their pursuits of power and position. While political speech receives the highest level of protection, it should also hold the highest level of punishment when the speech harms. When an elected official deliberately uses speech to harm or incite, then it forfeits the constitutional protection afforded under the First Amendment of the United States Constitution. As I stated in a previous law review article, "Voter Deception," "This right to speak freely, however, should not include the right to speak falsely."[54] Further, the United States Constitution does not protect the right to lie. The need for robust protections remains.

Although most state voter intimidation statutes contain language similar to the federal laws prohibiting intimidation—for example, "It shall be unlawful . . . to intimidate, threaten, or coerce"[55]—the best-structured laws that would encompass deception do not limit the illegal actions to those containing threats. Consequently, deceptive communications are considered more for the lack of truthfulness than the threatening statements.

Political Deception

The Founding Fathers made it clear that the ability to criticize elected officials should remain protected in our federal constitution. Yet, while the Founders could foresee the need to challenge power, it is sensible to consider that the Founders did not believe that government officials would maintain the right to spread false information as a constitutionally protected practice. Indeed, political deception falls squarely under the category of voter deception and intimidation. Consider, for example, President Trump's deception of presidential proportions in proclaiming, "In addition to winning the Electoral College in a landslide, I won the popular vote if you deduct the millions of people who voted illegally."[56] On that same day, four hours later, he added, "Serious voter fraud in Virginia, New Hampshire, and California—so why isn't the media reporting on this? Serious bias—big problem!"[57] After his inauguration, the claims escalated. "I will be asking for a major investigation into VOTER FRAUD," he declared.[58]

Since the 2016 presidential election, survey respondents expressed a palpable level of fear associated with the government.[59] Trump's comments that more than three million persons voted wrongfully tends to suggest to citizens that their right to vote was compromised and creates fear that the democratic process does not operate correctly. Consequently, I would characterize his comments after the election as political deception. Moreover, the president's statements, tweets, and so on were made to deceive, threaten, and deter citizens from participating in the electoral process.

The definition of voter deception includes knowing and intentional dissemination of misleading (false) information. The idea that three million people voted illegally in the 2016 election is akin to misleading statements that evidence voter deception. It is an attempt to deceive the voters into believing that the election system is fatally flawed. Voter deception is similar to voter intimidation. The only distinguishing factor is that intimidation includes threats, force, or interference in the voting process that affects the voter's ability to participate in the electoral process.[60] Political deception calls into question elected officials' immunity for speaking falsely when cognizable harm to voters occurs, as in the relationship of Trump's statements, the power to impact policy decisions, and the ability of voters to participate. A presidential commission designated to investigate fabricated claims gathers sensitive information about voters, places voters in a state of democratic limbo, and epitomizes political deception. When deception meets power, political deception occurs.

Deception and Intimidation 2.0

The Trump administration has committed and continues to commit many acts of political deception and intimidation. Its anti-immigrant policies, such as the Muslim ban, attempting to cancel immigration policies like DACA,[61] and the irresponsible and misleading statements suggesting that more than three million persons voted illegally in the 2016 election were meant to deceive voters. The administration's actions were deceptive, created fear, and intimidated voters.

Although Donald Trump won the Electoral College, he lost the popular vote by approximately three million votes. Unfortunately, he believed that the only way that he could have lost the popular vote was through fraudulent activity. In reality, the claims of three million illegal votes were false. The Brennan Center conducted a national survey on the issue of noncitizen voting or "illegal votes" in the 2016 election. It found that across forty-two jurisdictions, election officials who oversaw the tabulation of 23.5 million votes in the 2016 general election referred only an estimated thirty incidents of suspected noncitizen voting for further investigation or prosecution. In other words, improper noncitizen votes accounted for 0.0001 percent of the 2016 votes in those jurisdictions.

Forty of the jurisdictions—all but two of the forty-two studied—reported no known incidents of noncitizen voting in 2016. In the ten counties with the largest populations of noncitizens in 2016, only one reported any instances of noncitizen voting, consisting of fewer than ten votes, and New York City, home to two of the counties, declined to provide any information. In California, Virginia, and New Hampshire—the states where Trump claimed that the problem of noncitizen voting was especially acute—no official identified an incident of noncitizen voting in 2016.[62] It is well researched and widely accepted that voter fraud does not exist or at best is very rare.

Nonetheless, months after taking office, Trump empowered a cadre of persons who had exhibited one common purpose, that is, to suppress the right to vote, to question the authenticity of the democratic process, and to deem the votes of black and brown voters suspicious. The tainted viewpoint of the commission caused many citizens to respond in fearful ways.

Unprecedented Deception

The Presidential Advisory Commission on Election Integrity, also known as the Pence-Kobach Commission, was established to investigate claims that millions of votes were cast illegally in the 2016 election. As an initial act, the vice chair, Kris Kobach, requested voter data from all fifty states. As a result, states witnessed significant increases in voters deregistering to vote in different parts of the country. The commission's actions caused voters to remove themselves from the voter rolls, due to fear that the commission had nefarious goals. After Kobach and the commission sent an inquiry letter to the fifty states asking for specific identifying information from state election officials, many refused. Moreover, many voters, in unprecedented numbers, requested that their names be removed from the voter rolls.

In Colorado, after the announcement of the Pence-Kobach Commission, election officials witnessed a spike in the number of deregistrations. In that state, in less than a month after state election officials received the letter from the Pence-Kobach Commission, "3,738 voters cast off their franchise. The state has slightly more than 3.7 million registered voters. Looking at the party breakdown, far more Democrats than Republicans un-registered—to the tune of 2,037 to 367. As for unaffiliated voters, 1,255 unregistered to vote."[63]

Likewise, in Arapahoe County, Elections Chair Matt Crane stated, "We have no reason or data to suggest that the voters who have withdrawn their voter registration were not eligible electors. . . . I think any comments to the contrary are irresponsible and only further undermine our citizens' confidence in how our elections are conducted. It is regrettable that the President's Commission has brought out the worst in political activists from all sides. Once again, when this happens, it is our citizens that feel the negative effect of this irresponsible, fact-starved dialogue."[64] Voters deregistered for several reasons, including privacy concerns.[65]

In the perennial battleground state of Florida, after the announcement of the Pence-Kobach letter requesting voter information, the state saw a 117 percent spike in requests to unregister, as compared to the same period the previous year. In a twenty-day period, 1,715 Florida voters removed themselves from the registration rolls.[66] Voting rights advocates saw the letter as an "attempt at voter intimidation and suppression."[67] The Osceola County supervisor of elections, Mary Jane Arrington, reported that her office received seventy-six cancellations in the 2017 period, compared to thirteen in 2016 and nine in 2015. She believed that voters were concerned about the commission: "It really upsets people that their phone numbers, their email address—they give it to us to communicate about voting or absentee ballots—(will) become public record. . . . That bothers them immensely. We tell the voters when they're (canceling registration) that we can't guarantee their information is not going to be sent. People are upset. They want to know what it's going to be used for. We can't answer those questions."[68] In yet another county in Florida, Manatee County, within the twenty-day period of the Pence-Kobach letter, 253 persons requested removal from the voter rolls, which compares to three in 2016 and twenty-two in 2015.

This type of self-purging was unheard of particularly in the African American community, which had fought for decades to enjoy the right to vote, only now to find it threatened. The Pence-Kobach Commission's rabid insistence that the election was fraudulent and that the system warranted investigating, coupled with the president's ludicrous assertions concerning his losing the popular vote, caused fearful responses across the country. The statements that the president made and the backgrounds of the commission members called into question the commission's legitimacy. The commission has little power but much influence. Moreover, the attorney general of the United States wields broad authority to influence and enforce perceived and proven inequities. The unprecedented measure of assembling a commission to investigate an election that the candidate won implies that every vote cast against that candidate was somehow suspicious.

The commission did accomplish one of its primary goals, that being the removal of voters from the voter rolls. The mere presence of a federal commission to investigate actions of voters in an election that the candidate won causes many persons to question the authenticity of the commission. In many minds, the commission's sole purpose was to deceive, intimidate, and harass eligible voters. It claimed to be dedicated to increasing and assessing voter integrity, but the type of information requested violated privacy rights and, more importantly, made citizens nervous.

When politicians wield their power to cause citizens to lose the right to vote due to fear and intimidation, this constitutes political deception. Voters are fearful that the fight to vote is becoming meaningless. In years past, citizens had to fight to register to vote. We have witnessed mechanisms like the poll tax and voter ID limiting the number of persons who can actually cast a ballot. Accordingly, the self-purging that occurred in response to the Pence-Kobach Commission was unprecedented, particularly among groups of people who have only enjoyed the right to vote for less than a century. Citizens and present and former government officials were fearful regarding the purpose of the commission and its intentions. Aside from the unprecedented number of self-removals from the voter rolls, some believed that the commission ultimately sought to use the information to purge eligible voters.

Vanita Gupta, the former head of the Civil Rights Division at the Department of Justice in the Obama administration, maintained that the Pence-Kobach Commission was an "enormous voter suppression campaign through voter purges."[69] She suggested that the government would use the data to create a flawed national database that imperfectly identifies voters suspected of double voting. Her fears are well founded. Voters of color are overrepresented in the databases that list possible double voters. The United States Census indicates that people of color have eighty-five of the one hundred most common last names.

The director of elections in Denver, Colorado, wrote that after the Election Integrity Commission, it experienced a 2,150 percent increase in voter withdrawals, a 1,833 percent increase in walk-in transactions, a 790 percent increase in emails from voters, and a 247 percent increase in phone calls.[70] Denver's director of elections provided samples of voter statements that she received:

> "I have concerns that my individually-identifiable information would be misused for illegitimate purposes. I sincerely hope that the Denver Elections Division does not support, or respond to, any such requests involving private information in the future." . . . "I am officially requesting that you DO NOT release my name to the federal government, in terms of my act of voting, or my voting record, or any information at all. Voting should remain a citizen's private duty, and there is no need to do this." "I'm afraid to withdraw my voter registration because some law or rule may change in the interim that won't allow me to register again."[71]

Clearly, voters had concerns that the Election Integrity Commission would violate their privacy and share their information.

It turns out that voters' concerns were well founded. Vice Chair Kobach not only sent letters to all fifty states but also made unfounded accusations that New Hampshire's same-day registration process led to massive voter fraud and also accused New Hampshire officials of committing voter fraud.[72] His assertions were astoundingly misleading and untrue. One could argue that they were meant to defraud voters from participating in the electoral process. At the time of Kobach's statement, as a matter of law, New Hampshire did not require state residency to vote. It only required that the person lived in the state, even temporarily, as students normally do. College students who were residents of other states but present and living in New Hampshire for college could legally vote in New Hampshire and were not required to obtain a New Hampshire driver's license or register their vehicle in New Hampshire.[73] Accordingly, Kobach disingenuously compared the number of driver's licenses with the number of registered voters in the state. Indeed, New Hampshire officials rebuked Kobach's assertions as unfounded.[74]

While not the bloody and deadly encounters of the past, the president wielded his power in a manner that caused fear and intimidated eligible citizens into not participating in the political process. Accordingly, the falsehoods that serve as the root and branches of the political deception must be removed and the electoral process freed from the pain and fear of political death.

Prohibiting Deception

The nature of voter suppression and the ability to document examples of voter deception reinforce the need to prohibit the act of diluting the votes of eligible voters under the Equal Protection Clause. While congressional legislation explicitly addressing voter deception does not exist, the Department of Justice has a history of deploying federal government employees to observe national elections through its federal observer program contained in Section 4 of the Voting Rights Act. As a young Justice Department attorney, I participated in many federal election observations. The most harrowing one involved a small southern town where the black mayoral candidate's son had been shot outside the white mayor's home. The air was definitely very tense upon my arrival, and the federal government's presence was needed because the level of trust to conduct free and fair elections within the community was very low. As observers, federal employees cannot interrupt or conduct elections. The task of the federal observer was to watch and record Election Day activities. Observers were not allowed to intervene if a voting machine went down or if there was some discriminatory action such as asking only Latinx citizens for ID. Calls would be made to the appropriate city, county, or state authorities to seek correction before the election was closed. This occurred at a time when the federal government was believed to be a force of fairness. Often, we were asked to observe elections where tensions between white and black communities were extremely high, and the mere presence of a federal entity seemed to assuage fears and increase confidence in the community.

The Department of Justice worked with communities to serve as a protector of the right to vote and to provide opportunities for all citizens to participate free from intimidation. The George W. Bush administration thought the focus should no longer rest on voting rights enforcement but on voter fraud prevention. Resources were diverted from investigations involving racial minorities who were victims of racial discrimination. Additionally, since the *Shelby* decision, the DOJ has determined that it no longer has the authority to observe in locations where it does not have a court order, severely limiting the reach of the DOJ and further crippling voter confidence. In a post-*Shelby* statement, the DOJ described the impact of the election monitoring program this way: "when trained individuals travel to different locations to watch the election process and collect evidence about how elections are being conducted, they have a unique ability to help deter wrongdoing, defuse tension, promote compliance with the law and bolster public confidence in the electoral process. *Shelby County* significantly impacted the department's ability to watch for problems while elections are taking place."[75]

Instances of deception intended to intimidate and frustrate voters occur at the highest levels of government and cause harm to communities and our country. Congress's inability or unwillingness to address these threats to our democracy serve as yet another demonstration of a segmented complicity in order to achieve political benefits to the detriment of the democracy. In introducing H.R.1 in the 115th Congress, the chair of the Judiciary Committee, Congressman Jerrold Nadler, noted the need to quell political deception on the presidential level, citing yet another misleading and unfounded tweet.[76] Furthermore, Chairman

Nadler proclaimed that the "For the People Act of 2019" would "end voter intimidation, the dissemination of deceptive voting information, and other voter suppression tactics, by prohibiting such activities and adding, or increasing, criminal penalties for violations."[77] This is an omnibus bill that seeks to transform the way that Americans participate in the democratic process. It almost instantaneously received backlash from Republican lawmakers who called it a "political power grab" by Democrats.[78]

Contrast Germany, however, as a country that imposed fines and actively removed inaccurate and "illegal content" when it passed the Network Enforcement Act. In reference to the problem that Germany's legislation was meant to address, "the White House National Security Adviser H.R. McMaster said . . . [Moscow's] attempts to undermine the West . . . include a 'sophisticated campaign of subversion and disinformation and propaganda that is going every day to break apart Europe and that pit political groups against each other . . . to sow dissension and conspiracy theories.'"[79] Moreover, German academics understand that fake news is an attempt at voter manipulation through deception.[80] Unfortunately, the For the People Act of 2019 may go the way of the perennial Deceptive Practices and Voter Intimidation Acts of the past.

The Truth, the Whole Truth, and Nothing but the Truth

The harrowing events of the past surrounding the act of voting illicit fear. Today's threats, false assertions, and political pontifications cause eligible citizens to retreat from participating in the democratic process, not from fear of bodily harm but from a sense that voting is a perfunctory exercise that confirms their powerlessness, especially when the anger and hatred spew from the most powerful seat in the country, if not the world. Unfortunately, those feelings are not assuaged by the nation's primary legal entity, the Department of Justice. As a country, the Republicans have deceived Americans in proclaiming that the possibility of fraud is rampant. This exercise began in earnest during George

W. Bush's administration. I served as a deputy chief in the United States Department of Justice's Civil Rights Division, Voting Section. During the first term of President Bush, the DOJ began to train the United States attorneys' offices on the potential for voter fraud. Traditionally, we provided training on the existence and investigation of violations of federal voting rights statutes—for example, voter intimidation. The DOJ had neglected to file any voter intimidation cases under the federal law, even in the face of egregious acts committed in communities of color.

The elections in 2000 and 2016 led many Americans to doubt the authenticity and accuracy of the election process. Moreover, disparaging statements made during the campaign have led many to believe that the federal government cannot be trusted to serve as an impartial arbiter of fact or truth. As such, voters should push for the ability to sue on deception claims. Currently, only the federal government has that authority. Accordingly, it has only brought a paltry number of claims based on voter intimidation, not on deceptive practices.

The slow demise of the Voting Rights Act and its enforcement began during the Bush administration. Much to the disappointment of communities of color, the community could not look to the federal government for protection from voter intimidation or enforcement of federal voting statutes. It can do less so in the current administration. The aggression and reversals of the Department of Justice exacerbate the feeling of distrust. The current president of the National Association of Colored People believes that reliance on the federal government is misplaced. President Derrick Johnson encourages us to consider empowering ourselves on the state and local levels, particularly in the face of the many hypocrisies and reversals in this administration.

This distrust is also a product of a cyclical pattern from the Hayes Act and the removal of the federal troops to ensure that laws were followed, to all hell breaking loose in communities across the South for almost a century before passage of the Voting Rights Act of 1965. Beginning with *Brown v. Board of Education* and the monumental work that Charles Hamilton Houston and Thurgood Marshall forged to achieve a level of equality, the federal courts appeared to be our friends, even if they were slow to act. Indeed, the passage of the Civil Rights Acts and the VRA led folks to believe that the federal government could be relied on to do the right thing. However, in the fifty years since the VRA, we have witnessed a deliberate and steady erosion of the right to vote.

Moreover, the ability to find solace in the federal government has become virtually nonexistent in a very short period of time. Indeed, in some ways, the federal government has become the perpetrator of actions against communities of color. Indeed, federal courts tend to express greater concern about the potential for voter-initiated fraud than about protecting voters against intimidation and deception.[81]

What happens when elected officials make knowingly false statements? Could this be considered voter deception? Arguably, if the false statements were meant to deny the right to vote, yes! We have reached a point in our history when truth has become an individual commodity. People espouse "their truth." This truth need not have any factual basis. Moreover, one can possess and believe alternate facts that support one's truth. Unfortunately, for those of us who do not live in an alternative universe, the truth is not relative. When we consider the relationship between the right to vote and the democratic process, there are indeed quantifiable truths that do not bend toward alternative facts. The United States Constitution serves as a boundary for access to the ballot; age, gender, or citizenship status do indeed bar certain people from the polling place. However, when those who are entrusted with political office speak untruths that deter the voting process, does it reach constitutional proportions? As a country, we need a threshold for truth. While political speech is protected, outright politically motivated untruths should receive some penalty in order to create confidence in speech. Unfortunately, the political marketplace has provided its constituents with spoiled products that lack any government oversight to ensure its quality. The Founders hoped that the populace would have the ability to determine the truth, the whole truth, and nothing but the truth. However, the prevalence of lies on social media, the internet, and other media creates a devastating blizzard of information that is not easily dissected for its truth. When elected officials speak an abundance of lies, they undermine the constitutional underpinnings of our republic. Protections do exist, but those protections were intended for the public citizen, not the public official.

The fight for truth and justice is very real. Americans receive an enormous amount of information with limited ability to determine its veracity. Most turn to "trusted sources" that align with their view of the world. This type of response exacerbates the divisions and politicization[82] and does not bring unity but fear. Much like the violence during post-Reconstruction, the powerful proclamations that this administration makes cause injury to the many Americans who seek to participate in the democratic process. An effort to strengthen protections is needed that includes increasing access to unbiased information, restoring the authority of the attorney general, and giving the power to the public instead of elected officials.

5

Voter Purges

I earned the right to vote. . . . Whether I use it or not is up
to my personal discretion. They don't take away my right to
buy a gun if I don't buy a gun.
—Larry Harmon, a purged Ohio voter

Once upon a time, the right to vote felt more secure. Once upon a time, when you registered to vote, you were registered without fear of removal. The need to reregister only occurred when you moved or got married. Nonetheless, in this age of voter conspiracy theories, voters are finding that the right to remain on the voter rolls, if you have not voted in several years, has become uncertain.

The method of removing ineligible voters from state-compiled registered voter lists is called voter purge. States have the authority under the Elections Clause in the United States Constitution to determine the eligibility of voters. Although state governments have passed legislation that causes specific individuals, such as those declared mentally incompetent, to be designated as ineligible voters, voter purge can also cause the removal or invalidation of eligible and legal voters from voter registration lists.

Since states have the authority to maintain the voter rolls, election officials remove voters under the auspices of voter integrity, that is, governmental attempts to ensure that the voter rolls are "purged" of dead, mentally incompetent and disenfranchised felon voters. More often than not, however, these purges result in the disproportionate removal of voters of color, often with many inaccuracies. Additionally, state, county, and local entities embark on the task of cleaning the voter rolls in a less-than-transparent process and in varied ways.

Consequently, the purge process has become a tool in the voter suppression arsenal. The method of maintaining the accuracy of the voter rolls has become a thing of kabuki theater, a magical act: now you're registered, now you're not. For example, in 2014, the state of Georgia embarked on a voter purge. The storied hero of the civil rights movement Rev. Joseph Lowery, after viewing the list of common names in the African American community contained on the state's purge list, commented that it was a desperate political act and appeared to be "Jim Crow all over again."[1]

Purges in the Past

During a short period in US history, after the passage of the Civil War Amendments, we witnessed newly enfranchised citizens voting and electing representatives to local, state, and federal offices.[2] Voter participation, turnout, and involvement continued in great levels until it stopped. As mentioned in previous chapters, southern whites were so intimidated and threatened by the newfound independence of the former slaves that they established yet another compromise and removed the federal protections in the South that made new citizens able to participate in the franchise.[3] Once the southern states and the federal government negotiated a deal that removed military protection, whites began eliminating blacks from elected positions in legal and illegal ways, calling this scourge "redemption."[4]

During this period of "redemption," whites used violence as the primary means of ensuring that blacks did not participate in the voting process. The term "purge" is a reference to this violence used to enforce other suppressive measures, and the purging of people of color during the period of redemption was a complete elimination of voters of color from the voter rolls. Here is a historical account of the use of purges:

In 1896, in Louisiana, there were 164,088 whites registered and 130,344 Negroes. In 1900, the first registration year after the state adopted a new constitution, there were 125,437 whites and 5,320 Negroes registered. By 1904, Negro registration had declined to 1,718, and white registration was 106,360. This represented a 96 percent decrease in Negro registration, and a four percent decrease in white. In Alabama, Mississippi and South Carolina disfranchisement began earlier. In 1883, in Alabama, there were only 3,742 registered Negroes out of the 140,000 formerly registered. In South Carolina, Negro registration decreased from 92,081 in 1876 to 2,823 in 1898. In Mississippi, the decrease was from 52,705 in 1876 to 3,573 in 1898. Systematic exclusion continued up through the present time. Between 1920 and 1930 about 10,000 Negroes voted in Georgia out of a potential Negro electorate of 369,511, and in Virginia, the Negro vote at any time in that decade was 12,000 to 18,000 out of a voting-age-or-over and literate Negro population of 248,347.[5]

The Jim Crow laws and violence effectively killed the right to vote for the newly enfranchised citizen. The right to vote was no longer a reality, and democracy, a government for the people and by the people, ceased to exist. It took almost a century before the descendants of the former slaves would overcome the many obstacles set before them prohibiting access to the ballot in a meaningful way. An inability to register and vote existed across the South. Fear and intimidation were the recipes that

TABLE 5.1. Voter Registration Rates, 1965 and 1988

	March 1965			November 1988		
	Black (%)	White (%)	Gap (%)	Black (%)	White (%)	Gap (%)
Alabama	19.3	69.2	49.9	68.4	75.0	6.6
Georgia	27.4	62.6	35.2	56.8	63.9	7.1
Louisiana	31.6	80.5	48.9	77.1	75.1	-2.0
Mississippi	6.7	69.9	63.2	74.2	80.5	6.3
North Carolina	46.8	96.8	50.0	58.2	65.6	7.4
South Carolina	37.3	75.7	38.4	56.7	61.8	5.1
Virginia	38.3	61.1	22.8	63.8	68.5	4.7

Adapted from BERNARD GROFMAN, LISA HANDLEY & RICHARD G. NIEMI, MINORITY REPRESENTATION AND THE QUEST FOR VOTING EQUALITY 23–24 (1992).

southern segregationists used to ensure that voters of color could not enjoy the taste of full citizenship.

Barriers to voter registration existed until the mid-1960s. The passage of the Voting Rights Act opened the floodgates on access to the ballots. Moreover, the use of federal registrars also provided voter registration opportunities. The impact of the VRA was incredible.

Purge Prohibitions

In spite of the overwhelming success of the Voting Rights Act, our democracy needed more to increase voter registration and participation. In 1993, Congress passed the National Voter Registration Act (NVRA), commonly referred to as the "Motor Voter Law."[6] The purpose of the NVRA was (1) to establish procedures that would increase the number of eligible citizens who register to vote in elections for federal office; (2) to make it possible for federal, state, and local governments to implement the NVRA in a manner that enhances the participation of eligible citizens as voters in elections for federal office; (3) to protect the integrity of the electoral process; and (4) to ensure that accurate and current voter registration rolls are maintained.[7]

In developing the law, Congress believed that notwithstanding the success of the VRA in increasing registration and the number of black elected officials, more was needed to ensure that all citizens could access the right to vote. Congress found that some states were doing better than others regarding voter registration and assembled best practices for the country to implement to increase voter registration and participation. It chose practices to expand and improve the ability of citizens to register instead of limiting opportunities. Accordingly, based on best practices, Congress mandated states to provide voter registration opportunities at, among other things, the Department of Motor Vehicles, public assistance agencies, and veterans facilities. It also required uniform registration procedures at federal agencies and a voter registration form that citizens could use to register via a mail-in application. Congress also included proper protocols, or list maintenance procedures, for removing voters from the voter rolls.

States must follow the federal regulations to ensure uniformity and nondiscriminatory list maintenance procedures. Section 8 of the NVRA requires states to maintain voter registration lists for federal elections. The act also requires that election officials notify voters that their applications were accepted or rejected and keep accurate and current voter registration lists, including purging those persons who have died, have moved, or meet the state's felon disenfranchisement requirements.[8] Before removing persons or performing list maintenance procedures, the NVRA requires list maintenance programs that are uniform, nondiscriminatory, and compliant with the Voting Rights Act. Purges cannot occur ninety days before a federal election. Additionally, states cannot remove voters for the sole reason that they did not vote in several prior elections. The NVRA requires that the jurisdiction place these inactive voters on an inactive list only after adhering to the NVRA's fail-safe provisions, which allow for removal of voters from registration lists if they have "been convicted of a disqualifying crime or adjudged mentally incapacitated," according to state law.[9]

Despite Congress's measured approach, states challenged the NVRA as an unfunded mandate. As a young staff attorney at the Department of Justice, I worked on NVRA enforcement cases and successfully defended Congress's authority to pass this next step in the enfranchisement story.[10] Courts across the country held that the NVRA was constitutional and paved the way for states to again provide broad access to the electoral process by removing voter registration barriers.

Even with the attempt to federalize list maintenance procedures, no uniform approach to voter purges exists. Advocacy groups have criticized the method in which jurisdictions purge registered voters, particularly the questionable manner in which persons previously convicted are removed.[11] Although the stated purpose of the NVRA is to increase voter registration and participation, the Department of Justice is under attack for underenforcing the voter registration aspect of the act and overenforcing the voter purge requirements.[12]

Notwithstanding the difficulty of registering to vote, in most states, it remains the first step in gaining access to the voting process. Once registered, a person stays on the list until he or she moves, dies, or in some states commits certain criminal acts. States have the authority to ensure that voter rolls are accurate. The state, however, must operate within specific parameters, such as not violating the United States Constitution, the Voting Rights Act, and the National Voter Registration Act.

Although registration increased shortly after passage of the NVRA, table 5.2 shows that for the states listed in table 5.1, the registration rate has remained stagnant for decades, which suggests that more attention should be paid to increasing voter registration instead of purging registered voters.

TABLE 5.2. Voter Registration Rates, 1992–2016

State	1992 (%)	1996 (%)	2000 (%)	2004 (%)	2008 (%)	2012 (%)	2016 (%)
Alabama	77.1	73.8	73.6	72.6	69.7	71.1	68.0
Georgia	62.0	66.1	61.1	62.3	65.9	66.4	64.1
Louisiana	77.0	73.4	75.4	73.6	75.7	75.2	70.6
Mississippi	79.3	71.6	72.2	72.5	75.3	82.8	78.3
North Carolina	68.7	68.5	66.1	68.7	71.6	72.9	68.1
South Carolina	67.0	68.2	68.0	73.1	72.0	70.5	69.0
Virginia	65.4	66.5	64.1	64.1	69.1	69.1	69.4

Adapted from US Census Bureau, *Table A. Registration for Total Voting-Age Population, Presidential Elections: 1992–2016*, accessed January 2019, https://www.census.gov.

The purge process has become an unchecked method of removing eligible voters for reasons other than those stated in a state's legislation, or for voter registration cleanup procedures. Importantly, the NVRA explicitly refers to the right to vote as fundamental.[13] Congress considered the right to vote so vital that it limited the circumstances in which the states could remove citizens from the voter registration lists. Those prohibitions included but were not limited to mental incompetency and felony conviction.[14] Further, the NVRA specifically cautioned elected officials not to remove citizens for not voting. Indeed, it warned that citizens "have an equal right not to vote, for whatever reason."[15] It also recognized that states applied purges disproportionately against minority voters.[16]

In short order, the NVRA was successful in increasing voter registration. In June 1997, the Federal Election Commission produced a report on the impact of the NVRA on voter registration. It found that nationwide in 1996, a total of 142,995,856 persons registered to vote, which at the time equaled 72.77 percent of the voting-age population, the "highest percentage of voter registration since reliable records were first available in 1960."[17] Registering to vote at the Department of Motor Vehicles has become commonplace. Additionally, other community locations, such as libraries, Veterans Affairs offices, and social service agencies provide voter registration opportunities at sites throughout each state. Unmistakably, the NVRA served as a step in the right direction of ensuring that the chance to register to vote was accessible to all citizens.

In 2002, after the *Bush v. Gore*[18] catastrophe, Congress once again attempted to provide guidance and assistance to the states to improve voter participation and confidence. It passed the Help America Vote Act[19] (HAVA) to provide resources for antiquated election systems and established the Election Assistance Commission as the clearinghouse for information on election systems. Congress used the HAVA as a means to provide clarity on list maintenance. It is the combination of list maintenance functions in the NVRA and the HAVA that stands at the pinnacle of yet another attempt to reduce the voter rolls and decrease the number of voters of color. While these were laws meant to encourage citizens to vote, the United States Supreme Court and legislatures across the country are using them to make it easier for people to lose the right to vote.

Politicizing Purges

When I joined the Department of Justice as a staff attorney after the passage of the NVRA, I had the assignment to defend it against claims that it was an unconstitutional unfunded mandate.[20] States across the country argued that the NVRA required them to spend funds that they did not have and that it was an unconstitutional congressional act. DOJ attorneys in the Civil Rights Division, Voting Section, argued that Congress had the authority under the Civil War Amendments and the Elections Clause to enact the NVRA. This litigation was consistent with the first wave of cases challenging the VRA's constitutionality, followed by attempts to strip away protections contained within the act.

Years later, as I served in the George W. Bush administration as a deputy chief in the Voting Section, the narrative of bloated voter rolls and the propensity for widespread voter fraud was presented as an Orwellian fact that supported plans for increased pressure on states to make suspect voter purges. We have, unfortunately, watched this narrative grow exponentially in its reach across the country. Moreover, jurisdictions have utilized these unsupported charges to advocate for stricter voter ID and proof of citizenship laws, among others. Accordingly, we have seen an extensive increase in the number of election-related legal cases. Before 2000, election-related cases averaged less than 100 per year. In the period from 2000 to 2016, the average number of cases has increased to more than 250 each year.[21]

The politicization that began in a previous administration has exponentially advanced in this present age. The attorney general of the United States serves as a chief enforcer of these and other federal voting rights statutes. For more than two decades, the Department of Justice consistently interpreted the "Failure to Vote Clause" in the NVRA as explicitly prohibiting a voter's not voting as a rationale for his or her removal from the voter rolls.[22] Attorney General Jeff Sessions then switched DOJ's position on whether the NVRA allowed removal for not voting and urged the Supreme Court to reverse the Sixth Circuit Court of Appeals and enable Ohio to remove voters from the rolls.[23] This change was consistent with other DOJ positions against increasing voter access and championing various voter removal strategies. Former DOJ managers filed an amicus brief that explained to the court the long-standing view that the NVRA protected not only the fundamental right to vote but also the right not to vote.[24] Ohio is no stranger to voting rights litigation. As a battleground state, it is often a focal point prior to federal elections. From litigation over the weight of the paper used for voter registration to purges, Ohio provides many cautionary tales on prohibiting eligible persons from exercising the right to vote.

Ohio's Purge Process

Ohio sends notifications to those persons who choose not to vote within a two-year period, as part of the state's supplemental process. As I explained in a previous work, "Under the Ohio supplemental process, registered voters who have not engaged in specified voter activity, including voting for two years, are categorized as inactive voters and are sent a notice by the Board of Elections. If a voter fails to respond to the notice, and does not vote for four years thereafter, the state of Ohio removes the voter from its rolls."[25] The notification is generally used to determine if persons have moved from their previous place of residence.

For example, Ohio resident and Navy veteran Larry Harmon decided not to vote in the 2012 presidential election. He had regularly voted in presidential elections before. However, when he chose not to vote in 2012, after voting in 2008, the state of Ohio initiated the removal process. Mr. Harmon had not moved. Actually, he had maintained the same residence for more than sixteen years. Mr. Harmon does not recall receiving a notice, nor did he return a notice. When he decided to vote against a ballot initiative seeking to legalize marijuana, he learned that the state of Ohio had removed him from the voter rolls. As his statement that introduces this chapter evinces, Mr. Harmon was aggrieved. The state of Ohio had taken his right to vote away from him because he did not use it frequently.[26] His statement is profound.

If the right to vote is important to our country, then why does it not receive the same level of protection as other fundamental rights? Hence, organizations like the A. Philip Randolph Institute challenged Ohio's plan to conduct widespread purges based on a failure to vote. With this newfound advocate of voter removal, the state of Ohio sharpened the scheme that allowed it to remove voters for inactivity.[27] Interestingly, Ohio election officials interpreted the NVRA in conjunction with the HAVA to allow the removal of voters for the failure to vote.

The United States Supreme Court weighed in on the voter purge procedures in *Husted v. A. Philip Randolph Institute*, which challenged Ohio's purge process. Specifically, Ohio purged voters for failing to vote. The Supreme Court agreed with the state that failure to vote could serve as a reason for removing voters but could not serve as the sole reason for removal. Predictably, the Court aligned itself with the Republican view of allowing states to eliminate voters for a myriad of reasons, including flawed notice procedures. The Randolph Institute challenge was doomed with Judge Samuel Alito's opening statement that "[i]t has been estimated that 24 million voter registrations in the United States—about one in eight—are either invalid or significantly inaccurate. And about 2.75 million people are said to be registered to vote in more than one State." This statement, unfortunately, served as a clear indication that the Supreme Court would focus on the arbitrary process that Ohio developed instead of the impact that the purge had on eligible voters. Other justices discussed the important aspects of the process. Justice Sonia Sotomayor, in her dissent, recognized that this case was an important discussion on systematic discrimination. She highlighted the historical use of purges as a voter suppression method, stating, "[T]he majority does more than just misconstrue the statutory text. It entirely ignores the history of voter suppression against which the NVRA was enacted and upholds a program that appears to further the real disenfranchisement of minority and low-income voters that Congress set out to eradicate."[28]

Justice Stephen Breyer, however, issued a dissent that stated very plainly that Ohio was implementing a discriminatory purge process.[29] He also juxtaposed the practical implications and results of the Ohio supplemental process and the purpose of the NVRA. He noted the vast disparities in the number of notices sent and those returned compared to the number of persons actually known to have moved, finding,

[I]n 2012 Ohio identified about 1.5 million registered voters—nearly 20% of its 8 million registered voters—as likely ineligible to remain on the federal voter roll because they changed their residences. Ohio then sent those 1.5 million registered voters subsection (d) "last chance" confirmation notices. In response to those 1.5 million notices, Ohio only received back about 60,000 return cards (or 4%) which said, in effect, "You are right, Ohio. I have, in fact, moved." Also, Ohio received back about 235,000 return cards which said, in effect, "You are wrong, Ohio, I have not moved." In the end, however, there were more than 1,000,000 notices—the vast majority of notices sent—to which Ohio received back no return card at all.[30]

Further, according to the state of Ohio, nationwide only 4 percent of Americans actually move outside of their county annually, and in 2014, around 59 percent of Ohio's registered voters failed to vote.[31] Despite evidence demonstrating the ineffectiveness of Ohio's removal process, the Court found that Ohio could use a flawed purge process.

Unfortunately, the Supreme Court provided an opportunity for states to engage in risky behavior, that is, the removal of eligible persons from the voter registration rolls for not voting and other spurious reasons. Much like after the *Shelby County v. Holder* decision,[32] after which states almost immediately began implementing laws meant to disenfranchise voters, here states were anxiously awaiting the Court's decision. In fact, since *Shelby*, the nation has seen an increase in the number of purges, particularly in jurisdictions once covered under Section 5 of the Voting Rights Act.[33] According to a Brennan Center report, since *Shelby*, in the period of 2014 to 2016, nearly sixteen million voters have been removed from the voter rolls.[34] This represents a four-million-person increase, or 33 percent, when compared to 2006 to 2008. This increase exceeds the increase in registered voters and total population.[35] In Georgia, another state that used the failure to vote as a trigger for removing eligible citizens, approximately 750,000 more names were removed between 2012 and 2016 than between 2008 and 2012.[36] In Texas, more than 350,000 registrants were removed between 2012 and 2014, and in Virginia, approximately 380,000 were removed between 2012 and 2016.[37]

The Problem with Purges

Flawed purge procedures impact real voters. We have witnessed problematic purges throughout this millennium. Prior to the 2000 election, Florida Secretary of State Katherine Harris and Governor Jeb Bush hired Database Technologies to purge voters whose names matched or were similar to those of ex-felons. The result was the removal of 82,389 voters from the rolls. An investigation by Leon County Elections Supervisor Ion Sancho revealed that 95 percent of those who were purged in his county were, in fact, legally entitled to vote. Greg Palast of the BBC found that more than half of those who were wrongly purged were African Americans, even though African Americans represent only about 11 percent of the electorate, and that the purge list contained almost no Hispanics, notwithstanding Florida's sizable Hispanic population.[38]

In the Florida purge of 2000, "conservative estimates place the number of wrongfully purged voters close to 12,000": the purge "was generated in part by wrong matching criteria. Florida registrants were purged from the rolls in part if 80 percent of the letters of their last names were the same as those of persons with criminal convictions."[39].

In 2004, Florida planned to remove 48,000 "suspected felons" from its voter rolls. Many of those identified were, in fact, eligible to vote.[40] The flawed process generated a list of 22,000 African Americans to be purged but only sixty-one voters with Hispanic surnames, notwithstanding Florida's sizable Hispanic population. Importantly, the purge list overrepresented African Americans and mistakenly included thousands who had had their voting rights restored under Florida law.[41] Under pressure from voting rights groups, Florida ordered officials to stop using the purge list.[42] In 2006, the Kentucky State Board of Elections attempted to match names on its registration database against lists of voters in Tennessee and South Carolina and purged 8,000 voters as a result of the match—without notifying the voters and in violation of specific provisions of federal law.[43] In 2007, Louisiana election officials removed 21,000 persons, mostly African Americans, from the voter registration rolls of areas most devastated by Hurricane Katrina.[44] A voter could avoid removal only with proof that the registration was canceled in the other state. Documentation, however, would not be available to voters who never actually registered anywhere else.[45]

A report on voter roll purges includes an Ohio case study that says 416,744 registrants (5.3 percent of total registrants) were purged in 2006.[46] Similarly, the same report on voter roll purges includes a Washington State case study that says, "Between the close of registration for the November 2004 federal elections and the close of registration for the November 2006 federal elections, Washington deleted 503,151 registrants (15.4% of total registrants) from the state voter rolls."[47] In Georgia, college senior Kylla Berry received a letter from election officials challenging her status as an American citizen even though she was born in Boston, Massachusetts. Berry was informed that the election office "received notification from the state of Georgia indicating that [she was] not a citizen of the United States and therefore, not eligible to vote."[48] Berry was forced to file a provisional ballot. "It is still up to the county officials whether [her] ballot would actually count."[49] However, she did not have much confidence that it would be counted.

Further, reports have found that jurisdictions that were previously subject to Section 5 preclearance have engaged in more purges since the *Shelby* decision.[50] In 2008, some states were removing twice as many voters as they added,[51] and they were doing so within ninety days of a federal election.[52] Under federal law, election officials are supposed to use the Social Security database to check a registration application only as a last resort, if no record of the applicant is found on state databases, like those for driver's licenses or identification cards. The requirement exists because using the federal database is less reliable than the state lists and is more likely to incorrectly flag applications as invalid. Many state officials seem to be using the Social Security lists first. Officials of the Social Security Administration, presented with those numbers, said they were far too high to represent only cases in which names were not in state databases. They said the data seem to represent a violation of federal law and the contract that the states signed with the agency to use the database.

The United States lacks uniformity in conducting list maintenance. Some of the problems in the past US election occurred because of lack of uniform and transparent laws guiding elections at the national level and because the United States needs to make improvements in its election procedures and requirements.[53] As prior to the passage of the VRA, states have the autonomy to create voter purge procedures without the benefit of federal oversight or review. Purge proponents argue that they are needed to prevent voter fraud. Critics argue that the proclamations of vote fraud are a pretext for a broader agenda to disenfranchise Americans and "rig elections."[54] Others argue that the reason for elections is to "produce winners, decide who forms governments, and make the determination of winners and governments legitimate."[55]

Although the widespread removal of voters of color pales in comparison to the almost total elimination of black votes in the 1890s and the beginning of the twentieth century, voter-targeted fraud often presents a direct threat to the constitutional rights of American citizens, threatening not only their fundamental right to vote but also their First Amendment rights to political speech. Unfortunately, voter purges have been used as tools to ensure that fewer voters of color have the opportunity to participate. In 2000 in Florida, a high percentage of those on the list were African American. It is a common belief that the wrongful purge was instrumental in giving George W. Bush the US presidency. Martin Luther King III, the son of the slain civil rights leader, has argued that these methods were used with the sole purpose of tricking voters, saying, "I hate to characterize it as a trick [but] it really is. It really is about trying to control who can and cannot vote." Moreover, he lamented, "We purport to be the greatest in the world. But yet, in 2014, we are tying people's hands and keep—trying to keep them from voting? We should be making it easier."[56]

Critics have described the voter purges in Florida during the 2000 election as "wildly inaccurate voter purge lists that mistakenly identified 8,000 Floridians as felons thus ineligible to vote and that listed 2,300 felons, even though the state had restored their civil rights."[57] Moreover, in 2004, Florida once again embarked on an effort to cleanse the voter rolls, and it questioned the eligibility of more than 40,000 registered voters on the basis of felon status. Florida withdrew the list after advocacy groups and the media revealed that the list included persons who were eligible to vote and a disproportionate number of African Americans (22,000), while exempting large numbers of Hispanics.[58] The party affiliation of the alleged ineligible voters did not go unnoticed; the Republican administration sought to disenfranchise thousands of African American and likely Democratic voters once again.[59] Voters who want to challenge this method of purging bear the burden of proving that they have not been convicted of a disenfranchising offense.

Election officials routinely conduct voter purges. However, federal laws determine when the removals should not take place, for example, ninety days before an election. Additionally, who might get purged has limitations. The most significant issues when it comes to voter purges is accuracy. Unfortunately, Republican officials have been less concerned with accuracy and more concerned with removal.

In 2014, Vermillion County, Indiana, removed approximately four in ten registrants. The county clerk, Florinda Pruitt, asserted that the majority of the almost twelve hundred voters were removed due to death or change of address. She stated, "We really want people to vote. We really work at it. But if you don't want to vote, don't register. Don't clog our system."[60]

In Sparta, Georgia, population thirteen hundred, the majority-white Hancock County Board of Elections used public officials to determine whether black voters should be removed from the voter rolls. In a throwback to the post-Reconstruction voucher system, in which whites had to vouch for a black voter's character in order to allow him or her to vote, the board "sent teams block by block through Sparta looking for residents to vouch that their neighbors still lived where they were registered to vote."[61] On the basis of the "say-so" of neighbors, almost two hundred persons were slated for removal. One of the people listed for removal and his brother appeared in the removal hearing and observed the following: "They called name by name, and if they didn't answer, they'd just cross them off the list. . . . They got a kind of excitement out of what they were doing, by taking people's names off the list."[62] A majority of the purged voters were black.

Joe Helle, an army veteran and Ohio voter who was purged from the rolls for inactivity, stated,

> I was welcomed home to Ohio only to find out I had been purged from the voter rolls. I returned home from the military in 2011 and went to vote on a school levy measure in August. They couldn't find my name on the voting rolls, so I was forced to cast a provisional ballot. Thinking it was a one-time error, I went back to vote again in November 2011 and was barred from casting a ballot. The poll worker told me that they couldn't help me and I would have to go to the board of elections to fix the issue. . . . I joined the military to fight for our rights as Americans, and I don't think the right to vote should be taken away in these mass purges of the voter rolls. I learned that voter suppression can happen to anyone when I was blocked from casting a ballot, and I don't want one more eligible voter to be disenfranchised because of extreme voter purges.[63]

Jurisdictions primarily use two sources for list maintenance procedure: Crosscheck and Electronic Registration Information Center (ERIC). Crosscheck—which is used in Kansas and was developed by Kris Kobach, the attorney general of the state at the time—has been found to be less than reliable. The Advancement Project developed a comparison of the two systems, describing Crosscheck as a "state to state matching program that compares a state's voter list to lists from other participating states for the purpose of identifying 'possible double votes,' meaning, voters who allegedly cast ballots, in multiple states during the same election."[64] ERIC also matches data that compares voter lists from participating states. "Additionally, ERIC compares a state's voter list against a state's own databases and other databases. ERIC's purpose is to 'improve a state's ability to identify inaccurate and out-of-date voter registration records, as well as eligible, but unregistered residents.'"[65] Kobach's Crosscheck program is noted for its errors. Reports have demonstrated the rampant inaccuracies and racially skewed results.[66]

Also, Greg Palast has concluded that people of color are disproportionately "at risk of having their names scrubbed from the voter rolls [by Crosscheck]."[67] Palast's review of data from various states indicates that Crosscheck results are "heavily weighted with names such as Jackson, Garcia, Patel, and Kim."[68] He asserts that Crosscheck has put one in seven African American voters, one in eight Asian American voters, one in eight Latinx voters, and one in eleven white voters at risk of being unlawfully purged.[69]

Protecting from Purges

What protections exist for voters to remain on the voter rolls? The NVRA contains federal standards for the purge process and requires that states notify those persons who are removed. Voter access advocates should petition election officials to ensure that removed persons are notified and informed of the process of how to return to the active voter list. Additionally, the NVRA includes a private right of action. Thus, private citizens can bring claims under the NVRA. Although the Supreme Court has now authorized removal for reasons that the statute did not intend, because of the racially discriminatory impact of purges, advocacy groups should consider challenging voter purges that are violative of the discrimination prohibition in the NVRA and Section 2 of the Voting Rights Act.[70]

While the NVRA prescribes federal standards, states are encouraged to develop even more protections than the federal government provides. States that have constitutions with an affirmative right to vote may find it harder to remove citizens for not voting. In fact, every state except Arizona has an explicit and affirmative right to vote in its constitution.[71] The enumerated right to vote in state constitutions could serve as a basis to contest the removal of eligible persons from the voter rolls.

Purge proponents have wholeheartedly accepted the false notion that it is better to utilize a process that is proven to disenfranchise eligible voters than to invest in a system that ensures that the only voters removed from voter rolls are those persons who are deceased or one of a few exceptions for removal. Notwithstanding these obstacles, we have weapons to contest these formidable aggressions toward the right to vote.

Providing Notice

In the voter purge context, election officials should implement a standard due processe procedure that provides notice to voters and an opportunity for them to be heard prior to their removal. Jurisdictions could also disclose other methods they considered in determining the timing of conducting a voter purge and how to notify affected persons, as well as their coordination with other state agencies such as the Department of Motor Vehicles and Department of Vital Statistics.[72] Alternatives in the voter purge context would include proposals to gather the information and ensure that persons received the requisite notice prior to removal.

The Department of Justice could also serve as a barrier to inaccurate purges. Critics of voter purges suggest that instead of carrying out the primary function of the NVRA—increasing voter registration and participation—the Department of Justice's Voting Section is concentrating its NVRA enforcement priority on pressuring jurisdictions to trim the voter rolls.

Ensuring Accuracy

Advocacy groups have attempted to mandate accuracy prior to voters' removal from voter rolls. However, these efforts have generally been unsuccessful without an accompanying lawsuit. Advocates have asked that the data that jurisdictions use is complete and accurate and in compliance with the NVRA and VRA. Moreover, they routinely ask for uniform, nondiscriminatory list maintenance procedures and protections for privacy and from those who are seeking to arbitrarily challenge voters. State election officials must check for accuracy and potential errors before targeting a voter for removal.

Eliminating Reregistration

The decision in the *Husted* case now allows states to require removed citizens to reregister once they are alerted that their names were taken off the voter rolls. The burden of reregistering has placed an inordinate responsibility on voters for inaccurate removals. In the past, reregistrations have been used as a disenfranchising mechanism. For example, supposedly guided by state redistricting requirements, election officials in many Mississippi counties decreed that all registered voters, including those who had not yet voted, had to reregister in order to be able to participate in the fall elections—a decision that affected over 40 percent of Mississippi's registered black voters.[73] Indeed, for many African Americans, the courthouse served as a reminder of a time when blacks were not allowed to register to vote. These memories prevented many African Americans from undergoing the process of reregistering.

The requirement to reregister is problematic within African American culture, considering the many obstacles that African Americans had to overcome in order to have the right to vote. In some jurisdictions, federal employees were designated as federal registrars to register African Americans due to white citizens' refusal to do so. Moreover, the many altercations at the courthouse remain fresh in the memories of African Americans. Consequently, the requirement of reregistration can serve as an impediment to progress.

Failure to Vote

Unfortunately, *Husted* will allow states to use failure to vote as the trigger to place voters on an inactive list, which prematurely makes them susceptible to a purge. Accordingly, voters who only vote in presidential elections or every four years could find that the state has removed them from the voter rolls, which would require them to reregister to participate in the electoral process. Accordingly, voters could find themselves reregistering because they have chosen not to vote in a midterm election. This creates a nightmare for election officials, who already have inaccuracies on their lists of voters. The constant removal and updating of voters could lead to duplicate entries, removal of eligible voters, and voter apathy. We already know that the harder states make the voting process, the lower the turnout.

Additionally, if voters do not know that they are on the voter rolls, they are less likely to participate or have confidence in the electoral process. A lack of voter confidence leads to voter apathy. Politicians would then get what many of them want, that is, a select few voters determining the outcomes of significant local, state, and federal elections.

We can only hope that as a consequence of widespread purging, voters become more active to prevent removal. If citizens are aware that they could be removed for not regularly casting a ballot, the threat of removal could compel them to vote in elections on a more regular basis. Essentially, *Husted* could create a means for compulsory voting. In other countries, such as Australia, citizens are penalized for not voting.[74] Indeed, one could consider removal as a penalty that citizens could seek to avoid by going to the polls. Same-day registration would allow citizens to register and vote on the same day. In most states, voters must register twenty or thirty days before an election in order to be eligible to vote. In fact, most states' voter registration laws have a more extended waiting period to vote than to buy a gun. Accordingly, we must heighten the right to vote to the fundamental status that it is accorded in the United States Constitution.

Shifting Burdens

Instead of burdening voters with the responsibility of ensuring that they remain on the voter rolls, the burden should shift to the state or other jurisdiction conducting the purge.[75] This shift could remedy the discriminatory purge procedures and increase the level of minority registration and participation. Jocelyn Benson argues that legislatures should not only adopt reforms of conventional purge systems that would permit them to survive strict scrutiny but also consider alternative methods of fraud prevention that would minimize infringement on the right to vote.[76] She maintains that the burden of maintaining updated voting rolls should fall on the state even if the state does not take an affirmative role in registering voters. Accordingly, state agencies should provide updated death records and changes of address to the registrars' offices. Moreover, it is important that the state implement a system that allows agencies to communicate changes in voter status. For example, the state could require that data on deaths and changes of addresses from the various agencies (including the US Post Office, motor vehicle departments, benefits offices, and bureaus of deaths and statistics) go to the registrars' office in the voter's former and present precincts, which would then cancel and transfer registrations.

Pressing toward the Mark

The Voter Education Project (VEP) testimony before the Civil Rights Oversight Subcommittee of the US House of Representatives summarized the feeling of isolation and frustration felt throughout the South:

> Black people have a sense of hopelessness because they feel they have nowhere to turn for justice. For one fleeting moment, in the sixties, blacks found encouragement and a sense of hope from the intervention of the federal government. Since those days, the weight of the federal government has not been felt in a meaningful way. Although hundreds of thousands of blacks still face registration difficulties and more serious difficulties in casting a meaningful vote, the federal government refuses to address itself to these needs. It is time for a public rededication of effort and commitment on the part of federal enforcement agencies to an affirmative program of enforcement.[77]

Although this statement was made shortly after the passage of the Voting Rights Act, the feeling that African Americans do not have a federal government that aggressively enforces civil rights is an unfortunate modern-day reality. Just as the Supreme Court is complicit in the removal of eligible registered voters, the DOJ also has a responsibility in the questionable process. The DOJ sent letters to jurisdictions encouraging them to "clean up" their voter rolls, which leads to more purges. Moreover, without Section 5, the necessary protections to vet the purge process no longer exist. The DOJ has aligned itself with those who are seeking to limit voter access. Actions such as those exhibited in Ohio and Georgia do not necessarily "clean" the registration lists. They remove large swaths of eligible voters from the voter lists, cause confusion, and encourage voter apathy. The DOJ's list maintenance threats to states, its lack of enforcement of civil rights statutes, and the removal of federal protections under *Shelby* could lead African Americans to have little hope. However, the continuing fight to advance the franchise should provide encouragement to a people who have remained steadfast and unmovable on their right to vote.

Voter Purges

Key Points

It has been estimated that 24 million voter registrations in the United States—about one in eight—are either invalid or significantly inaccurate. And about 2.75 million people are said to be registered to vote in more than one State.[78]
—Justice Alito, *Husted* majority opinion

[T]he majority does more than just misconstrue the statutory text. It entirely ignores the history of voter suppression against which the NVRA was enacted and upholds a program that appears to further the very disenfranchisement of minority and low-income voters that Congress set out to eradicate.[79]
—Justice Sotomayor, *Husted* dissenting opinion

The United States Supreme Court's decision in *Husted v. A. Philip Randolph Institute* epitomizes the battle between voter integrity and voter access. Registrars have a commitment to ensure the accuracy of the voter rolls. However, in an effort to achieve that end, many jurisdictions employ questionable and flawed mechanisms that disproportionately impact voters of color. Wide-scale voter purges have increased since the *Shelby* decision. Moreover, proponents of these types of removal programs have argued the necessity to prevent voter fraud. The author of *The Myth of Voter Fraud*, Lorraine Minnite, describes this as "a form of suppression in the guise of an integrity issue."[80]

Key Needs
- A National Voter Registration Act "to establish procedures that will increase the number of eligible citizens who register to vote in elections for Federal office; to make it possible for Federal, State, and local governments to implement [the NVRA] in a manner that enhances the participation of eligible citizens as voters in elections

for Federal office; to protect the integrity of the electoral process; and to ensure that accurate and current voter registration rolls are maintained."[81]

- In particular, any voting list maintenance must be uniform, nondiscriminatory, and in compliance with Sections 2 and 5 of the VRA.
- State election officials must check for accuracy and potential errors before targeting a voter for removal.
- Privacy for those who are identified for investigation must be protected to the fullest extent of the law.
- If a voter is improperly targeted, he or she must be fully reinstated, encouraged to vote, protected against challenges, and able to vote a regular (not provisional) ballot.

6

Felon Disenfranchisement

Citizenship is not a [right] that expires upon misbehavior.
—*Trop v. Dulles*

Race, gender, age, and criminal conviction as the basis for disenfranchisement are all vestiges of a white-supremacist movement that decided that only white males should enjoy the unfettered right to vote. This sentiment has lasted for centuries and had its origin in the founding of our country. One by one, these shackles of disenfranchisement have fallen off of the United States' democratic conscience. One prominent constraint that remains is today's felon disenfranchisement laws.

Felon disenfranchisement is the process of denying the right to vote to persons who have previously committed felonies. The state designates a penalty of losing the right to vote either temporarily or permanently. The types of disenfranchising crimes vary from state to state. Likewise, the time period for losing the right to vote—while incarcerated, on parole, or probation or a period of years after serving one's sentence—and the process of restoring the right to vote also vary from one state to another.

Consider the following adapted experience, which is exemplary of felon disenfranchisement laws across the country:

> At nineteen years old, Stephanie Stevens made the unfortunate decision of shoplifting from a grocery store in Baltimore, Maryland. She was unemployed and needed to provide food for her young child. The state of Maryland charged her with shoplifting. Stephanie's punishment consisted of ninety days in jail and a $2,500 fine. As a result of Stephanie's felony conviction, she also received the penalty of disen-

franchisement during her sentence and was unable to vote in the 2008 presidential election. In some other states, shoplifting does not disenfranchise persons. Once Stephanie completed her sentence, the state of Maryland restored her right to vote. A few years later, Stephanie was encouraged through community outreach to exercise her right to vote, and she voted in Maryland's 2014 gubernatorial election. Six years after her conviction, Stephanie was a far cry from her teenage self. She had gotten married, had another child, and worked as an assistant manager for a shipping company. She received a promotion and was relocated to her company's Tampa, Florida, office. After moving, Stephanie went to the Department of Motor Vehicles in Florida to register her car, obtain a new license, and register to vote. A few months later, Stephanie received a letter from the state of Florida that notified her that she was ineligible to register to vote because of her felony conviction from Maryland. Under Florida law, Stephanie was permanently disenfranchised due to her previous felony conviction. In order to regain the right to vote, Stephanie would have to petition the governor and appear before a clemency committee. The average wait for an interview was two years, and the rate of approval was abysmal. After six years, ninety days in jail, $2,500 paid in fines, and 945 miles, Stephanie was now receiving additional punishment for a crime for which she had fully paid her debt to society. She was now repaying her debt to society, again, and was denied the right to vote in the 2016 presidential election. By moving to Florida, she became one of the 1.54 million people that the state of Florida has disenfranchised.

Stephanie's experience, while illustrative, is rooted in the reality of felon disenfranchisement laws and its varied applicability from state to state. This system of disenfranchising citizens has been called a "crazy quilt" of laws. Indeed, these laws are only stitched together by their connection to previous discriminatory law and its modern-day impact. The craziness ensues in its severity and the continuation of the punishment, in some states, from crime to grave.

A History of Disenfranchisement

Felon disenfranchisement remains one of the oldest and most entrenched mechanisms to ensure that voters of color and African Americans in particular are barred from the ballot box. Voter ID is a relatively recent phenomenon, arriving on the scene in this millennium with clear connections to the past. However, felon disenfranchisement dates back to post-Reconstruction, when the stated intended purpose of the law was to stop newly enfranchised former slaves from voting. Just like the ghosts of Jim Crow, the effects of these laws continue to haunt the African American community. Indeed, today's felon disenfranchisement laws serve as a modern-day three-fifth compromise.

Founding Fathers and the First Disenfranchisement

From the outset of the drafting of the United States Constitution, African Americans were considered less than full citizens. Their status as slaves provided a conundrum for the new and struggling United States of America. During the 1787 Constitutional Convention, the Founding Fathers sought to address the large numbers of enslaved persons in the South and the need to apportion representation to the new government. This Congress decided three issues pertinent to the lives of slaves during the 1787 Convention:

1. Congress could not interfere with the slave trade for twenty years,[1] thus allowing states to import black bodies without federal intervention and as such providing states with the authority to determine whether slave trading would continue in each state during that time frame.
2. Congress also established Fugitive Slave Laws that allowed a slave owner to recapture an escaped slave located in another state.[2]
3. The three-fifths compromise was an agreement between the North and the Southern slaveholding states that was used for apportioning the members of Congress.

These constitutional compromises placed some notable Founders betwixt two opinions regarding slavery and the benefits they received from free labor. The primary drafter of the Declaration of Independence, Thomas Jefferson, and the first president of our country, George Washington, owned slaves. Neither of them advocated for the abolition of slavery, although they recognized that the United States' peculiar institution could one day destroy the young country. These political compromises reflected the observation of the Virginia Constitutional Convention delegate (and future US president) James Madison that "the States were divided into different interests, not by their . . . size . . . but principally from their having or not having slaves."[3] Thus, from the beginning, the black man's freedom was subordinate to the white man's independence. The idea that "all men were created equal" presented a fallacy from the start.

The three-fifths compromise provided the following: "Representatives and direct Taxes shall be apportioned among the several States which may be included within this Union, according to their respective Numbers, which shall be determined by adding to the whole Number of free Persons, including those bound to Service for a Term of Years, and excluding Indians not taxed, three fifths of all other Persons."[4]

Not surprisingly, the South wanted to count slaves for purposes of apportioning the members of Congress, because it provided an advantage to the region in controlling the federal government. The states agreed to count their enslaved persons for representation but refused to acknowledge their humanity in any way. Additionally, the South agreed to the compromise of counting an enslaved person as three-fifths of a person primarily because if slaves were counted equally, the slave owners would be taxed at a much higher rate. Therefore, the compromise allowed for a diminished count for apportionment and provided a discounted tax rate to those who were in the business of slavery. In 1793, the South had forty-seven Representatives due to the compromise. Without the compromise, it would have had thirty-three, almost a third fewer representatives. Accordingly, the South was overrepresented in the presidency, the House of Representatives, and the Senate. By the 1800s, abolitionists noted that the compromise allowed the South and slaveholders to "dominate" the new government.[5]

The compromise was clearly a win for the Founding Fathers and a complete loss for persons living as slaves in the home of the free and the disenfranchised. The idea that states knew best led the Founding Fathers to determine that the slave issue was better left to the individual states rather than the new federal Congress. Accordingly, with this compromise, the Founding Fathers established that black bodies should only count for three-fifths of white persons. The permanence of second-class citizenship, as reflected in the three-fifths compromise, served as a reminder of the impact of racial dominance and the distribution of power in the US system.

From the Founders to the Fourteenth Amendment

The impact of the three-fifths compromise was dramatic. It allowed the South to control the new Congress for most of its first century. From the 1787 Constitution to the passage of the Fourteenth Amendment, the desire to keep black citizens out of the ballot box persisted. As the Founders predicted, the ability to own slaves served as the basis for the demise of the Union. While Abraham Lincoln is commonly referred to as the president who freed the slaves, his only intention was to save the country from division. He stated, "If I could save the Union without freeing any slave, I would do it: if I could save it by freeing all the slaves, I would do it; and if I could do it by freeing some and leaving others alone, I would also do that. What I do about slavery and the colored race, I do because I believe it helps to save this Union; and what I forbear, I forbear because I do not believe it would help to save the Union."[6]

After the Civil War, Congress passed the Fourteenth Amendment, which maintains that all persons were to be treated equally under the law. Section 2 of the Fourteenth Amendment reads,

Representatives shall be apportioned among the several states according to their respective numbers, counting the whole number of persons in each state, excluding Indians not taxed. But when the right to vote at any election . . . is denied to any of the male inhabitants of such state, being twenty-one years of age, and citizens of the United States, or in any way abridged, except for participation in rebellion, or other crime, the basis of representation therein shall be reduced in the proportion which the number of such male citizens shall bear to the whole number of male citizens twenty-one years of age in such state.[7]

The amendment also contained an exception for "rebellion or other crime." While arguably the drafters did not intend for this clause to apply to the newly enfranchised former slave, the conveners of southern constitutional conventions had one goal in mind: to keep the newly enfranchised citizens from casting ballots.

Black voters, nonetheless, exercised the right to vote and achieved political success. After the passage of the Fifteenth Amendment, black men like my great-great-grandfather, who lived on the Oakland Plantation in Bermuda, Louisiana, realized the importance of the vote. Whites, however, feared that if blacks were given access to the franchise, it would threaten the "natural laws" of white supremacy. With much dedication, after the passage of the Civil War Amendments and the end of Reconstruction, white southerners purposed to eliminate the ability of former slaves to register and to vote and used felon disenfranchisement to do so.

From the Fourteenth Amendment to Felon Disenfranchisement

Identifying crimes that blacks were most likely to commit was one of the tools used to keep the newly freed citizens out of the polling place. In Florida, Governor David Walker addressed the 1865 legislature, making his sentiments clear: "Of course we could never accede to the demand for negro suffrage, should it be made. . . . [W]e could not give either an honest or a conscientious assent to negro suffrage."[8] The legislature rejected efforts to extend the franchise to its new citizens: "We must be shorn of our representation or give the inferior and unintelligent race the supremacy in the State government."[9]

In 1890, Mississippi changed its disenfranchising law from including "any crime" to including particular crimes that its white participants believed black men were more likely to commit, crimes such as bigamy, forgery, burglary, arson, and perjury.[10] The Mississippi Supreme Court revealed its racist rationale when it refused to add violent crimes such as rape and murder: "Restrained by the federal constitution from discriminating against the negro race, the convention discriminated against its characteristics and the offenses to which its weaker member was prone. . . . Burglary, theft, arson, and obtaining money under false pretenses were declared to be disqualifications [from voting], while robbery and murders, and other crimes in which violence was the principal ingredient, were not."[11] Other states followed.

In 1901, Alabama changed its constitution to include noncriminal acts as disenfranchising actions. John B. Knox served as the president of the Alabama Constitutional Convention and stated that "manipulation of the ballot" was justified to avoid "the menace of negro domination." Further, delegate John Field Bunting did not hide his intentions in his statement that "the crime of wife-beating alone would disqualify sixty percent of the Negroes."[12]

Likewise, during the 1903 Virginia Constitutional Convention, delegate Carter Glass proclaimed that the "central purpose of the convention" was to "eliminate the darkey as a political factor in this State in less than 5 years, so that in no single county . . . will there be the least concern felt for the complete supremacy of the white race in the affairs of government."[13] Delegate R. L. Gordon stated, "I told the people of my county before they sent me here that I intended, as far as in me lay, to disenfranchise every negro that I could disenfranchise under the Constitution of the United States, and as few white people as possible."[14]

It took less than two decades for another political compromise to pave the way for political oppression. Much like the three-fifths compromise to appease white slave owners in the South during this country's infancy, the Hayes-Tilden compromise, almost a century later, sought to satisfy whites' need for manufactured supremacy to the detriment of and with blatant disregard for the impact on the newly emancipated black man, in the name of achieving national unity. "To achieve 'national unity'— the consolidation of power among White citizenries of the North and South—disparate, conflicting groups of Whites resolved the problem of fractured governance and Democratic-Republican political strife by abandoning Reconstruction, and thus, the recently emancipated slaves to White-supremacist retribution. In exchange for support in electing President Hayes, Republicans agreed to give Democrats 'home rule' under the auspices of 'equal sovereignty of the states,' the same limiting principle invoked by the majority opinion in *Shelby County v. Holder*, more than a century later."[15]

Modern-Day Disenfranchisement

While many of the disenfranchising statutes have changed, the primary impact of felon disenfranchisement in many states remains the disqualification of people of color. Felon disenfranchisement serves as a modern-day three-fifths compromise. Just as the three-fifths compromise counted black citizens for the purpose of representation as less than white citizens, felon disenfranchisement discounts black citizens and their votes in the same way. Legislation across the country has designated a specific group of people as ineligible regarding the rights and responsibilities accorded citizens, on the basis of crimes that were chosen in many states arbitrarily and with discriminatory intent.

In most states, once you are convicted of a felony, four civil rights are taken away: (1) the right to vote, (2) the right to hold public office, (3) the right to serve as a juror, and (4) the right to serve as a notary public. Today, a remarkable 6.2 million Americans are prohibited from voting due to laws that disenfranchise persons with former felony convictions. In most states, the system remains punitive, denying returning citizens their dignity, humanity, and ability to reenter society and operate within society. Moreover, felon disenfranchisement policies disproportionately impact communities of color due to racial disparities in the criminal justice system.

In large part, incarceration is used to deny the right to vote. However, two states allow persons who are in prison to vote. Consequently, in forty-eight states and the District of Columbia, disenfranchisement laws deprive convicted offenders of the right to vote while they are in prison. In thirty-five states, convicted offenders may not vote while they are on parole, and thirty of these states disenfranchise felony probationers as well. In ten states, a conviction can result in lifetime disenfranchisement.[16]

Disenfranchising crimes vary among states. For example, the Mississippi Voter Registration Application lists the following disenfranchising crimes: "Arson, Armed Robbery, Bigamy, Bribery, Embezzlement, Extortion, Felony Bad Check, Felony Shoplifting, Forgery, Larceny, Murder, Obtaining Money or Goods under False Pretense, Perjury, Rape, Receiving Stolen Property, Robbery, Theft, Timber Larceny, Unlawful Taking of Motor Vehicle, Statutory Rape, or Carjacking."[17] Mississippi, like other states, includes an attestation that the voter has "never been convicted of a disenfranchising crime, or [has] had [his or her] rights restored as required by law, [has] not been declared mentally incompetent by a court. Furthermore, [the applicant must] certify that [he or she has] answered all questions on this application for registration and that [he or she] will faithfully support the Constitution of the United States and of the State of Mississippi and will bear true faith and allegiance to the same."[18]

Kentucky and Iowa are now the only states that permanently disenfranchise previously convicted persons. In Alabama, Arizona, Delaware, Florida, Georgia, Maryland, Mississippi, Missouri, Nevada, Tennessee, and Wyoming, some persons continue to suffer from permanent disenfranchisement. For example, persons who committed certain election-related crimes are permanently disenfranchised. All others, in these states, have their right to vote restored once they are no longer incarcerated. Alaska, Arkansas, Georgia, Idaho, Kansas, Minnesota, New Jersey, New Mexico, North Carolina, Oklahoma, South Carolina, South Dakota, Texas, Virginia, Washington, West Virginia, Wisconsin, and Virginia allow those persons who have completed their sentence, including prison, parole, and probation, to vote. Likewise, California, Colorado, Connecticut, and Louisiana provide automatic restoration of voting rights once the person is no longer incarcerated or subject to parole. Louisiana has a five-year waiting period. The remaining states allow for the automatic restoration of voting rights upon release from prison. Finally, two states, Maine and Vermont, do not disenfranchise persons who commit felonies and allow all persons, even those who are incarcerated, to cast a ballot.

Changing Felon Disenfranchisement Laws

In considering felon disenfranchisement laws, invariably two views persist. One argues that disenfranchising laws are needed to demonstrate that persons who commit crimes have forfeited their ability to exercise the rights of citizenship, including the right to vote. Others argue that once a person who has previously been convicted of a felony has completed probation and/or parole, the debt to society is paid, and the person should have his or her right to vote restored. President Barack Obama advocated, "[W]hile the people in our prisons have made some mistakes—and sometimes big mistakes—they are also Americans, and we have to make sure that as they do their time and pay back their debt to society that we are increasing the possibility that they can turn their lives around. . . . [I]f folks have served their time, and they've reentered society, they should be able to vote."[19] Conversely, Florida Attorney General Pam Bondi believes that "felons earned the designation of convicted felon by breaking the law, so they should also earn the restoration of civil rights by abiding by the law and applying. . . . The 'paid their debt' argument also wrongly suggests that completion of a criminal sentence signals rehabilitation."[20]

Challenges to state felon disenfranchisement laws have been brought under the First Amendment, under the meaning of "rebellion or other crime" in the Equal Protection Clause, under the Privileges and Immunities Clause, and under various rights prescribed in state constitutions.[21] Courts have overwhelmingly upheld states' ability to determine the disqualifying measures for convicted persons. In *Richardson v. Ramirez*,[22] the Court upheld the state's ability to disenfranchise persons who were previously convicted of a felony pursuant to Section 2 of the Fourteenth Amendment. In *Johnson v. Bush*, a challenge to Florida's disenfranchisement law, the court found that the state's "discretion to deny the vote to convicted felons is fixed by the text of § 2 of the Fourteenth Amendment."[23] These laws, however, cannot discriminate based on race. State laws and regulations cannot, for example, "disenfranchise similarly situated blue-eyed felons but not brown-eyed felons."[24]

In *Hunter v. Underwood*,[25] the Supreme Court ruled that the Alabama constitutional provision disenfranchising those who were convicted of "any crime . . . involving moral turpitude" violated the Equal Protection Clause of the Fourteenth Amendment.[26] Alabama's facially neutral law, which produced undisputed disproportionate impact based on race, was deemed to be unconstitutional. The Court found that the disenfranchising crimes contained in the Alabama constitution were originally enacted with discriminatory intent. Compare, however, *Farrakhan v. Gregoire*,[27] in which a lower court found a discriminatory disparate impact between blue-eyed and brown-eyed disenfranchised persons. Nonetheless, the appellate court held that challenges to a state's felon disenfranchisement regime must show intentional discrimination. Here, Mr. Farrakhan's claims that disenfranchisement of people convicted of "infamous crimes" violated Section 2 of the Voting Rights Act was insufficiently supported by statistical evidence of racial disparities in the state. Accordingly, the court did not accept the wide disparities in the criminal justice system as enough to condemn the disenfranchisement process in Washington State. Consequently, the courts have not served as a place for successful challenges. Since courts have found the felon disenfranchisement laws consistent with the United States Constitution, other ways to combat felon disenfranchisement have evolved.

Restoration

If the states can lawfully disenfranchise, how can affected persons regain their right to vote? How long are persons who previously committed felonies barred from the ballot box? At what point should we grant access to the vote for persons who commit crimes? Nicole Austin-Hillery worked diligently as director of the Brennan Center's Washington, DC, office to support efforts to restore voting rights on the federal level. She maintains that restoration helps with rehabilitation and decreases recidivism. Notwithstanding her hard work, attempts to pass federal legislation have been a continuing failure. The Democracy Restoration Act highlighted three areas worthy of federal intervention:

(A) the lack of a uniform standard for voting in Federal elections leads to an unfair disparity and unequal participation in Federal elections based solely on where a person lives;

(B) laws governing the restoration of voting rights after a criminal conviction vary throughout the country and persons in some States can easily regain their voting rights while in other States persons effectively lose their right to vote permanently; and

(C) State disenfranchisement laws disproportionately impact racial and ethnic minorities.[28]

Congress has yet to debate the efficacy of the Democracy Restoration Act. Accordingly, we still lack direction from the federal government on the issue of felon disenfranchisement and restoration.

Without a federal standard, the crazy quilt of felon disenfranchisement laws continues the flawed idea that the Founding Fathers instituted when they allowed the states to determine whether they would continue slavery and when they allowed states to determine the path to the vote.

States have rolled over the fundamental right to vote like a steamroller on pavement, changing requirements, polling places, and methods of voting with frequency. The nod to the states has allowed the fundamental right to vote to become less than fundamental.

While the impact of felon disenfranchisement on the African American vote is undeniable, the wound to our democratic process is life-threatening. Three states are illustrative of ways to remove the stain of second-class citizenship from returning citizens. In these states, advocates have attempted various approaches, including litigation, legislation, and ballot initiatives to restore the right to vote.

Virginia

Virginia has a history of racial disenfranchisement. Its post-Reconstruction disenfranchisement process followed the rest of the South in its efforts to eliminate the African American voter. The state implemented poll taxes, literacy tests, and extremely complicated registration requirements.[29] Until 2016, Virginia had one of the strictest and most difficult restoration processes in the country. It had the distinction of being one of four of the harshest states on former felons. Approximately 7.34 percent of its population lost the right to vote due to a felony conviction, which is more than 450,000 persons. In Virginia, less than 100,000 of those persons were incarcerated or under parole or probationary status, which equates to approximately 350,000 persons who were no longer incarcerated but were denied the fundamental right to vote.

African Americans constitute 19.4 percent of Virginia's population, per the 2010 Census, yet they comprise 45.9 percent of the 206,000 people that were disenfranchised prior to Governor Terry McAuliffe's 2016 executive order changing the law.

The political impact of this high-level disenfranchisement is enormous. An average Virginia Assembly district is composed of 80,000 residents, and a Senate district has approximately 240,000 residents. Consequently, the number of disenfranchised persons could constitute at least one Senate district and as many as three Assembly districts.

Further, in this era of too-close-to-call elections, every vote counts. In the 2014 US Senate election in Virginia, Mark Warner won by 0.08 percent, or less than 18,000 votes. Likewise, in 2014, Florida Governor Rick Scott won reelection with only 60,000 more votes than his opponent. Florida disenfranchises 1.5 million people, or 10 percent of its population. Of that 1.5 million, 23 percent are African American, or 520,521 citizens.

This is the type of disparity that Governor McAuliffe's order sought to address. He believed that completing the term of imprisonment, probation, and parole was enough to regain the right to vote. In Virginia, proponents of felon disenfranchisement argued that the governor's actions were political, that is, a ploy to help Democratic candidates. Nonetheless, after the Virginia Supreme Court found that alterations to the restoration of the right to vote were consistent with the state's constitution, Governor McAuliffe restored voting rights to approximately 200,000 formerly incarcerated persons—a feat that has not gone unnoticed and arguably had an effect on the 2017 state elections.[30]

Until the 2016 change, Virginia was one of the only states that permanently stripped individuals of their voting rights upon a felony conviction. Its harsh felony disenfranchisement law disproportionately impacted people of color, particularly African Americans, essentially silencing the political voice of entire communities. Fortunately, reforms over the past three years helped streamline the process by which Virginians may apply to restore their voting rights. The Advancement Project, a national racial justice organization, works on restoration of rights work in Virginia, Louisiana, and Florida. Sabrina Kahn, an attorney at Advancement Project, worked on the organization's rights of restoration campaign in Virginia. She describes the experience of helping formerly incarcerated people obtain the right to vote as follows:

Richmond resident Viola Marie Brooks cast the first ballot of her life after getting her voting rights restored in 2016. Clutching her restoration order with tears in her eyes, she stated, "Now I feel whole." Ms. Brooks tragically passed away soon afterwards in January 2017. Advancement Project was grateful to have had the honor of immortalizing her words in our amicus brief in *Howell v. McAuliffe* [full cite omitted]. The right to vote is fundamental to our humanity; it is intrinsically linked to our dignity and confirms that society values our voices. In an effort to illustrate the deeply personal nature of felony disenfranchisement, we lifted up the stories of those directly impacted by the law. As the fight charges onward to eliminate felony disenfranchisement, we hope to continue humanizing this issue through the power of story-telling.[31]

Richie Canady is one of the many persons who received the restoration of voting rights during Governor McAuliffe's term. He stated,

> I did something wrong, and I have paid for it. I completed my restitution in 2011. When I found out I was eligible to vote, I was elated because I am a taxpaying, law-abiding citizen and I should have the right to dictate who represents me. When I found out that there was a challenge to my right to vote, I thought it was really sad and shameful. Being able to vote is an important part of being American. It is important for me to have the right to vote because my family was active in the Civil Rights movement and experienced discrimination when I was growing up. I want to vote because I don't believe a person can be silent when they are struggling so much. When I came out of prison, I had very little, and I have been trying ever since to make myself whole again.[32]

In Virginia, the Secretary of the Commonwealth provides testimonials from restored returning citizens on its website. For example, Lynette states, "I was able to vote for the first time in almost 30 years. Having my rights restored was the final piece to feeling like I completed my sentence. I feel like I can finally live as a whole citizen and have [a] say so in issues that affect my life and my family's and neighbors' lives."[33]

Florida

In states like Florida where permanent disenfranchisement served as a long-standing rule, one in four African American men were denied the right to vote due to a former felony conviction. Florida's restoration process assessed punishment even after one had completed probation and parole, ensuring that former felons would not reintegrate into society. The Florida disenfranchising statute was challenged under Section 2 of the Voting Rights Act, the Fourteenth Amendment, and the First Amendment of the United States Constitution.

The restoration process varies among the states. It was arguably the most difficult in the state of Florida. The Florida statute provided, "(a) No person convicted of a felony or adjudicated in this or any other state to be mentally incompetent shall be qualified to vote or hold office until restoration of civil rights or removal of disability."[34] A federal court found Florida's restoration process arbitrary and violative of the United States Constitution. In fact, the judge in the First Amendment challenge to Florida's felon disenfranchisement law characterized Florida's restoration process in the following manner:

> Florida strips the right to vote from every man and woman who commits a felony. To vote again, disenfranchised citizens must kowtow before a panel of high-level government officials over which Florida's Governor has absolute veto authority. No standards guide the panel. Its members alone must be satisfied that these citizens deserve restoration. Until that moment (if it ever comes), these citizens cannot legally vote for presidents, governors, senators, representatives, mayors, or school-board members. These citizens are subject to the consequences of bills, actions, programs, and policies that their elected leaders enact and enforce. But

these citizens cannot ever legally vote unless Florida's Governor approves restoration of this fundamental right.

Florida's Executive Clemency Board has, by rule, unfettered discretion in restoring voting rights. "We can do whatever we want," the Governor said at one clemency hearing. One need not search long to find alarming illustrations of this scheme in action. In 2010, a white man, Steven Warner, cast an illegal ballot. Three years later, he sought the restoration of his voting rights. He went before the state's Executive Clemency Board, where Governor Scott asked him about his illegal voting. "Actually, I voted for you," he said. The Governor laughed. "I probably shouldn't respond to that." A few seconds passed. The Governor then granted the former felon his voting rights.[35]

While this legal challenge was ongoing, the people of Florida attempted to take the decision-making process away from the governor and give it back to the people through a ballot referendum that restored the right to vote to the state's more than 1.5 million disenfranchised individuals. The ballot initiative, Amendment 4, would automatically restore voting rights to previously convicted persons once they complete their sentences. The amendment did not include the restoration of rights for those who were convicted of sexual offenses or murder. Those persons would have to comply with Florida's current system, which requires a five-year waiting period and approval from the governor and the clemency board. Former governor Rick Scott believes that previously convicted persons should demonstrate their worthiness to regain the right to vote. The previous governor restored the right to vote to more than 155,000 persons in a four-year period. In eight years, Governor Scott only restored approximately 4,000 persons. Trevon Simmons is one of the 4,000 persons who received restoration from Governor Scott. Mr. Simmons has been out of prison since 2005, having served seven years for armed robbery. At his clemency hearing before the governor, the police chief, the sheriff, and other officials supported his petition. He took responsibility for his actions and had demonstrated his ability to serve as a good citizen. "'No matter your past, who you are and where you're headed means a lot more,' Simmons said. 'I wanted to vote in every election but couldn't. It was like having to sit on the sidelines and watch a game you want to play in.'"[36]

In November 2018, the people of Florida voted overwhelmingly to change Florida's constitution and provide for the automatic restoration of rights for its citizens. Approximately two months later, many of the 1.5 million disenfranchised Florida citizens went to their county's registrar to register to vote. A voter in Jacksonville, Florida, who lost his right to vote for driving with a suspended license was one of the first in line to register. According to the *Florida Times Union,*

> He dressed up for the occasion in a red sweater over a button-down shirt. He, too, talked about how he had wanted to vote in 2008 for Obama as the first African-American president. But an earlier felony conviction of driving with a suspended license prohibited him. "I didn't have a whole lot of confidence in the voting process," he said. But "now the people making laws and writing laws are going to be listening to me." He said he hopes legislators know that his top priorities for them are focusing on re-entry services for people who have been incarcerated and sentencing reform. "People with molestation charges who have a lot of money get less time than someone caught driving with a suspended license. It's time to level the playing field."[37]

Louisiana

As in Virginia and Florida, formerly convicted persons in Louisiana seek to participate in the democratic process as a testament to their ability to make contributions to society. The Louisiana Constitution denies the right to vote to persons "under an order of imprisonment for conviction of felony."[38] The interpretation of this clause has been challenged in the state courts and the Louisiana legislature. The legislature interpreted the clause to mean a sentence of confinement, "whether or not suspended, whether or not the subject of the order has been placed on probation, with or without supervision, and whether or not the subject of the order has been paroled."[39] Thus far, legal challenges have been unsuccessful in convincing the courts that the constitutional intention was limited to the plain meaning of the term "imprisonment," that is, while confined in a penal institution.[40]

In Louisiana, Voice of the Experienced (VOTE) is a Louisiana non-profit founded by ex-offenders that works for and with formerly incarcerated persons and their families. It promotes civic engagement and works for sustainable social change. In 1987, a group of paralegals who were incarcerated at the Louisiana State Penitentiary at Angola recognized through their research that the Louisiana Constitution provided the right to vote once a person was no longer in prison. After they were released from prison, they established VOTE to continue to educate formerly incarcerated persons and their families about their rights.

One of the founders of VOTE is Norris Henderson. He was wrongfully incarcerated for twenty-seven years. Upon his release in 2003, Mr. Henderson continued his work educating formerly incarcerated persons. His work has been recognized throughout the country. He is a former Soros Justice Fellow and a highly regarded and awarded individual who fervently believes that "those who are closest to the problem are closest to the solution."[41]

According to the complaint in *VOTE v. Louisiana*, 60 percent of the organization's staff was formerly incarcerated. The named plaintiffs in the lawsuit have incredible stories: Kenneth Johnston is a sixty-seven-year-old African American man who resides in New Orleans and who served his country in the army for three years, including eighteen months in Vietnam. Mr. Johnson suffered from posttraumatic stress disorder (PTSD) and an addiction to heroin. He served twenty-two years in prison and had been released for twenty-four years. As part of his sentence, he must serve a lifetime of parole. Under Louisiana's interpretation of "under imprisonment," Mr. Johnson will never gain the right to vote. Mr. Johnson works as a paralegal and is a responsible citizen and father. Under the challenged interpretation of the Louisiana Constitution, "[d]espite his service to his country, his successful transition back to the community, his contribution to the federal and state governments by paying his taxes, he will never have the opportunity to vote and participate in the democratic process before he dies."[42]

Bruce Reilly is the deputy director of VOTE and works tirelessly to educate and inform previously incarcerated individuals and their families. Bruce was convicted of crimes that were committed in 1992 in Rhode Island. He was released in 2005 and placed on parole. In 2006, the Rhode Island Constitution was amended by popular ballot, and Mr. Reilly's voting rights were restored. In 2010, he completed parole and began serving a twenty-five-year probationary term. Mr. Reilly moved to New Orleans to attend Tulane University Law School. Unfortunately, the laws of Louisiana stripped Mr. Reilly of his right to vote in that state. In 2014, he graduated from Tulane Law School. Yet, under the current interpretation of the Louisiana Constitution, he remains outside the ballot box.

VOTE, with the support of Advancement Project and local civil rights attorneys, challenged the interpretation of the Louisiana Constitution and its meaning of "under an order of imprisonment." While not having success in litigation, VOTE was successful in lessening the penalty through the Louisiana legislature. In the 2018 legislative session, VOTE lobbied the state legislative members to pass H.B. 265, which would allow people with felony convictions to vote if they have not been incarcerated within the past five years. The numbers vary, but this measure could restore the right to vote to between 15,000 and 40,000 returning citizens.

Impact of Felon Disenfranchisement

African Americans and the criminal justice system have a long and sordid history. Works by noted authors, Douglas A. Blackmon's *Slavery by Another Name: The Re-enslavement of Black Americans from the Civil War to World War II* and Michele Alexander's *The New Jim Crow: Mass*

Incarceration in the Age of Colorblindness, chronicle the US system of mass incarceration as a continuation of the slave industrial complex from the end of the Civil War to the present. I have witnessed the overabundance of black bodies in prisons, which requires them to work and live in deplorable conditions.

Before working for the Department of Justice, I represented death-row inmates and brought prison condition cases in Alabama and Georgia as a staff attorney with the Southern Center for Human Rights in Atlanta, Georgia. In this capacity, I visited prisons that were exemplary of others across the country in their horrific conditions. The disparities are written into the formula for imprisonment. The disenfranchising statutes were intended to exacerbate those disparities and cripple the African American community in its ability to participate in the governing process. The genesis of the disenfranchising laws was meant to eliminate the African American from the process. More than two centuries later, the struggle for the emancipation of formerly incarcerated individuals continues.

Christopher Uggen, Angela Behrens, and Jeff Manza are experts on felon disenfranchisement and found that the rate of African Americans in prisons and jails has consistently exceeded white incarceration rates since the 1800s. They considered information from the 1950s to the new millennium and found that states with large numbers of African Americans were most likely to have felon disenfranchisement statutes when compared to those with smaller African American populations. "The expansion of citizenship to racial minorities, and the subsequent extension of suffrage to all citizens threatened to undermine the political power of the white majority," Behrens, Uggen, and Manza wrote. "By restricting the voting rights of a disproportionately nonwhite population, felon disenfranchisement laws offered one method for states to avert [the changes]." "The sharp increase in African American imprisonment goes hand-in-hand with changes in voting laws," they continued. "Felon disenfranchisement provisions offered a tangible response to the threat of new African-American voters that would help preserve existing racial hierarchies."[43]

The report notes that the percentage of blacks in prison doubled from 1850 to 1870 in certain southern states. In 1850, Alabama's black prison population constituted 2 percent of the overall prison population. However, twenty years later, after the passage of the Thirteenth Amendment, 74 percent of persons incarcerated in Alabama were people of color. The authors found a direct correlation between the emancipation of former slaves and the exponential increase in black incarceration and lessened freedom. This increase is stark compared to the reality that the black population during this period only increased slightly.

Here, as with other disenfranchising tools, the fear of black voting power serves as the rationale to maintain criminal convictions as a means of impacting the ballot box. The dispensation of justice has often been unjustly applied to people of color. Law enforcement has been used as a tool against, instead of help for, communities of color. Moreover, felon disenfranchisement has an impact on election outcomes. In December 2010, 2.23 million of disenfranchised Americans were African American. Felon voting bans have wide-ranging effects on elections. It is believed that the 2000 presidential election and seven US Senate elections could have been altered if persons who were previously convicted would have been allowed to vote.[44]

In comparison to other countries, the United States is abysmal on this issue. Twenty-one countries allow their citizens to vote while they are in prison. Additionally, ten countries allow some prisoners to vote while restricting others. Ten countries ban voting when persons are in prison but allow those persons to cast a ballot once they are released. The United States, Armenia, Belgium, and Chile ban persons from voting once they are released. The United States also allows the states to determine which crimes merit losing the right to vote. Clearly, we are the least progressive and the most stringent on the issue of felon disenfranchisement. Thankfully, the winds of change are blowing in this arena. Victories in states like Florida, Virginia, and Louisiana demonstrate what steps we need to take to eliminate felon disenfranchisement.

The Way Forward

The efforts in Florida, Virginia, and Louisiana serve as beacons of light on the path to true emancipation. While litigation is an important tool, it has proven to be the least effective in the felon disenfranchisement arena. However, legislative victories in states like Louisiana illustrate the need to engage and educate our elected officials. Moreover, the massive victory in Florida showed us all how a grassroots effort can rise from the ashes and prove that the people united can never be defeated. The implementation of these rule changes poses another level of challenges: educating not only formerly incarcerated persons but also elected officials on laws, practices, and procedures that are available to assist formerly incarcerated persons to seamlessly reenter society as contributing persons without the ever-present reality of continuing punishment. Additionally, we must educate citizens and help to dispel the fear of retaliation and incarceration for exercising the right to vote. The prevalence of voter fraud narratives has placed fear in the hearts of many who hope to register but have questions about eligibility.

One approach to this conundrum has emerged in Colorado, where the legislature passed the Voter Registration Individuals Registration Act, which requires parole officers to provide persons on probation with information on their voting rights.[45] The legislation provides that

(b) [T]he division of adult parole shall provide, at the initial meeting with the individual, information regarding how he or she may preregister to vote. . . .

(c) Prior to an individual being discharged from parole, the division of adult parole shall provide, at the last meeting the officer has with him or her, information regarding:

(I) The individual's voting rights;

(II) How the individual may register to vote or update or confirm his or her voter registration record;

(III)   How to obtain and cast a ballot; and

(IV)   How to obtain voter information materials.[46]

Further, "[a] person who is otherwise qualified to register and is on parole may preregister," and once released from parole, "the individual shall be automatically registered to vote."[47] This legislation places the burden on the Department of Corrections to inform and preregister individuals on parole to ensure that they reintegrate into the voting process. One of the legislators supporting the bill stated, "I think if we believe in a rehabilitative system of justice, we should strive for reintegration. . . . [W]hen we have people who have paid their debt to society back on the voter roll, they have a vested interest in the community."[48]

Colorado can serve as a model for other departments of corrections to place the burden on the governmental entity to provide voter registration information and opportunities to persons under their control. Moreover, in providing the opportunity to preregister and to automatically register persons discharged from the parole system provides for their integration into the democratic process. It removes the fear of being prosecuted for mistakenly registering to vote because of eligibility questions. In Texas, Crystal Mason, a woman on probation, was prosecuted for mistakenly casting a provisional ballot and sentenced to five years in prison. She said that she did not know that she was not eligible to vote.[49] The uncertainty around eligibility keeps previously convicted persons who are eligible to vote from registering and participating in the democratic process. Punishments for voting when not eligible can range from a fine to a year or, as in Ms. Mason's case, years of incarceration. Marc Meredith, an associate professor at the University of Pennsylvania, has observed, "Even in states that allow felons to vote, . . . their turnout rate lingers between 10 to 20 percent in a presidential election year, far below the general population."[50] Instead of taking the risk of mistakenly voting, many choose not to engage. A system like the one in Colorado that provides the information from the Department of Corrections on eligibility and the process for registration can alleviate those fears, while at the same time expanding the electorate.

Felon disenfranchisement is analogous to the three-fifths compromise in that it diminishes the representational capacity of African Americans. Under the three-fifths compromise, 60 percent of African Americans were counted toward apportionment. Under Florida's felon disenfranchisement laws, only 60 percent of its African American citizens had the right to vote—different century, same result.

Just as the three-fifths compromise allowed states to count blacks as less than whites, in many states, black votes are worth less than those of whites. The sheer number of persons affected and the geographical scope remains consistent with the three-fifths compromise. The disparities were written into the founding formula. The work continues in removing felon disenfranchisement and its widespread impact on the election process and African Americans. More than two centuries later, that mission has been accomplished. Yet efforts across the country, like those in Florida, Virginia, and Louisiana, are attempting to lift this country up where it belongs with other industrialized nations that allow persons who are no longer incarcerated the opportunity to register and vote.

While felon disenfranchisement serves as one of the last bastions of widespread disenfranchising tools, we are seeing that its impact and import is diminishing. However, it is important to continue to be vigilant to ensure that new measures are not adopted that would once again disenfranchise large swaths of people of color in a way that is unrelated to the election process itself. Legislation and other policy changes have been the most successful ways to break the system of felon disenfranchisement. Unfortunately, without congressional action on this issue, a state-by-state attack has proven to be the most effective route to the franchise. The first Congress constricted the franchise. In the future, Congress can choose to expand the franchise through eliminating the lack of uniformity that currently exists. This would eliminate the crazy quilt of felon disenfranchisement that currently exists and replace it with a blanket of freedom.

Key Stats

6.2 million Americans cannot vote due to a previous felony conviction.

2.6 million disenfranchised persons have completed their sentences, constituting 45 percent of the total disenfranchised population.

2 states allow persons convicted of a felony never to lose the right to vote, including while they are incarcerated.

48 states and the District of Columbia have disenfranchisement laws that deprive convicted offenders of the right to vote while they are in prison.

In 14 states, returning citizens can vote once they are no longer incarcerated.

In 34 states, previously convicted persons cannot vote until they have completed either parole or probation; in some states, returning citizens must complete both probation and parole before regaining voter eligibility.

Felon disenfranchisement operates as a modern-day three-fifths compromise.

1 in 56 nonblack Americans are disenfranchised.

1 in 13 black adults are disenfranchised nationally.

2.2 million black citizens are banned from voting, which represents 7.7 percent of black adults; compare this to 1.8 percent of the nonblack population.

7

Changing Demographics

As demographics change, social and cultural change occurs
in this country. . . . This is a battle that is fighting for who belongs here [and] on what basis. We are in a battle where they
are asking us to forget the fact we are here because they were
there. They were in our countries.
—Marisa Franco, cofounder of Mijente

This country has a history of suppressing the electoral power of
people of color. As illustrated in previous chapters, efforts such as
Reconstruction and the passage of the Voting Rights Act were met
with aggressive and violent efforts to squash the electoral involvement
of people of color. The fight to vote has for centuries focused on the
plight of African Americans to obtain free and fair access to the ballot.
However, Native Americans, Asian Americans, and Latin Americans
have all been involved in the struggle for the right to vote.

To be clear, the suppressive efforts used to thwart African American
access was wielded against other communities of color throughout
this country's history. Losmin Jimenez,[1] an immigrant rights attorney,
reminds us that literacy tests were also targeted at Mexican Americans, Chicanos in the Southwest, and Puerto Ricans in the Northeast.
She recalls that her grandmother Maria Luisa Jimenez, who migrated
to the United States from Puerto Rico in 1951, in order to vote in
1966 had to take a literacy test, which was administered by the State
University of New York. The certificate read, "Be it Known that the
person whose name and address are entered herein, having met the
requirements prescribed in Section 168 of the Election Law, and rules
and regulations of the Regents of the State of New York, and having

made the signature appearing herein in the presence of the examiner, is herewith granted a CERTIFICATE OF LITERACY."[2] From the 1860s to the 1960s to this millennium, voters of color endured poll taxes, literacy tests, grandfather clauses, violence, and murder as significant barriers to the ballot box. Arguably, the goal from the Founding Fathers' three-fifths compromise to post-Reconstruction Jim Crow to poll taxes, vouchers, felon disenfranchisement, and modern-day voter suppression tactics has always been limiting access to the franchise by people of color.

Yet, the demographics in our country are changing. Because of those changes, we see and hear a number of derogatory statements and events in once-sacred venues that are targeting broader communities of color. Some people believe that this onslaught of racial degradation is directly related to the projected increase in the number of people of color, particularly in the Latinx community. Judith Brown-Dianis, the Advancement Project's executive director, offers that it is this fear of becoming a minority that compels the present administration to conduct a "racial purge" in order to maintain the status quo as long as practicable. In explaining the term "racial purge," Judith Brown-Dianis states,

> The "shitholes" comments, through [Trump's] attack on Latinx people . . . made it clear that this was just about people of color and getting them out of our country. He didn't talk about Australians, Brits, or Russians . . . but how do we get rid of what he considered to be the people who would bring our country down and all targeting people of color. But it makes sense that in a time when we are fighting over who this country will grow up to be and looking at becoming a majority people of color country, that the only way that you get to stop it from being that is to slow the growth of people of color. Either you slow it or you throw out the ones you got. The targeting of people of color plus the voter suppression tactics make sure that the power shift doesn't happen.[3]

Marisa Franco is cofounder of Mijente, which serves as a central resource for Latinx and Chicanx organizing. She explains, "We're going to see increasing changing of the rules in respect in who can vote in this country, who can have any level of political power, who can be here under what circumstances, under what kind of jobs can you have. And I think it's important, then, when you situate what's happening with immigration and someone was like, "Ahh, I'm not really sure that's my core issue." It is in fact all connected because there is a backlash that has taken hold, and it's not just in Arizona, it's not just in Texas, it's not just in Alabama; it is all over this country.[4]

By the Numbers

Numbers never lie. The numbers tell us that the United States will soon become an even more diverse country with a majority of people of color. The black-white binary used over the past forty years will soon become obsolete in the face of current population growth. The United States Census Bureau projects that in the year 2050, Latinxs will constitute 30 percent of the nation's population.[5] In the 2010 census, the Latino population increased 3.1 percent and accounted for much of the growth in the country's population.[6] Between July 1, 2008, and July 1, 2009, for example, more than one of every two people added to the country's population was Latinx.[7] The Census Bureau projects that people of color will be the fastest growing demographic in the country, when compared to "an aging, slow-growing and soon to be declining white population."[9] New statistics find that the United States will become a minority white country as early as 2045. In that year, whites will constitute 49.8 percent of the population, in contrast to 24.6 percent for Hispanics, 13.1 percent for blacks, 7.8 percent for Asians, and 3.8 percent for multiracial populations. The Brookings Institution found that the white population will increase slightly throughout 2023 and then experience a consistent decline through 2060. During this decline, whites will experience more deaths than births.[9]

With this level of growth, a number of issues arise regarding access to democracy. This new explosion of Latinx population has caused a considerable increase in legislation requiring proof of citizenship and anti-immigrant laws.[10] While immigration tends to serve as the primary focus, the voting rights of naturalized and native-born Latinx citizens will also become a source of possible litigation.

Over and Under

What do these developments mean in the voting context? Because of voter suppression tactics, such as inaccurate purges, voter ID, and felon disenfranchisement, "whites have been consistently overrepresented among voters in both presidential and midterm elections for the past 36 years. Even as their share of the population has declined, their overrepresentation has actually increased, going from a 7-point gap in the 1980 and 1982 elections to a 10- and 14-point gap in 2012 and 2014. This is notable because we generally expect representation gaps to grow as a population grows and to shrink as a population shrinks."[11]

While whites were overrepresented, voters of color were dramatically underrepresented. In federal elections between 1980 and 1994, African Americans experienced a –2 point gap in representation. An improvement occurred after 1996 and especially in 2008 and 2012 during the election of President Barack Obama: African Americans were in parity with whites in 2008 and slightly overrepresented in 2012. The Latinx community, however, has experienced further declines in recent years. For example, "in 1980 and 1982, there were representation gaps of –3 and –4 points, respectively; by 2012 and 2014, these gaps had grown to –8 and –10 points. This makes Hispanics the racial group that is most underrepresented as well as the group that has seen the largest increase in their underrepresentation over time."[12]

The Brookings Institution suggests that the representation gaps will continue throughout most of the twenty-first century. It found,

[T]he steady overrepresentation of whites during these years was mir-
rored by the underrepresentation of communities of color. For blacks,
the underrepresentation gaps in presidential and midterm elections
hovered around –2 points between 1980 and 1994. However, after 1996,
these gaps began to shrink, especially for presidential elections. During
the election and re-election of America's first black president, Barack
Obama, we saw underrepresentation reduced to essentially zero in 2008
and actually flip to a slight overrepresentation in 2012. There's been a
similar movement in the past two midterm elections, where we saw
black representation gaps move above –1 for the very first time. In contrast to whites and blacks, Hispanics' representational fortunes have
moved in the opposite direction.[13]

Brookings predicts that white overrepresentation will decline about
3 points for presidential and midterm elections by 2060, which would
bring whites' representation levels down to levels found in 1980. For African Americans, Brookings believes that over a forty-four-year period,
their overrepresentation will rise to approximately 1.4 points but will
continue to experience some underrepresentation through 2030. Over
the next forty-four years, Latinx will also improve in presidential and
midterm elections. Generally, despite dwindling in numbers, whites
will maintain a level of overrepresentation while African Americans
and Latinx levels will increase but will find it difficult to meet the levels
of whites.[14]

To offset the white population decline, we will experience a system
shift akin to the redemption period. Because of the increase of people
of color, especially the higher birth rate of Latinx communities when
compared to whites, these communities become natural targets of anti-
immigrant sentiment. It is important to remember that during redemption white supremacists wore red shirts as a symbol of their political
ideology. In this century, the red Make America Great Again (MAGA)
hats and other paraphernalia are employed to advocate for similar poli-

cies to extricate our country and the democratic system from unwanted people of color. Accordingly, instead of red shirts, the symbol of white supremacy is a red hat. These MAGA hats are representative of the sentiments that the administration espouses depicting people of color as menacing and criminal, unworthy of the benefits of citizenship.

While whites enjoy overrepresentation at the ballot box, minority communities are younger and growing faster than white communities. According to Brookings, since 1980, whites have fewer people in the zero to seventeen age group than do Hispanics and African Americans, who will have "larger and larger portions of their population age into the voting age population. Asians/others will continue to see their age gap increase, but the change will be less dramatic than what we've seen in the last three decades."[15] Consequently, the gaps will begin to shrink, particularly in the Hispanic community, where immigration increased in the 1980s but the citizenship rate did not. However, growth in this community is due to native births in this community instead of stalled immigration policy. Losmin Jimenez points out that this theory does not consider the relationship of the United States and Puerto Rican migration to the mainland or the forced migration from Central America due to failed US foreign policies. Nonetheless, according to Brookings, "Even absent any legislative action," the institute expects "the citizenship gaps of both Hispanics and Asians/others to return to their 1980 levels in the 2030s and 2020s, respectively. By the 2050s, both these groups will have effectively zeroed out their eligibility issues."[16]

A reason for this overrepresentation could cause us to consider disproportionate registration rates. According to the Pew Research Group, "[N]ational registration rates . . . are substantially lower for minority citizens than the registration rate of majority citizens. Based on 2014 data, for example, only 48.8% of Asian American citizens, 51.3% of Latino citizens, and 63.4% of African-American citizens reported being registered to vote—rates that fall below, and in some cases, significantly below the 68.1% reported registration rate for White, non-Hispanic citizens."[17]

Historical Significance

Throughout US history, the country has experienced periods with an influx of immigrants, whether from European nations or Central and Latin American countries, plus population increase because of conquest and colonization, as in Mexican annexation and the Spanish-American War. Judith Browne-Dianis believes that we have seen this before in our country. She says, "I just think it's history repeating itself. . . . any time there's been an influx in immigrants. . . . There were efforts to make sure they couldn't vote, start to put the clamp down on that because white Anglo-Saxons are worried about their property, their power, and their money. I just think it's just . . . using every tool that they possibly can."[18]

We also see, in regard to voter suppression, a purge based on religion, ethnicity, and race. Previous and present administrations' decisions to purge the country of these persons and certainly remove them from the possibility of achieving the right to vote is consistent with the founding of our country in the idea that some people should be allowed to access the franchise and others should not. It was and continues to be an effort to purify the ballot box. Whites have feared the political power of people of color more so than voters of color have recognized their power. By 2045, the United States will no longer be a majority white country. Whites will be 49.8 percent, and 24.6 percent will be Latinx, 13.1 percent black, 7.8 percent Asian, and approximately 4 percent multiracial.

Indeed, Ms. Franco saw this coming. In 2010, while in Arizona, she noted, "You had the highest number of white people over sixty-five and the highest number of brown people under eighteen. . . . This is actually not just about one state. This is a foreshadowing about what this country will have to face."[19] Accordingly, this threat of whites being in the minority serves as the impetus for the racial purge and voter suppression from the executive branch of the federal government to state legislatures.

Executive Deterrents to a Diverse Populace

The executive branch of the United States government is entrusted with great authority. Article II of the United States Constitution provides that the president "shall take Care that the Laws be faithfully executed."[20] Historically, presidents have utilized their power to issue impactful decisions through use of the executive order. These orders have the power of expanding the power of the president. They are often challenged legally. Almost every president has used executive orders to address executive concerns. We have seen presidents use the executive orders to suppress immigrant communities. Most notably, in 1942, President Franklin Delano Roosevelt issued Executive Order 9006, which authorized Japanese internment camps. It required the relocation of persons in states with large populations of persons with Japanese ancestry. The encampments affected approximately 117,000 persons, most of whom were US citizens. Contemporaneously, the executive order and executive-level decisions are used as a weapon against immigrants and cast a shadow over their status and ability to live free and potentially become citizens of this country.

DACA

We see the administration's efforts toward purging and impacting the inevitable changing demographics in the executive proclamation to end the Deferred Action for Childhood Arrivals (DACA), which allows persons who migrated to the United States as children to experience deferred action status. In June 2012, President Barack Obama announced this policy, which allowed certain immigrants to receive a work permit for two years that was renewable with good behavior. President Obama stated, "Put yourselves in [the Dreamers'] shoes. Imagine you've done everything right your entire life, only to suddenly face deportation to a country you know nothing about with a language that you do not speak."[21] DACA recipients had to be younger than thirty-one at the time of the executive announcement and had to have arrived in the country when they were younger than sixteen. The DACA recipients, or immigrant youth, were required to register with a federal agency for a fee. This registration permits DACA registrants to live and work in the United States without fear of deportation. In August 2012, shortly after President Obama's executive order, the Pew Research Center estimated that this policy could potentially impact 1.7 million people.[22] DACA did not provide a path to citizenship, only deferred action on possible deportation.

DACA authorization operated similarly to compromises of another era. The recipients were expected to live and work in this country but could not enjoy the benefits of citizenship. Essentially, the country would accept and expect immigrant labor but would not provide the benefits of citizenship. DACA registrants could not vote in the United States, and the measure did not provide a path to citizenship.

In September 2017, President Trump announced his intention to eliminate DACA protections. This pronouncement sent shock waves through the country. It was clear that the new policy would adversely affect more than 800,000 people who entered the country as children and had only known life in the United States. President Trump had indicated his disdain for DACA when, as a presidential candidate in August 2016, he stated, "We will immediately terminate President Obama's two illegal executive amnesties, in which he defied federal law and the Constitution to give amnesty to approximately 5 million illegal immigrants,"[23] suggesting an end to DACA and the Deferred Action for Parents of Americans and Lawful Permanent Residents. Consequently, the millions of undocumented people feared that it was merely a matter of time before the administration sought to remove or purge them from the populace.

Temporary Protective Status

Another revocation of liberty and an attempt to purge the country of people of color came with the removal of Temporary Protective Status (TPS), affecting persons from countries in Central America, Africa, and Asia. TPS is a Department of Homeland Security designation of a foreign country "due to conditions in the country that temporarily prevent the country's nationals from returning safely, or in certain circumstances, where the country is unable to handle the return of its nationals adequately. USCIS [US Citizenship and Immigration Services] may grant TPS to eligible nationals of certain countries (or parts of countries), who are already in the United States. Eligible individuals without nationality who last resided in the designated country may also be granted TPS."[24] In order to become TPS designated, the following temporary conditions must exist: a civil war or ongoing armed conflict, or environmental disaster or other extraordinary and temporary conditions. Some countries, like El Salvador, enjoyed TPS for approximately thirty years. The abruptness of the administration's decision caused a ripple effect of fear in these communities. Many had spent decades in the United States. Moreover, more than 300,000 persons possessed TPS status. Nonetheless, the president proposed eliminating TPS status for El Salvador, Honduras, Haiti, Nepal, Sudan, and Nicaragua.[25]

This revocation occurred in close proximity to President Trump's comment, "Why do we want all these people from 'shithole countries' coming here?"[26] The statement was a clear disparagement of persons who immigrate to the United States from economically disadvantaged countries. Again, these initiatives serve as a racial purge with the uncontroverted purpose of eliminating people of color and the threat of minority status or the loss of power.

Proof of Citizenship

In addition to the revocation of TPS status and a renunciation of DACA, on the state level operatives have attempted to implement measures that marginalize naturalized and native-born citizens from immigrant communities from participating in the electoral process. Specifically, states have developed proof of citizenship laws that target the increase of persons of color. In these states, citizens must provide documentary proof of citizenship. This type of proof requires a birth certificate or naturalization papers as documentary evidence that a person is a citizen of the United States. Title 42 of the Code of Federal Regulations, Section 435.407, outlines acceptable forms of documentary evidence of citizenship, which include a US passport, certificate of naturalization, birth certificate, or under some circumstances a valid driver's license issued with the last four digits of a Social Security number or other form of proof of citizenship.[27]

Arizona and Kansas have been leaders in the documentation effort. In a case challenging the Kansas legislation, according to the complaint in *Fish v. Kobach*, more than 35,000 voters were on the suspension list due to the documentary proof of citizenship requirement. They constituted approximately 14 percent of all individuals who, as of that date, had attempted to register to vote since the Kansas Documentary Proof of Citizenship law went into effect on January 1, 2013. These voters are disproportionately young: as of December 11, 2015, voters between the ages of eighteen and twenty-nine constituted more than 44 percent of the voters on the suspension list due to purported failure to provide documentary proof of citizenship, a percentage that far outstrips their share among eligible or registered voters. Most of the suspended voters are also unaffiliated: almost 54 percent of voters on the suspension list due to purported failure to provide documentary proof of citizenship were unaffiliated with any political party.

In 2014, Steven Wayne Fish attested that he was a US citizen who lived in Lawrence, Kansas. He was born on a US military base in Illinois that was no longer active. Mr. Fish attempted to register to vote in Kansas while renewing his driver's license. He did not, however, have documentary proof of citizenship like a birth certificate, because it was not needed to renew his driver's license. Due to his lack of documentary proof of citizenship, he was not allowed to register and was placed on a suspended voter registration list. Because the military base had closed, Mr. Fish was not aware of how to obtain his birth certificate and was unable to locate a copy of the document. Unfortunately, because Mr. Fish did not submit the requisite documentary evidence within ninety days of his voter registration application, Mr. Fish remained on the suspension list and was unable to vote.[28]

Similarly, Ralph Ortiz also attempted to register to vote while renewing his license, to no avail. He, too, neglected to provide documentary proof of citizenship during the renewal or within the ninety-day period. Mr. Ortiz is a US citizen and a veteran who served thirteen years in the US Air Force. Nonetheless, his inability to provide documentary proof of citizenship allowed the state to place him on the suspension list and ultimately to purge him from the voter rolls.[29] Likewise, *Fish v. Kobach* plaintiffs Marvin and JoAnn Brown are US citizens who attempted to register in Kansas using the federal voter registration form, which does not require documentary proof of citizenship. Because of Kansas's documentary proof of citizenship requirement, they were subsequently denied the opportunity to register and vote.[30]

In *Fish v. Kobach*, the court found that Kansas mistakenly argued that 129 noncitizens had registered or attempted registrations since 1999. In fact, approximately 67 instances had occurred; only 39 of those, or 0.002 percent of all registered voters, successfully registered to vote, and several of those cases were the result of state employees' errors and/or applicants' confusion. The court weighed the burden of documentary proof of citizenship and the benefit of denying the ballot to eligible citizens due to 0.0002 percent of incorrect registrations and determined that Kansas's proof of citizenship law was harmful and burdensome to citizens.

The stated purpose of documentary proof of citizenship laws is to root out noncitizen voters. Much like voter ID laws, proof of citizenship laws are a solution in search of a problem and are more harmful to the democratic process than they are helpful. It is widely accepted and proven that widespread voter fraud and noncitizen voting does not exist.[31] This misconception leads to the unfounded assertion that proof of citizenship laws are needed to prevent voter fraud. In reality, these mechanisms cause harm and unduly burden eligible voters in their exercise of the franchise.

Citizenship Question

Another way in which noncitizens are targeted to ensure white political power is evident in the United States Census Bureau's proclamation that it would include a question regarding citizenship on the 2020 Census form. The bureau's press release on the topic stated, "On December 12, 2017, DOJ requested that the Census Bureau reinstate a citizenship question on the decennial census to provide census block level citizenship voting age population (CVAP) data that is not currently available from government surveys. DOJ and the courts use CVAP data for the enforcement of Section 2 of the VRA, which protects minority voting rights. Having citizenship data at the census block level will permit more effective enforcement of the VRA, and Secretary Wilbur Ross determined that obtaining complete and accurate information to meet this legitimate government purpose outweighed the limited potential adverse impacts."[32]

The census counts the number of people in the country as of April 1 of the decennial census. The census, however, does not capture citizenship status. It does capture a myriad of information, including the education and ages of members of the household. For apportionment purposes, the Census Bureau takes the number of people and divides that number by 435 to determine the appropriate number of persons comprised in each district for the US House of Representatives. The number that the Census Bureau uses to ensure equal representation for federal elections includes citizens, noncitizens, children, the elderly, educated, and uneducated. It is extremely important for representation and economic purposes that the Census Bureau has an accurate count of the persons in the United States. The citizenship question has provided a surplus of concerns, including the fear that many individuals will opt not to complete the census. If this occurs, the country will experience a severe undercount, which could lead to the underrepresentation of communities and the underfunding of schools, roads, and other vital projects. Moreover, a severe undercount could occur in states that have large numbers of noncitizens and mixed-status families. The concern is that in communities that are already subject to a severe undercount, such as people of color or people who move frequently, if the citizenship question remains, persons who are not citizens may not complete the census forms. If the forms are not completed and returned, the states could potentially lose federal funds and/or congressional seats. The census's total count of persons in the states is used to apportion the 435 seats in the House of Representatives. If a state like California or Texas that has large numbers of noncitizens does not increase in population but decreases according to the census, it could potentially lose not only congressional seats but money for much-needed projects, such as schools, roads, and hospitals. Adding a citizenship question that chills responses will lead to a severe undercount and harm communities, locally, regionally, and nationally.

The Department of Justice has proffered that adding the citizenship question is needed in order to ensure effective enforcement of the Voting Rights Act. In reality, this assertion sought to reverse engineer an outcome that disenfranchisement proponents could not get through litigation. In *Evenwel v. Abbott*,[33] the appellants challenged the method of using total population for redistricting purposes. Texas, like all other states, used total population, meaning the total number of persons in the state are counted regardless of citizenship status or voter eligibility. The appellants argued that states should use the number of voter-eligible citizens in apportioning districts. This calculation would have been detrimental to communities with large percentages of persons under eighteen and noncitizens including those persons in the United States on legal visas, permanent residents, or otherwise.

Indeed, the state of Texas drew its legislative districts on the basis of total population to ensure that each district contained the same number of people. The Texas Constitution requires that the state legislature reapportion its Senate districts during the first regular session after every federal census. After the 2010 census, the legislature created a redistricting plan that was signed into law. The appellants argued that Texas's districting based on total population as opposed to the voter-eligible population diluted their votes in violation of the Equal Protection Clause. The United States Supreme Court found that a state drawing its legislative districts on the basis of total population does not violate the Equal Protection Clause, which requires that state-legislature districts be apportioned so that each district has the same number of people. The unequal distribution of representation in legislative districts is called malapportionment. A state may use any population baseline to avoid malapportionment, so long as the decision is rational and nondiscriminatory. The Court found that "[a]dopting voter-eligible apportionment as constitutional command would upset a well-functioning approach to districting that all 50 States and countless local jurisdictions have followed for decades, even centuries. Appellants have shown no reason for the Court to disturb this long-standing use of total population."[34]

The effort to change the method of apportioning districts to voter-eligible districts was a modern-day approach to treating persons who do not meet the eligibility requirements as second-class citizens. In a 277-page opinion, a federal trial court judge stated, "While the court is unable to determine—based on the existing record, at least—what Secretary Ross's real reasons for adding the citizenship question were, it does find, by a preponderance of the evidence, that promoting enforcement of the [Voting Rights Act] was not his real reason for the decision. Instead, the court finds that the V.R.A. was a post hoc rationale for a decision that the secretary had already made for other reasons."[35]

In the legal challenges to the citizenship question, petitioners argued in part that adding a citizenship question would violate the United States Constitution. Moreover the Administrative Procedure Act interprets the Constitution to require an actual enumeration. These suits argue that the Census Bureau did not follow protocol in determining whether the addition of the citizenship question was proper. Additionally, they suggest that adding this question is unconstitutional and is otherwise illegal and that the citizenship question will certainly undermine the federal government's obligation to conduct an accurate count. The Court's opinion reinforced the ideal that legislators represent all people in a district, not only eligible voters.

It was widely understood that the citizenship question would not aid in enforcing the VRA.[36] In fact, this DOJ has neglected to file *any* lawsuits enforcing the Voting Rights Act, and the reason for doing so is not associated with the US Census. Clearly, the proposed rationale serves as a pretext for suppression. Indeed, it would impede the enforcement of the act on behalf of voters of color. Many advocacy groups opposed the Census Bureau's inclusion of the citizenship question. Terri Ann Lowenthal, a consultant on Census 2020 issues, described the inclusion of the question as "a pretense to achieve a political goal through the census." She added, "The pieces of the puzzle are starting to fit together, going back to when President Trump took office."[37] Consequently, the citizenship question becomes another tool in the arsenal of voter suppression. It is widely seen as an attempt to alter the census count and arguably will worsen the already difficult task of counting certain communities. Further, critics argue that including the citizenship question attempts to take the United States back to a pre-civil-rights era, when voting was reserved primarily for whites, to the exclusion of people of color.[38]

Denaturalizations

Unfortunately, we are indeed experiencing a purge, and it is racially based. We have seen an increase in the number of denaturalizations. In less than two years, the Trump administration authorized ninety-five denaturalization cases for the Department of Justice, more than any other administration in such a short period of time. The average per year from 1990 to 2017 was eleven. Additionally, the US Immigration and Customs Enforcement (ICE) requested funds in its 2019 budget to review the files of 700,000 US citizens for potential denaturalization procedures. The proposed budget and the exponential increase in denaturalization evince an erosion in due process and fairness and minimize the value of US citizenship. The degrading, racist remarks, the repeal of DACA, TPS, and the denaturalization of naturalized citizens evince efforts to offset a desperate and aging white electorate.

The denaturalization threat has particularly impacted people who are from Muslim countries and naturalized.[39] Amanda Frost, a law professor at American University's Washington College of Law, suggests, "The message that's being sent, whether they intend it or not, is to chill and frighten naturalized citizens. . . . The broader the government's power and ability to denaturalize, the more at risk it puts the 20 million people in this country who are naturalized citizens and the more it renders them second-class citizens. Unlike a native-born American they have to fear that they might become the target of the government's denaturalization campaign."[40] All of these measures send the message that immigrants from certain countries need not apply to become citizens of the United States. The executive branch has been used to decrease and dissuade instead of expanding the opportunity of citizenship and the rights that are afforded therein.

The Way Forward

If the goal of a democracy is to have a representative government, that is, a government that reflects the racial, political, religious, and other diversity of its inhabitants, then the efforts to make voter registration and access to the ballot more difficult have a different goal, which is exclusion instead of inclusion. The methods' names may have changed from era to era, but the impact is the same. As demonstrated throughout this text, from the nation's founding to the latest suppression tools, the goal has been expanding the franchise for whites and reducing the opportunities to participate for people of color. The exercise of power to exclude citizens from the democratic process is antithetical to American democracy. The increasing numbers of people of color and particularly the births of US citizens to immigrants should lead to an expansion of democracy, not its contraction. Improved access to voter registration, an accurate census count, and renewal of DACA, TPS, and/or a path to citizenship for these immigrants demonstrate the ways in which we could welcome diverse opinions into our society and politics. In years to come, we should experience an increase in the number of young Asian American and Latinx citizens, who will have reached the age of eligibility. We must contextualize the proof of citizenship laws as yet another attempt to disenfranchise already-underrepresented groups. These newly envisioned methods will further disenfranchise citizens and widen the gap between white overrepresentation and the underrepresentation of people of color.

To combat these erosive issues, we have examples of inclusion across the country. In determining what inclusion might look like, it is illustrative to consider Takoma Park, Maryland, where noncitizens and returning citizens—those formerly incarcerated—can vote in local elections. Takoma Park also allows residents to register and vote if they are citizens of the United States, are at least sixteen years old, are only registered as a resident of Takoma Park, are not incarcerated or "under supervision due to a felony conviction," did not buy or sell votes, and are a resident of the city of Takoma Park for "at least 21 days before the election."[41] Additionally, eleven states allow nonresidents—second home or business owners—to vote in local elections.[42] Three states allow nonresidents to vote in local, municipal elections, and eight states allow nonresidents to vote in special district elections, like water and utility districts.[43]

Noncitizen voting has a significant history. The Founding Fathers allowed noncitizen property owners to vote in elections. The rationale exists that persons who are not citizens live in communities, pay taxes, and contribute to society in many ways. Citizenship status should not serve as an impediment to participation in democracy. Persons who live in a jurisdiction should have a voice regarding governance. We should follow the lead of some local jurisdictions and give noncitizens an opportunity to participate in governing themselves. Opening the process to residents makes for an inclusive process and allows noncitizens to express their concerns to elected officials without fear of deportation or other harm.

The reign of terror that we have experienced with the focus on non-citizens has made a mockery of US citizenship. Democracy demands inclusion of various viewpoints. When we quiet voices that are not like our own, we silence democracy. Elected officials make decisions that impact the lives of persons living in their jurisdictions. These persons come from different countries and are different races, religions, ethnicities and status. Increasing the representative form of governance to include non-citizens is a very American thing to do and should be expanded beyond a few local jurisdictions to the state and federal levels.

8

This Too Shall Pass

The greatest mistake of the movement has been trying to organize a sleeping people around specific goals. You have to wake the people up first, then you'll get action.
—Malcolm X

The question for our consideration is, What will it take for the United States to wake from its slumber? What will it take for the United States to return to its pursuit of progressive and emancipating principles? History seems to be repeating itself in the reentrenchment of bigotry, greed, and hate. In the late 1800s, the Hayes-Tilden compromise led the nation down a path of hatred and denial. The constitutional conventions that led to the widespread disenfranchisement of millions of Americans in the post-Reconstruction era are similar to the voter suppression methods that quickly emerged in the post-Obama era. The *Shelby* decision marked a pivotal moment in our nation's history, similar to *Plessy v. Ferguson*, in the dismantling of hard fought gains. The torches in Charlottesville, Virginia, remind us of the potential for violence and hate focused on preserving a culture of oppression and white supremacy. We are in a crisis of voter suppression, but there are forces fighting to beat back the hands of oppression and lift us to a truly democratic society with increased opportunities to participate.

Those of us who believe that the United States can ascend to higher heights must unrelentingly use the many resources that we have available to us—litigation, legislation, social media, community building, organizations, and social, professional, and religious alliances—to converge on this quest for liberation and emancipation like never before. We are not where we once were; in fact, we have more tools available to us today than at any point in our nation's history. We have seen the mountaintop and must claim the higher ground of civility, justice, and humanity.

Can America indeed achieve greatness? The country missed an opportunity to be great when the Founding Fathers refused to treat all human beings equally, to abolish slavery, to give all persons the right to vote. Our country can be great, only if it recognizes the importance of eliminating barriers to fundamental freedoms like the right to vote. Let us not miss this present opportunity to be a nation that provides unfettered access to the ballot box and expands the notions of freedom and the franchise. We must, however, wake first and have a clear plan of action to achieve these lofty but necessary goals.

Come Too Far to Turn Back Now

In the context of the Voting Rights Act, we can consider that it certainly brought us from 1965 to the present. It is evident, however, that the VRA has become less viable to eradicate discrimination based on race. While *Shelby* destroyed Section 5 of the Voting Rights Act, we know that Section 2 of the act is currently in the crosshairs of those who seek to completely dismantle the gains made in the past fifty years. Derrick Johnson, president of the NAACP, warns that we have become too reliant on the Voting Rights Act. He continues, "I think we should be looking at new approaches to protect the right to vote. Not that we give up on the Voting Rights Act unless we don't fight to protect it. But the reality is it's under attack, and if the Supreme Court goes the way that I believe it's going to go, Section 2 [of the Voting Rights Act] will be the next thing on the chopping block. So we would have this shell of an act without the two most important sections in the act."[1]

Indeed, the United States Supreme Court has a chief justice and at least two associate justices who could vote to end Section 2 of the VRA because of their disdain for race-based remedies. These remedies, however, are needed because of the many historical examples of discrimination in voting and the many contemporaneous examples of disenfranchisement. If we do suffer from an overreliance on the VRA, the question remains as to whether we should use our efforts to restore the lost or vulnerable parts of the Voting Rights Act. Scholars and advocates tend to disagree on the way to address the demise of Section 5.

In 2010, when the *NAMUDNO* decision was handed down by the Supreme Court, advocates discussed the landmines involved in asking a democratic Congress to address the concerns that the Court had regarding the Section 5 coverage formula. The overwhelming consensus was that the potential for harm severely outweighed any possible gains. Accordingly, the advocacy groups did not make a major push for Congress to clarify or adjust the coverage formula. Recall that this decision was made when the country had a Democratic president and a Democratic-controlled House and Senate. Consequently, once the Republican sweep occurred in 2010, any thoughts of asking Congress to address Section 5 concerns seemed ludicrous for fear that the entire Voting Rights Act would be mangled into a paper tiger with no real authority or ability to impact change. What has transpired since that fateful time, however, has left the VRA in shambles and communities with little protection from discriminatory election practices and procedures. We have witnessed an increase in voter purges, voter deception, polling place closures, voter intimidation, and other suppressive voting practices and procedures not just in formerly covered jurisdictions but throughout the country. With these new suppressive measures, voter confidence in the system dwindles and democracy suffers.

Kareem Crayton believes that the case law "signals a hostility, or at least a mild indifference, to the problems that people cited even as recently as 2006, that gave rise to the renewal of Section 5. As a civil rights attorney, I recognize the benefit that the federal judiciary offers and has provided in the past half century. We are currently, however, experiencing a pendulum swing to a much more conservative federal judiciary. The infiltration of conservative, politicized judges will make it very difficult to receive an impartial decision on voting rights and other civil rights issues. The *Shelby* decision is just the latest example of the Supreme Court's activism and Congress's inactions. The people have little trust that Congress will address the potential fallout around the VRA. There once was a time when men and women of honorable intentions could seek an impartial and just decision from the federal judiciary. The politicization of the bench, however, has made the judiciary's decisions, especially at the highest levels, somewhat predictable along party lines and disruptive to common ideals of justice, fairness, and order.

When I was a deputy chief in the George W. Bush administration, the politicization and marginalization of career attorneys was apparent and verified in an inspector general's report finding discrimination and high levels of politicization in the Civil Rights Division, Voting Section. Attorneys were routinely reprimanded for seeking to enforce, follow, and advocate for enforcement of the federal voting rights laws. Moreover, the Bush administration treated vote fraud as a much-larger problem than political exclusion.

At this time, we need legislation that recognizes an official obligation to make sure all citizens who are eligible to vote are placed on the voting rolls and that elections run smoothly and accurately.[2] We can have a political system that works only when the Department of Justice (DOJ) attorneys who enforce voting rights are not themselves partisan activists. Further, the Department of Justice is not the president's lawyer; it is the nation's law firm. Its purpose is to enforce the laws of the United States, not to serve the president. Its purpose is to serve the people. When the DOJ is no longer operating in the manner that it was made to function, chaos ensues. A DOJ focused on enforcing the laws and working on behalf of the people of the United States affords an opportunity for public service and for justice. In the Civil Rights Division, Voting Section, the lack of authority under Section 5 of the Voting Rights Act severely limits enforcement opportunities. Nonetheless, discrimination in voting continues to occur, and the DOJ must use the tools entrusted to it for the benefit of all people.

The Trump administration's efforts, however, have risen to new levels that have gone beyond discouraging enforcement to using executive actions to achieve antidemocratic objectives. The Pence-Kobach Commission and departmental decisions to roll back enforcement even further than previous administrations, along with the lack of federal oversight, a Congress that refuses to act on behalf of its constituents, and a Supreme Court that is complicit in the rollback of civil rights, have allowed jurisdictions to implement disenfranchising measures with complete disregard for the impact on voters, especially voters of color. Moreover, false narratives of the need for citizenship questions on the census must be disavowed. Currently, no part of the federal government—executive, legislative, or judicial—is seen as a friend to civil rights issues, but eventually the pendulum will swing from this extreme to normalcy. We the people must demand as much.

The Voting Rights Act certainly brought us here, but it may take a courageous act of Congress to determine how to address racial and social inequities in the area of voting. Invariably, the question for Congress is, Can you develop a law that addresses racial discrimination in voting as it exists today and will evolve tomorrow? What we have witnessed is the ability of legislatures and jurisdictions, not just in the South, to pass laws that appear neutral but severely impact voters of color. If Congress lacks the ability to pass an adaptive version of the VRA, then it should look carefully at historical and contemporaneous disenfranchising mechanisms and develop laws that prevent discrimination in voting despite what we might call the disenfranchising device of the time, for example, poll tax or voter ID. Congress's attempts to do so in the Voting Rights Amendment Act were feeble attempts at a regurgitation of Section 4 that did not fully address the issue of race discrimination in voting. Dr. Crayton suggests that Congress must ask, "Can you reorganize a tool to deal with race discrimination in a way that achieves, and this is the key, that links to voting rights in a bipartisan way? A clear national statement that certain kinds of decisions are just going to be unacceptable in our politics?"[3] Agreed. Can we develop laws that make it unacceptable to discriminate based on race or language ability, laws that squarely and clearly say that we are a country that will not tolerate racial discrimination or laws that suppress communities of color in the exercise of the electoral process?

It is highly questionable that Congress has the will to address these issues. In the meantime, we are left wanting and waiting on remedies that work to eliminate the current climate of despair. However, we do not have to wait and wonder. The Voting Rights Act only became law because the people were awakened to the injustices that had occurred over the preceding century. We cannot wait a century for the next action from Congress. We, the people, must make a demand.

If we are relying too heavily on the VRA, the courts, and Congress, then where should we look for refuge? NAACP president Derrick Johnson suggested that "we begin to think about voting rights differently and expand the notion of how we open up opportunity for individuals to exercise their franchise, and not simply connected in the foursquare box that we've always been thinking about these arguments."[4]

Imaginative and creative solutions to address the crisis of voter suppression are sorely needed. I believe and have previously argued that "not only should we pursue so-called race neutral measures, but we must also recognize the need for racially aware legislation that corrects for past historical discrimination that continues to have contemporaneous effects on the right to vote. . . . In order to address the gap between the racial reality that we currently live in and the rampant attempts to limit voter access requires a dose of what I call 'voting realism.'"[5] This approach implores us to

> think imaginatively about what the laws should be without ignoring the role that racism plays in the process. It suggests that instead of abandoning racially aware remedies, we should acknowledge the impact that the existing laws have on racial and ethnic minorities and their ability to access the ballot to develop laws that address concerns. Voting realism highlights that race neutral laws can and often do have racial effects and adversely impact people of color and other groups. . . . However, voting realism offers that racial effects should serve as a key consideration in any

legislation affecting the right to vote. . . . Voting realism attempts to envision the possibilities of a system that is free from race discrimination, yet does the work of mitigating its influence.[6]

It is understood that this is a monumental task. A dramatic shift is important to slow the cyclical consequences of voter suppression. Creative and aggressive solutions are necessary to address the current state of the right to vote. We must, among other things, seek structural changes within the election system, such as depoliticizing the administration of elections, namely, by removing partisan operatives from key election administration positions, such as the secretary of state, to prevent the appearance of partisan gamesmanship. While alarming, this situation is not new. People of color have faced hostile courts and elected officials on the state and federal levels before and overcame those obstacles.

We Shall Overcome

It took an act of the people to persuade Congress and a president to sign the VRA. An elder from another era, Frederick Douglass, proclaimed, "If there is no struggle there is no progress. Those who profess to favor freedom and yet deprecate agitation are men who want crops without plowing up the ground; they want rain without thunder and lightning. They want the ocean without the awful roar of its many waters. This struggle may be a moral one, or it may be a physical one, and it may be both moral and physical, but it must be a struggle. Power concedes nothing without a demand. It never did and it never will."[7]

The current climate of oppression has led many people to become more involved in civic activities. Many people are finding their voices and raising them in an effort to achieve racial, economic, and gender equality. "Fighting the powers that be" resonates on issues that we face as a nation and in particular among younger generations. Movements, such as "MeToo" and "Black Lives Matter," are fighting for the same things: equality. How do we harness the winds of change and steer them in the direction of truth and justice? The next thing will come from the people demanding that their representatives on the local, state, and federal levels actually represent the people's interests. Accordingly, we must press for change and innovation in the way that we experience the right to vote. The hope is that these other mechanisms will eliminate the opportunity for suppressive tactics to take root. The goal of those who are working to expand the franchise is to adopt measures that reinforce a secure, fair, accurate, and nondiscriminatory path to political participation. Additionally, those efforts should make the process easier, not harder.

The suppressive measures outlined in this book illustrate the levels that people go to make voting harder. In *Crawford v. Marion*, the Supreme Court's voter ID case, Justice Ruth Bader Ginsburg wondered why voting is a difficult experience, stating,

> I'd like you to concentrate on the one group of people where I think you can make a facial challenge . . . , and that's the indigent people who can't get—don't have the photo ID. They don't drive, and they can't get up the money to get the birth certificate or whatever else. They do have a burden that, it seems to me, the State could easily eliminate if they want those people to vote, and that is to say okay, do the affidavit, the whole thing in your local precinct; we'll make it easy for you and not send you away, send you off to the county courthouse to get it validated. Why—why, if you really wanted people to vote, wouldn't you do it that way?[8]

We have the power to increase participation and thus have a more representative democracy. We have many ways to achieve this end.

Right to Vote Amendment

An example of imaginative thinking involves advocating for an affirmative right to vote in the United States Constitution. Currently, the Constitution has more amendments addressing the right to vote than any other fundamental right. Indeed, it prohibits voting discrimination based on race,[9] sex,[10] and age.[11] It also contains prohibitions against poll taxes.[12] However, it does not grant the right to vote. As the noted scholar Lani Guinier explains,

> The Constitution itself, as drafted by the framers, never explicitly granted the fundamental constitutional right to vote to anyone. The Constitution created no voters. Rather, it said that the voters would be the people that the states determined could vote. And then you had amendments to the Constitution, which simply state that the state or the United States cannot deny or abridge the right to vote on the grounds of race or the grounds of sex or the failure to pay a poll tax. But those are negative proscriptions. They are not an affirmative guarantee that we really want all citizens of the United States to participate in making the decisions that affect their lives.[13]

Moreover, organizations like Advancement Project argue that the lack of a right to vote (RTV) amendment continues to make the right to vote vulnerable to suppressive measures.[14] The US Supreme Court in *Bush v. Gore* informed us that "the individual citizen has no federal constitutional right to vote for electors for the President of the United States."[15]

A right to vote (RTV) amendment undercuts the debate around race-conscious and race-neutral solutions in the area of voting rights. Arguably an affirmative right to vote secures this fundamental right for all eligible persons. It would also limit the circumstances in which states could develop ways to disenfranchise voters. This type of amendment could eliminate barriers to the ballot box on the basis of race and ethnicity. Without an explicit right to vote, states are free to grant and revoke the right on the basis of various conditions, such as previous criminal convictions, competency, presenting a particular form of identification, or payment of a fee. Some scholars contend that an RTV amendment would not add to our current protections to the right to vote, primarily the antidiscrimination attributes of the present amendments.[16] How-

ever, an RTV amendment would go further than the present set of protections and set a ceiling instead of a floor for the fundamental right to
vote. As I have maintained, "an RTV amendment that simply guaranteed
citizens an explicit constitutional right to vote would rise to the level of
other protected rights such as the right to free speech and to practice
the religion of your choice. An explicit right makes it much harder for
states to employ divisive tactics that inhibit the exercise of the franchise.
An RTV amendment eliminates the massive differences in accessing the
ballot that occur across the country. The 'crazy quilt' of felon disenfranchisement requirements would no longer exist if the RTV amendment
granted the right to vote to all citizens."[17] An RTV amendment propels
this country into another democratic dimension. The present-day barriers to the ballot could not exist in the presence of a federal right to
participate in the electoral process.[18]

Voter Engagement

Nicole Austin-Hillery believes that we should undertake massive civic
education programs and stress civic engagement. She says,

> We have to do a few things. One, we're going to have to—now when I
> say we, I mean the community organizations that work on democracy
> issues—we are going to have to undertake a huge public education effort
> because voters, black and brown, are going to have to understand that the
> best way to protect their interest is for them to be engaged voters, to re-
> ally take part in the electoral process. They cannot be discouraged by or
> become disinterested. . . . And that's really one of the issues: public educa-
> tion undertaking. Secondly, I think nationally as a country, we're going to
> have to start to focus more on the fact that our biggest problems in this
> country really are not—and I tell people this all the time—our biggest
> problems are not voter ID. Our biggest problems are not disenfranchise-
> ment. And that's not to say that those aren't problems. But the biggest

problems we have are that we do not have enough Americans who engage in the voting process. When you look at the numbers of Americans that actually participate—and you can look at it at all levels, from primary elections to special elections to general elections for national office—the numbers are abysmal. So our biggest problem is getting our citizenry even focused on the importance of voting.[19]

As a country, we have a lower voter turnout rate when compared to other countries. The level of engagement could and should certainly improve with public education campaigns.

Voter Education

Certainly, we hear an abundance of persons reiterating the need for involvement. It is important that we emphasize that involvement is more than voting every two or four years. It is knowing your local, state, and national representatives. It is engaging in the electoral process in ways that inspire others to learn more about the process and work to change it. It is about truly having a representative government, one that reflects the city, state, or nation in its diversity. Austin-Hillery characterizes it this way: "Voters have to get more informed." You can get people registered, but I think we have to start teaching our citizenry that you have an obligation to not only register to vote but to also learn about the issues, learn about the candidates, learn about what's important. It is simply not enough to register, but you want to make informed decisions."[20] She continues, "So I think the effort has to be a bifurcated one. It has to be an effort to get more people registered but also to help people understand that the power to impact change lies in their hands and that the way that they empower themselves is by becoming educated about the issues, about the candidates, and to make informed decisions based on that education."[21] In essence, we must stress that civic engagement is about more than casting a ballot. While we must work to utterly destroy all barriers to the ballot box, we must also ensure that individuals have the power and knowledge needed to make sure that elected officials are effectively representing them after Election Day.

Compulsory Voting

The United States Supreme Court decision *Husted v. APRI*, involving Ohio's voter purge law, could prompt a move toward an informal system of compulsory voting.[22] Essentially, voters would vote more often in order to avoid the penalty of removal from the voter rolls for a failure to vote in a short time period, usually two to four years. In other countries, like Australia, citizens are penalized or fined for not voting. Certainly, one could consider removal from the voter rolls as a penalty that citizens could seek to avoid by going to the polls. If we truly wanted a more representative democracy deciding elections, some measure of compulsion would be acceptable without infringing on our deeply ingrained sense of liberty. NAACP president Derrick Johnson proclaimed, "You look at voting rights in Australia, we're talking about 96% of the electorate votes. In Canada, we're talking about 93%, and Germany is around 92%. They have different forms of compulsory voting; it is a state obligation to ensure folks vote."[23] If the state took ownership of ensuring participation in elections instead of penalizing and burdening voters, we might enjoy a more representative electoral system. In 2016, 56 percent of voting-age persons participated in the federal election. In the 2018 midterm, almost 50 percent of eligible voters participated, which was a dramatic increase from previous midterm contests. If we want a more representative democracy, then we must increase participation.

Eliminating Restrictive Voting Precincts

Derrick Johnson also believed that we should eliminate restrictive voting precincts. He pointed to our experience during early voting periods, in which voters go to a central location, for example, a courthouse, and cast a ballot regardless of whether the courthouse is their actual voting precinct. Generally, what happens outside of the early voting process, voters who happen to go to the wrong precinct are informed of the proper polling site or offered a provisional ballot that may or may not get counted. In essence, jurisdictions restrict voters to voting only within their precincts in order for their votes to count. NAACP president Johnson was correct that we have demonstrated the ability to conduct elections without connection to a particular polling place in the early voting process and could extend this practice to Election Day. Surely, we have become technologically advanced enough to provide voter registration information outside of an assigned precinct such that voters can vote at any polling place, just as they do during early voting. President Johnson maintained, "There is no reason why someone should get off work and drive past three, four, five voting precincts before they get to their designated precinct to cast their ballot, when the technology allows people to vote from wherever they exist, and the correct ballot can be produced. Early voting at courthouses demonstrate that every election cycle."[24]

National Holiday

Advocates continue to advance the proposition that federal elections should serve as a national holiday. Most states conduct elections on a weekday, and many close schools in order to utilize those facilities for the election. Indeed, Senator Bernie Sanders has suggested that we should make Election Day a national holiday. He has proposed "Democracy Day" to address low turnout in federal elections.[25] However, Senator Sanders's bill and others like it have not received much congressional support. When Barack Obama was president, he entertained a campaign to declare Election Day a paid holiday for federal workers. Although he decided not to implement this change, he stated, "Everything we can do to make sure that we're increasing participation is something that we should promote and encourage."[26] This proposal does have its detractors, who believe that declaring a national holiday would do little to increase turnout and would only benefit wealthier voters.[27] They question whether workers would actually use the day to vote or go shopping. In my opinion, a national holiday for elections will not solve the problem in total but should help lift some of the burden.

Other Modes of Modernization

Many voting rights groups advocate for modernization of the voting process. We certainly learned from our experience in the 2000 presidential election that our various voting methods were somewhat antiquated. Groups are pushing for automatic and same-day registration and online voting and registration. These measures will change the whole dynamic of how we vote and possibly moot current issues, such as the need for voter ID. Austin-Hillery says that "if registrations are automatically renewed, if people's registrations are following them—which portability is an aspect of the whole voter registration modernization concept— those things are going make these efforts like voter ID moot . . . , I think, eventually empower even more voters. That's also what will work to protect minority voters, who are the ones who are really at the core of these attacks."[28]

ONLINE VOTER REGISTRATION. Most states have a form of online voter registration. Internet voting can make it easier for a tech-savvy generation to register. However, persons who do not have reliable internet access or cannot afford access to the internet would not benefit from this innovation. Nonetheless, it is important to have numerous ways to register and to vote to increase access and to maintain the integrity of the ballot box.

AUTOMATIC VOTER REGISTRATION. Automatic voter registration would require election officials to increase the number of registered voters and the ease of registering to vote. Oregon was the first state to adopt automatic voter registration. Fifteen other states and the District of Columbia have also approved the policy. If the remaining states adopted this one policy, it could add fifty million people to the voter rolls.

SAME-DAY VOTER REGISTRATION. This method of registering would allow voters to register on Election Day, including early voting days. Seventeen states and the District of Columbia have same-day voter registration.

Certainly, modernization could help in the fight to vote and eliminate many of the attacks via voter challenges and inaccurate purges. Modernization would most help, in my opinion, millennials to engage in the electoral process. Turnout among this group of voters is abysmal. We have a turnout crisis based on age, socioeconomic level, and race. Marcia Johnson-Blanco, the codirector of the Election Protection Program housed at the Lawyers Committee for Civil Rights under Law, admonishes millennials to encourage each other to get engaged and participate in the political process. According to the Pew Research Center, Generation Xers and Millennials constitute approximately 59 percent of the electorate. However, "in the 2014 midterm election, which had a historically low turnout, these younger generations accounted for 53% of eligible voters but cast just 36 million votes—21 million fewer than the Boomer, Silent and Greatest generations, who are ages 54 and older in 2018."[29] Alarmingly, only 20 percent of eighteen- to twenty-four-year-olds voted in the 2014 midterm election. Again, modernization is not a silver bullet, but it stands to reason that if we increase access to registration and casting a ballot, participation would also increase. It is important to emphasize that "the fix" for our system will involve many innovations that are tailored to particular groups, regions, and demographics.

A 2016 study on turnout found that "a mix of strategies" would work best toward the goal of increasing turnout. It also found that a change of focus could well be in order away from turnout and that "[i]mproving the representativeness of the electorate, and knowledge about policies at stake, may be a more important (and realistic) goal than dramatically increasing overall turnout."[30] If we truly want people to participate, then we must provide the mechanisms for them to do so without fear or unnecessary encumbrances.

Cycles of Change

It is not coincidental that extreme voter-suppressive measures are introduced after periods of minority electoral success. It is interesting to note that the proliferation of voter ID laws were introduced and passed after another substantial demonstration of minority voters' cohesiveness. After the election of the nation's first African American president and a record turnout among minority and young voters, voter ID catapulted to the top as an antifraud and certainly an antiparticipation device. These changes coincidentally occurred after a period of great success, that is, an energized electorate, record-breaking turnout, and increased participation. The rules change, but we must continue to play the game. As such, it is imperative that our country does not dismiss the timing of these measures and sleep on the potential for entrenched and repeated voter marginalization.

With the vast number of disenfranchising mechanisms utilized in today's society, one can suffer from battle fatigue. This weariness of the soul leads to a disconnect from political participation, where we tend to relegate the decisions to a group of persons who may not have our interests in mind. The great historian John Hope Franklin concluded,

> Since all other issues were subordinated to the issue of "the Negro," it became impossible to have free and open discussion of problems affecting all the people. There could be no two-party system, for the temptation to call upon blacks to decide between opposing factions would be too great. Interest in politics waned to a point at which only professionals,

who skillfully deflected the interest from issues to races, were concerned with public life. The end result was an impoverished, pale imitation of democracy, one that placed government heavily under the control of a small elite class of propertied white males.[31]

These suppressive ebbs and flows are likened unto cycles. We have experienced cycles of progress and cycles of regress. One of my research assistants thought it akin to a J-curve, where you have exponential growth before an abrupt stop and significant drop. This concept is applicable to efforts that the United States has made toward social progress when there is exponential growth—for example, after the Civil War during the Reconstruction period in the late 1800s; after World War II during the Industrial Age in the 1940s and 1950s; after the civil rights movement in the 1960s and 1970s; after the reinforcement of NATO, NAFTA, and domestic policies that promoted economic growth and stability in the 1990s; and after the election of the first African American president of the United States in 2008. However, when efforts to impede social progress dominate—like slavery before the Civil War, Nazi Germany before World War II, Jim Crow before the civil rights movement, national isolation before international trade agreements, the great recession before the Obama administration, the current administration's attempts to stoke division and fear—growth stops, and a significant loss occurs.

The Voting Rights Act was created during a time of exponential growth: the civil rights Movement. Recent efforts to dismantle and possibly destroy it indicate that the peak of the J-curve may have been reached and that the United States is in store for a significant loss—unless we awake and make demands of ourselves, our communities, our elected officials, and our nation. Dr. Martin Luther King Jr. said, "one of the great liabilities of life is that all too many people find themselves living amid a great period of social change, and yet they fail to develop the new attitudes, the new mental responses, that the new situation demands. They end up sleeping through a revolution."[32] It may take a revolution to ensure that we do not experience an elongated period of repression.

Finally, it is important for all Americans to understand that voting is not a black and white issue and that it is not a Republican or Democrat issue. It is a fundamental democratic issue. It is the responsibility of all Americans to protect the integrity and promote access to the ballot box. The measures that opponents of democracy have developed to ensure political supremacy can be overwhelming. It is a fight to vote in this country. It is a right preservative of all others and must be held in high esteem for the sheer power that resides in it. It is incumbent on us all to value the right to vote and to fight to ensure that all Americans may truly possess it and the power therein.

Conclusion

When Hate Wakes, Justice Cannot Slumber

Voting fights in this country have ebbed and flowed from its inception. My grandmother's almost one hundred years have witnessed victories and defeats, progress and regress, hard-fought battles, with more battles to come. MaDear often encouraged me to keep my eyes on the prize. Here, the prize is freedom, emancipation, not returning to a darker time in our history. For this reason, we continue to fight for the right to vote regardless of race, ethnicity, language ability, gender, or criminal conviction. We fight.

The spiral of hatred, white supremacy, and black oppression took nearly one hundred years to address through the landmark civil rights acts of the 1950s and '60s. Blacks in the South, like my grandmother, parents, siblings, and other relatives, experienced this throughout their lifetime. Things did not change until the country was embarrassed by its own actions: killing four little girls in church on Sunday morning, water hoses ripping the skin off children in Birmingham, billy clubs bashing in the brains of freedom fighters, bombings of churches, bombings of buses, bombings of homes, beating people for voting and attempting to vote, killing people for marching, and then Selma, Lord, Selma. All of these actions personified the black existence. Yet hiding in plain sight were the huge disparities in voter registration rates and educational achievement gaps. These gaps perpetuated and soothed white-supremacist thoughts/beliefs on blacks' abilities. People fighting for equality forced the country to change. Strategic policies and lives lost lifted a nation from the pit of social and political polarization.

My father used to love to sing the old Sam Cooke song "A Change Is Gonna Come." Cooke composed this song in 1964 after getting turned away from a whites-only hotel in Louisiana.

> Then I go to my brother
> And I say, "Brother, help me please."
> But he winds up knockin' me
> Back down on my knees
>
> There been times that I thought I couldn't last for long
> But now I think I'm able to carry on
>
> It's been a long, a long time coming
> But I know a change gon' come, oh yes it will[1]

When my father sang the song, it had a sound of hope, of struggle, of battles fought and won.

In this new millennium, we are still looking for a change that unites, that does not weary, that empowers. It is that belief that allows my father and others to continue to work to change our country into a loving, compassionate image of a nation that beckons, as my former pastor often recited, "the least, the less, and the lost." This change from suppressive and regressive laws and outcomes to sustained progress will not be easy. My father often said, "Anything worth having is worth fighting for." We fight. We make progress, and then we fight for more. We cannot get satisfied. We cannot expect the system to change without our continued efforts to change it from a system that excludes people of color from obtaining and maintaining power to one of inclusion and recognition. It is this faith that compels us to continue to move forward toward a more just society. It starts with recognizing the quagmire that we are in and the impact our decisions have on the democratic system. The rise of hate in this century has solidified around the right to vote. While we do not have literacy tests, grandfather clauses, or vouchers, the modern-day mechanisms of voter ID and felon disenfranchisement, among others, operate in the same manner.

One could argue that hate has awoken, but justice cannot slumber. In this cyclical game of progress and regress, we are headed down the slippery slope of regression. It is important that at this time in our history we not only recognize our state of being but also fight to ensure that we do not continue to lose ground. We have the tools to complete the victory. This generation has more opportunities to right the ship of democracy in our lifetime. Recognizing the present cycle and fighting to push the pendulum toward justice and progress is within our reach. The struggle indeed continues. We are more than equipped to win the fight. However, it will take sustained effort and sacrifice to battle the forces of voter suppression. We do not have one hundred years. We do have the benefit of the wisdom of the elders and the fortitude of the foreparents that we will not return to a darker time when people of color are subordinated to second-class citizenship.

MaDear would say, "These times they are a-changing." Yet, through her eyes, these times are eerily familiar. The times are changing such that people of color will soon constitute the majority of persons in this country. The attempted purge will fail. The suppressive measures will fail. MaDear has seen this before. She witnessed a time when the power of the people changed the direction of the country. We have the power to ensure that the winds of change blow in the direction of progress and justice. These are critical times, but we are not sleeping. We press forward to our change. It is going to come.

Yes, it will.

ACKNOWLEDGMENTS

I would like to acknowledge the enormous support that I have received throughout the drafting, submission, and writing process. I am grateful to New York University Press, the University of Baltimore School of Law (UB), and the Colored Girls Group, consisting of my sisters in arms at UB, who read early drafts and provided valuable suggestions. I would also like to thank my many research assistants for their help on this work, including Sumbul Alam, David Bana, Ike Mpamaugo, Shaneel Myles, Candace Parker, and Ned Richardson. My former colleagues at the Department of Justice, especially Bruce Adelson, who encouraged and challenged me every step of the way, and my comrades at Advancement Project also deserve acknowledgment for their support. I am grateful to the Get Out the Boat Girls—Beverly, Carmen, and Cheryl—who constantly reminded me that if I wanted to walk on water, I had to get out of the boat. To the multitude of friends, encouragers, and folks who are too numerous to name who pushed me to write, were excited to hear about the book, kept me accountable, and provided an astute eye or a listening ear, *thank you.*

I would like to express my overwhelming gratitude for my siblings—Priscilla, Walter Jr., and Deidria—and a host of aunts, uncles, nieces, nephews, and cousins. My beloved grandmother passed away on February 15, 2019, in Kansas City, Kansas. She was laid to rest near Cane River in Louisiana, where her grandparents were enslaved. She has passed the mantle on to my generation and future ones to walk in dignity, strength, and faith. I am forever indebted to my parents and parents-in-law for sharing their stories and supporting me on this journey. Their examples have shaped me in ways that I could not have imagined.

Words cannot express the love that I have for my husband and children and for their unwavering support and sacrifice. The innumerable hours spent at Panera Bread, Busboys and Poets, the library, my office, and other venues were hours that I did not spend with you. Thanks for understanding and celebrating the milestones along the way. Thank you for allowing me to get the work done. All of my heart belongs to Laurence, Lauren, and William.

Finally, to all those who believe that the people are a sleeping giant, whose slumber has come to an end, let us continue to march toward the mark of the high calling of justice and peace and create the change that we want to see. For generations to come are relying on us to make this world a better place.

Onward!

NOTES

INTRODUCTION

1. The place where my maternal grandmother's grandparents were slaves, the Oakland Plantation in Natchitoches Parish, Louisiana, is a national historic site: National Park Service, *Oakland Plantation History* (last updated May 31, 2018), www.nps.gov.
2. Spencer Overton, *Voter Identification*, 105 MICH. L. REV. 631 (2007) (arguing that more empirical evidence is needed prior to adoption of voter ID laws.).
3. The poll tax for voting was outlawed in the Twenty-Fourth Amendment. In *Harper v. Virginia State Board of Elections*, 383 U.S. 663, 666 (1966), the Supreme Court found that "a State violates the Equal Protection Clause of the Fourteenth Amendment whenever it makes the affluence of the voter or payment of any fee an electoral standard."
4. According the United States Census Bureau, "The terms 'Hispanic' or 'Latino' refer to persons who trace their origin or descent to Mexico, Puerto Rico, Cuba, Spanish speaking Central and South America countries, and other Spanish cultures. Origin can be considered as the heritage, nationality group, lineage, or country of the person or the person's parents or ancestors before their arrival in the United States. People who identify their origin as Hispanic or Latino may be of any race." *Hispanic Population of the United States*, UNITED STATES CENSUS BUREAU (2012), www.census.gov. Nonetheless, *Latinx* is a gender-neutral term used as an alternative to *Latino* or *Latina* that refers to persons from Latin American countries. *Merriam-Webster's Dictionary* included the term in 2018. Both terms, *Hispanic* and *Latinx*, are used throughout this book.

CHAPTER 1. HISTORY REPEATS ITSELF

1. 347 U.S. 483 (1954).
2. In 1957, civil rights leaders, entertainers, and others organized the "Pilgrimage" to encourage federal officials to realize the promise of the then three-year-old *Brown v. Board of Education* Supreme Court decision. More than 20,000 people listened to three hours of speeches. Dr. King spoke last and focused his comments primarily on the need to ensure voting rights to the disenfranchised Southern Negro.
3. *Id.*
4. Avidit Acharya, Matthew Blackwell, and Maya Sen, *The Political Legacy of American Slavery*, 78 J. POLITICS 621 (2016).

5. *Id.* at 621.

6. Dr. Martin Luther King Jr., excerpt from *Give Us the Ballot*, speech, Washington, DC, May 17, 1957.

7. The hurry to impose restrictive voter ID laws began in the states after the passage of the Help America Vote Act. Georgia and Indiana, which had Republican-majority legislatures, were the first two states to adopt voter ID laws that severely limited access to the ballot. See, e.g., Joshua Douglas, *Introduction: The History of Voter ID Laws and the Story of* Crawford v. Marion County Election Board *(March 4, 2016)*, in ELECTION LAW STORIES (Joshua Douglas & Eugene Mazo eds., 2016).

8. Theophilus Eugene "Bull" Connor was commissioner of public safety for the city of Birmingham, Alabama, during the very violent 1960s. He publicly fought against efforts to enfranchise African Americans.

9. ACLU Pennsylvania, Applewhite, et al. v. Commonwealth of Pennsylvania, et al., Applewhite Petition for Review, http://aclupa.org.

10. *See* chapter 3, *infra*.

11. President Abraham Lincoln, Gettysburg Address, 1863. ("It is for us the living, rather, to be dedicated here to the unfinished work which they who fought here have thus far so nobly advanced. It is rather for us to be here dedicated to the great task remaining before us . . . that this nation, under God, shall have a new birth of freedom—and that government of the people, by the people, for the people, shall not perish from the earth.").

12. After the Civil War, in 1870, Congress passed the Fifteenth Amendment, which granted the right to vote, regardless of "race, color or previous condition of servitude." The Fifteenth Amendment of the United States Constitution states, "The right of citizens of the United States to vote shall not be denied or abridged by the United States or by any State on account of race, color, or previous condition of servitude. The Congress shall have power to enforce this article by appropriate legislation." US CONST. amend. XV, §§ 1–2.

13. *See* LA STATE CONST., Law Library of Louisiana, http://lasc.libguides.com.

14. Richard L. Engstrom, Stanley A. Halpin Jr., Jean A. Hill, and Victoria M. Caridas-Butterworth, *Louisiana*, in QUIET REVOLUTION IN THE SOUTH: THE IMPACT OF THE VOTING RIGHTS ACT 1965–1990, at 105 (Chandler Davidson & Bernard Grofman eds., 2006).

15. *See* ERIC FONER, RECONSTRUCTION: AMERICA'S UNFINISHED REVOLUTION 1863–1877, at 352 (Henry Steele Commager & Richard B. Morris eds., 1988).

16. *Id.*

17. 1866 Civil Rights Act, 14 Stat. 27–30 (Apr. 9, 1866), Chap. XXXI, An Act to protect all Persons in the United States in their Civil Rights, and furnish the Means of their Vindication.

18. Steven G. Calabresi and Andrea Matthews, *Originalism and* Loving v. Virginia, 2012 B.Y.U.L. REV. 1393, 1403.

19. Excerpt from TROUBLE THEY SEEN: THE STORY OF RECONSTRUCTION IN THE WORD OF AFRICAN AMERICANS (Dorothy Sterling ed., 1994).

20. The Fourteenth and Fifteenth amendments were ratified in 1868 and 1870, respectively.

21. Civil Rights Cases, 109 U.S. 3 (1883).

22. George Henry White, a Republican member of the United States House of Representatives, first elected in 1896, was the last African American to leave Congress during the period of Reconstruction. See *George H. White—Biography*, DOCUMENTING THE AMERICAN SOUTH, http://docsouth.unc.edu (citing DICTIONARY OF NORTH CAROLINA BIOGRAPHY (William S. Powell ed., 1996)).

23. RAYFORD W. LOGAN, THE BETRAYAL OF THE NEGRO, FROM RUTHERFORD B. HAYES TO WOODROW WILSON 91 (1997).

24. See J. MORGAN KOUSSER, THE SHAPING OF SOUTHERN POLITICS: SUFFRAGE RESTRICTION AND THE ESTABLISHMENT OF THE ONE-PARTY SOUTH, 1880–1910 (1974) (providing a history of the Southern Constitutional Conventions). Convention participants openly argued for the discriminatory removal of African American voters. In the Virginia convention, one delegate proclaimed, "Discrimination! . . . that, exactly, is what this Convention was elected for . . . with a view to the elimination of every negro voter." See REPORT OF THE PROCEEDINGS AND DEBATES OF THE CONSTITUTIONAL CONVENTION, STATE OF VIRGINIA 3076 (1906).

25. ALEXANDER KEYSSAR, THE RIGHT TO VOTE: THE CONTESTED HISTORY OF DEMOCRACY IN THE UNITED STATES (2000) (explaining that many of these measures "technically" did not violate the Fifteenth Amendment).

26. *Id.* at 112 ("In short order, other states followed suit, adopting—in varying combinations—poll taxes, cumulative poll taxes, . . . literacy tests, secret ballot laws, lengthy residence requirements, elaborate registration systems, confusing multiple voting-box arrangements, and eventually, Democratic primaries restricted to white voters. Criminal exclusion laws also were altered to disfranchise men convicted of minor offenses, such as vagrancy and bigamy.").

27. Major v. Treen, 574 F. Supp. 325, 340 (E.D. La. 1983).

28. HANES WALTON JR., BLACK REPUBLICANS: THE POLITICS OF THE BLACK AND TANS 90, 83 (1941); see also Sheryll D. Cashin, *Democracy, Race, and Multiculturalism in the Twenty-First Century: Will the Voting Rights Act Ever Be Obsolete?*, 22 WASH. U. J.L. & POL'Y 71, 105 (2006).

29. *See* WALTON, *supra* note 28, at 84.

30. *See* Cashin, *supra* note 28, at 79–84 (citing JOHN HOPE FRANKLIN & ALFRED A. MOSS JR., FROM SLAVERY TO FREEDOM: A HISTORY OF AFRICAN AMERICANS 285 (8th ed. 2000)).

31. Guinn v. United States, 238 U.S. 347 (1915).

32. *See, e.g.*, John Lewis & Archie E. Allen, *Black Voter Registration Efforts in the South*, 48 NOTRE DAME L. REV. 105, 122 (1972) (citing BLACK PROTEST: HISTORY, DOCUMENTS, AND ANALYSES 111 (J. Grant ed., 1968) In Louisiana in 1896, there were 164,088 whites registered and 130,344 Negroes. In 1900, the first registration year after a new constitution had been adopted, there were 125,437 whites and 5,320 Negroes registered. By 1904, Negro registration had declined to 1,718, and white registration was 106,360. This represented a 96 percent decrease in Negro registration and a 4 percent decrease in white registration.

33. Major v. Treen, 574 F. Supp. 325, 340 (E.D. La. 1983).

34. Interview with Beetrice Perry-Soublet, Robert Perry's daughter, October 2018.

35. Recounted by Mrs. Jones's daughter, Cassandra Jones Havard, October 7, 2018.

36. Interview with Rufus and Blanche Daniels, September 15, 2018. My father-in-law, Rufus Daniels, passed away on June 3, 2019, only a few days away from his eighty-second birthday.

37. *See generally* 347 U.S. 483 (1954).

38. Rufus Daniels interview.

39. *Id.*

40. *Id.*

41. 364 U.S. 339 (1960) (finding that a district drawn by the legislature to disenfranchise the predominantly African American citizens in Tuskegee, Alabama, violated the Fifteenth Amendment of the United States Constitution).

42. Founded in 1881, Tuskegee University enjoyed prominence and prestige under the leadership of its first president, Booker T. Washington, and scholars like Dr. George Washington Carver. The famed Tuskegee Airmen were trained at the Tuskegee Institute. Find out more, including contemporary developments, at www.tuskegee.edu.

43. *See* Fred Gray Sr., *Opening Remarks*, 10 T.G. JONES L. REV. 1, 5 (2006) ("In 1939, Dr. C. G. Gomillion, who was then a professor at Tuskegee Institute, which is now Tuskegee University, and other persons who worked at the Veteran Affairs Hospital . . . in Tuskegee formed the Tuskegee Civic Association. That Association later developed into a legal arm that those citizens used to secure the rights under the Thirteenth, Fourteenth and Fifteenth Amendments. In addition to them filing suit in *Gomillion v. Lightfoot* [364 U.S. 339 (1960)], . . . that organization caused other lawsuits to be filed.").

44. *See* Lee v. Macon County Board of Education, 221 F. Supp. 297 (M.D. Ala. 1963) (challenging school segregation in Macon County, Alabama; court ordered the desegregation of the schools and required the superintendent to present the plan).

45. *See* Henderson v. Macon County Agricultural Stabilization and Conservation Service, 317 F. Supp. 430 (M.D. Ala. 1970) (holding that the federal government could not discriminate in disseminating farm subsidies).

46. *See* Mitchell v. Johnson, 250 F. Supp. 117, 123–24 (M.D. Ala. 1966).

47. *See generally Gomillion*, 364 U.S. 39.
48. *Id.*
49. Excerpt from *Gomillion* Supreme Court transcript, www.oyez.org.
50. President Dwight D. Eisenhower created the Civil Rights Commission in the Civil Rights Act of 1957.
51. The Civil Rights Act of 1957 created the United States Commission on Civil Rights, transferred the Civil Rights Section to a more powerful Division with an Assistant Attorney General, and proposed that civil rights cases, including voting cases, be removed from state courts to federal courts. Civil Rights Act of 1957, Pub. L. 85-315, 71 Stat. 634 (codified as amended at 42 U.S.C. § 1995 (2006)). It was, however, seen primarily as a symbolic measure with little enforcement.
52. *See* South Carolina v. Katzenbach, 383 U.S. 301, 313 (1966), a case challenging the constitutionality of the Voting Rights Act. The Supreme Court noted,
    In recent years, Congress has repeatedly tried to cope with the problem by facilitating case-by-case litigation against voting discrimination. The Civil Rights Act of 1957 authorized the Attorney General to seek injunctions against public and private interference with the right to vote on racial grounds. Perfecting amendments in the Civil Rights Act of 1960 permitted the joinder of States as parties, gave the Attorney General access to local voting records, and authorized courts to register voters in areas of systematic discrimination. Title I of the Civil Rights Act of 1964 expedited the hearing of voting cases before three-judge courts and outlawed some of the tactics used to disqualify Negroes from voting in federal elections.
53. PRESIDENT LYNDON B. JOHNSON, SPECIAL MESSAGE TO THE CONGRESS: THE AMERICAN PROMISE (Mar. 15, 1965).
54. Voting Rights Act Amendments of 1982, S. Rep. 97-417, at 4 (1982).
55. President Lyndon B. Johnson, *Remarks in the Capital Rotunda at the Signing of the Voting Rights Act, August 6, 1965, available at* http://lbjmuseum.com.
56. President Lyndon B. Johnson called the Voting Rights Act of 1965 "one of the most monumental laws in the entire history of American freedom." DAVID J. GARROW, PROTEST AT SELMA: MARTIN LUTHER KING, JR., AND THE VOTING RIGHTS ACT OF 1965, at 132 (1978).
57. *See, e.g.*, BERNARD GROFMAN, LISA HANDLEY & RICHARD G. NIEMI, MINORITY REPRESENTATION AND THE QUEST FOR VOTING EQUALITY 23–24 (1992) (indicating that the gap between white and African American voters decreased significantly and in some instances disappeared in some southern states between 1965 and 1988).
58. The number of African American elected officials stood at 1,469 in 1970. In 2000, 9,040 African Americans held elected office in the United States. See DAVID BOSITIS, BLACK ELECTED OFFICIALS: A STATISTICAL SUMMARY, 2000, at 5 (2002), www.jointcenter.org.

59. *See* Bernard Grofman, Lisa Handley & Richard G. Niemi, Minority Representation and the Quest for Voting Equality 23–24 (1992).

60. Voting Rights Act of 1965, *available at* www.ourdocuments.gov (last visited Nov. 15, 2011).

61. *Id.*

62. *Id.*

63. Michael Ross, *The Voting Rights Act Turns 40*, MSNBC.com (Oct. 4, 2005), www.msnbc.msn.com.

64. From 1970 to 1998, the number of black elected officials increased from 1,469 to 8,868. Theodore Caplow, Louis Hicks & Ben J. Wattenberg, The First Measured Century: An Illustrated Guide to Trends in America, 1900–2000, at 186 (2001).

65. Voting Rights Act of 1965.

66. Bernard Grofman and Lisa Handley, *The Impact of the Voting Rights Act on Black Representation in Southern State Legislatures*, 16 Legislative Studies Q. 111 (1991).

67. *See* Bositis, *supra* note 58, at 5.

68. The police jury is likened unto county commissioners. The police jury's members are called jurors, and they serve as the legislative and executive governing body for the parish.

69. Interview with Walter and Betty Williams, October 1, 2018.

70. This data is limited to six states because it is the only enumeration conducted before 1984. See Rodolfo O. de la Garza and Louis DeSipio, Reshaping the Tub: The Limits of the VRA for Latino Electoral Politics (cited by David Epstein et al., The Future of the Voting Rights Act 142 (2006)).

71. Caplow, Hicks & Wattenberg, *supra* note 64, at 186.

72. The senator was Barack Obama, who became president of the United States in 2008.

73. *See* Daniel P. Tokaji, *Early Returns on Election Reform: Discretion, Disenfranchisement, and the Help America Vote Act*, 73 Geo. Wash. L. Rev. 1206, 1209–13 (2005) (describing the many reports that evolved after the 2000 election detailing voting irregularities).

74. From 2000 to 2002, the United States saw an increase in election reform laws. In state legislatures, approximately 3,643 election-related bills were introduced; 492 were passed into law. The number of election reform bills continued to increase as jurisdictions sought to comply with the Help American Vote Act of 2002 (HAVA). National Conference of State Legislatures, The States Tackle Election Reform: Summary of 2003 Legislative Action (May 11, 2004), www.ncsl.org.

75. Spencer Overton, *Voter Identification*, 105 MICH. L. REV. 631, 653–63 (2007) (addressing the need for more reliable data and empirical studies on voter fraud and the impact of fraud-preventing legislation).

76. US CIVIL RIGHTS COMMISSION, VOTING IRREGULARITIES IN FLORIDA DURING THE 2000 PRESIDENTIAL ELECTION (June 2001), www.usccr.gov.

77. *Id.*

78. HAVA, Pub. L. No. 107-252, 116 Stat. 1666. The HAVA is codified at 42 U.S.C. §§ 15301–15545 (Supp. III 2003).

79. H.R. Rep. No. 107-730 at 1 (2002) (Conf. Rep.).

80. *See generally* Crawford v. Marion Cty. Election Bd., 553 U.S. 181 (2008).

81. *See* South Carolina v. Katzenbach, 383 U.S. 301, 329–30 (1966) (upholding Section 5 and finding the coverage formula "rational"); City of Rome v. United States, 446 U.S. 156, 173 (1980) (upholding pre-1982 amendment version of Section 5 as constitutional); County Council of Sumter County, S.C. v. United States, 555 F. Supp. 694, 707 (D.D.C. 1983) (upholding statute and rejecting the challenge to the coverage formula because jurisdictions argued that more than 50 percent of their citizens were registered to vote); Northwest Austin Mun. Utility Dist. No. One v. Holder, 557 U.S. 193, 129 S. Ct. 2504, 174 L.Ed.2d 140 (2009) (in which the Supreme Court used the doctrine of constitutional avoidance and interpreted the bailout provisions as allowing any covered jurisdiction to apply for a bailout).

82. 570 U.S. 529 (2013).

83. THE LEADERSHIP CONFERENCE EDUCATION FUND, WARNING SIGNS: THE POTENTIAL IMPACT OF *SHELBY COUNTY V. HOLDER* ON THE 2016 GENERAL ELECTION (2016), www.aclu.org.

84. Shelby County., Ala. v. Holder, 570 U.S. 529, 558, 133 S. Ct. 2612, 2631, 186 L. Ed. 2d 651 (2013).

85. For Reconstruction citations, *see* FONER, *supra* note 15; KOUSSER, *supra* note 24; KEYSSAR, *supra* note 25.

86. Northwest Austin Utility District Number One v. Holder, Oral Argument Trial Tr. vol. 1, 41–42 (Apr. 29, 2009), www.oyez.org.

CHAPTER 2. THE VOTING RIGHTS ACT

Chapter subtitle: In 1980, Sheyann Webb, Rachel West, and Frank Sikora published a book of memoirs entitled *Selma, Lord, Selma: Girlhood Memories of the Civil-Rights Days*. Subsequently, Disney turned the book into a movie. The title of the book and the subtitle of this chapter refer to the magnitude of the events in Selma, Alabama, and the United States Supreme Court decision involving Shelby County, Alabama. *Epigraph:* North Carolina General Assembly, House, Audio Archives, July 25, 2013, www.ncleg.net. Eighty-three-year-old Mickey Michaux had been elected in 1972 as Durham's first black representative and appointed in 1977 as the South's first black US attorney since Reconstruction. In 2013, he was the longest-serving member of the North Carolina General Assembly. "I want you to understand why this means so much to so many people," he said on the house floor with tears in his eyes.

1. Zak Cheney-Rice, *Fear of a Black North Carolina*, NEW YORK MAG., Dec. 1, 2018, http://nymag.com.

2. In the "White Hands" advertisement, the commercial begins with a white male—showing only his hands—opening a letter and then throwing it away. The announcer then says, "You needed that job, and you were the best qualified. But they had to give it to a minority because of a racial quota. Is that really fair? Harvey Gantt says it is. Gantt supports Ted Kennedy's racial quota law that makes the color of your skin more important than your qualifications. You'll vote on this issue next Tuesday. For racial quotas, Harvey Gantt. Against racial quotas, Jesse Helms." *Jesse Helms "Hands" Ad*, YOUTUBE (Oct. 16, 2006), www.youtube.com. After airing the "White Hands" political advertisement, Senator Helms moved up considerably in the polls and ultimately won the election.

3. N.C. State Conference of NAACP v. McCrory, 831 F.3d 204, 214–15 (4th Cir. 2016).

4. Alexis Allston, *Q&A with Rep. Mickey Michaux on Durham Life and History*, DURHAM VOICE (Spring 2017), https://durhamvoice.org.

5. Sam Fullwood III, *A Voting Rights Story: Injustice in North Carolina*, CTR. FOR AM. PROGRESS (July 22, 2016), www.americanprogress.org.

6. *McCrory*, 831 F.3d at 216.

7. *See also* SL 2013-381, H.B. 589, 2013 Gen. Assemb. (N.C. 2013); 2013 N.C. SESS. LAWS 381.

8. In 1969, William Clay Sr. became the first African American elected from a former slave state since Reconstruction. US House of Representatives, *Clay, William Lacy, Sr.*, HISTORY, ART & ARCHIVES, http://history.house.gov (last visited June 2018).

9. In 1971, Parren Mitchell became the first African American elected from a former slave state since Reconstruction. US House of Representatives, *Mitchell, Parren James*, HISTORY, ART & ARCHIVES, http://history.house.gov (last visited June 2018).

10. *See* Adam Liptak, *Supreme Court Invalidates Key Part of Voting Rights Act*, N.Y. TIMES, June 25, 2013, www.nytimes.com.

11. *See* Derrick Bell, Brown v. Board of Education *and the Interest Convergence Dilemma*, 93 HARV. L. REV. 518 (1980).

12. 42 U.S.C. § 1973 (2006) at § 1973c(a).

13. *See* Fannie Lou Hamer, Rosa Parks, and Coretta Scott King Voting Rights Act Reauthorization and Amendments Act of 2006, Pub. L. No. 109-246, 120 Stat. 577. The VRA's most prominent temporary provisions include Sections 5 and 203, which govern which jurisdictions must report all voting changes to the attorney general and designate those jurisdictions required to provide election materials in certain minority languages. 42 U.S.C. § 1973(c) (Section 5); 42 U.S.C. § 1973aa-1a (Section 203).

14. 42 U.S.C. § 1973 (2006). Section 2 of the VRA prohibits voting practices and procedures that discriminate on the basis of race or color. Traditionally, Section 2 cases have involved challenges to at-large methods of election. However, Section 2's nationwide prohibition against racial discrimination in voting applies to any voting standard, practice, or procedure, including redistricting plans.

15. *Id.*

16. Voting Rights Act, Pub. L. No. 94-73, 89 Stat. 400 (amended 1975); Voting Rights Act, Pub. L. No. 91-285, 84 Stat. 314 (amended 1970); Voting Rights Act, Pub. L. No. 97-205, 96 Stat. 131 (amended 1982).

17. *See* S. Rep. No. 97-417, at 1 (1982).

18. *Id.* at 4.

19. In 1982, Congress eliminated the "intent to discriminate" requirement devised in *Mobile v. Bolden*, 446 U.S. 55 (1980). Voting Rights Act, Pub. L. No. 97-205, sec. 3, § 2, 96 Stat. 131, 134 (amended 1982) (codified as amended at 42 U.S.C. § 1973 (2006)).

20. Section 203 of the VRA, another temporary provision of the act, establishes coverage for jurisdictions with significant language minorities and requires those jurisdictions, among other things, to provide election materials and assistance in the covered language. 42 U.S.C. § 1973aa-1a (2006).

21. Section 208 provides that a person who needs assistance to vote due to blindness, disability, or illiteracy may have an assistant of his or her choice, provided that the person is not an agent or officer of the voter's employer or union. 42 U.S.C. § 1973aa-6.

22. Fannie Lou Hamer, Rosa Parks, and Coretta Scott King Voting Rights Act Reauthorization and Amendments Act of 2006, Pub. L. No. 109-246, secs. 4–5, §§ 4(a)(7)–(8), 5, 120 Stat. 577, 580–81 (codified as amended at 42 U.S.C. §§ 1973b(a)(7)–(8), 1973c(b) (2006)) (extending the temporary provisions for another twenty-five years).

23. *Id.* at sec. 2; 120 Stat. at 577–78.

24. H.R. Rep. No. 109-478, at 6 (2006) (footnotes omitted).

25. *Id.* at 2 (2006); see also Pub. L. No. 109-246, sec. 2(b)(9), 120 Stat. at 578.

26. H.R. Rep. No. 109-478, at 2.

27. In the 2006 reauthorization, Congress also made what is referred to as "the Ashcroft fix," amending Section 5 to overrule the Supreme Court's decision in *Georgia v. Ashcroft*, 53 U.S. 461 (2003), which held that states could replace majority-minority districts with "coalition" districts.

28. South Carolina v. Katzenbach, 329, 86 S. Ct. 803, 819 (1966).

29. Shelby Cty., Ala. v. Holder, 133 S. Ct. 594 (2012).

30. Shelby County, Ala. v. Holder, 133 S. Ct. 2612, 2631 (2013) ("We issue no holding on § 5 itself, only on the coverage formula. Congress may draft another formula based on current conditions.").

31. Shelby County, Ala. v. Holder, 570 U.S. 529, 535 (2013).
32. Currently, covered jurisdictions include all or part of the following states: Alabama, Alaska, Arizona, California, Florida, Georgia, Louisiana, Mississippi, New York, North Carolina, South Carolina, South Dakota, Texas, and Virginia. It also covers select townships in Michigan. *Section 5 Covered Jurisdictions*, US DEP'T OF JUSTICE, www.justice.gov (last visited Sept. 7, 2013).
33. Congress changed the bailout provisions in 1982 to enable more jurisdictions to seek to use the procedure. In *NAMUDNO*, the Supreme Court expanded the ability to seek release from Section 5's requirements through the use of the bailout provision. Nw. Austin Mun. Util. Dist. No. One v. Holder (*NAMUDNO*), 557 U.S. 193, 210–11 (2009). Since 1967, more than fifty jurisdictions have successfully "bailed out" of Section 5. For a list of jurisdictions and require-ments, see *Section 4 of the Voting Rights Act*, US DEP'T OF JUSTICE, www. justice.gov.
34. See *NAMUDNO*, 557 U.S. at 210–11 (broadening the definition of "political subdivision" under Section 5 to expand eligibility for bailout).
35. *Shelby*, 133 S. Ct. at 2619.
36. *NAMUDNO*, 557 U.S. at 203.
37. Thom File, *Voting in America: A Look at the 2016 Presidential Election*, PEW RESEARCH (May 10, 2017), www.pewresearch.org.
38. Dr. Crayton is the executive director of the Southern Coalition for Social Justice, an organization that works with "communities of color and economically disadvantaged communities in the South." SOUTHERN COALITION FOR SOCIAL JUSTICE WEBSITE, www.southerncoalition.org. A former law professor and a consultant, Crayton conducts research and writing in the area of voting, working on issues involving redistricting and its interaction with the Voting Rights Act, particularly in the US South. He clerked in the District of Columbia Circuit Court and interned in the Department of Justice, Civil Rights Division Voting Section.
39. Interview with Kareem Crayton, August 2018.
40. *About Section 5 of the Voting Rights Act*, DEP'T OF JUSTICE, www.justice.gov (last updated Dec. 4, 2017).
41. US Atty. Gen. Eric Holder, speech at the National Urban League, Philadelphia (July 25, 2013), www.justice.gov.
42. 163 U.S. 537 (1896).
43. *See infra* chapter 3 (discussing recent decisions in voter ID cases).
44. Richard Fausset, *Georgia County Rejects Plan to Close 7 Polling Places in Majority-Black Area*, N.Y. TIMES, Aug. 23, 2018.
45. Section 2 of the Voting Rights Act serves as a nationwide prohibition against voting practices and procedures that discriminate on the basis of race, color, or membership in a language-minority group. To prove a violation of Section 2, you must demonstrate "that a certain electoral law, practice, or structure interacts with

social and historical conditions to cause an inequality in the opportunities enjoyed by black and white voters to elect their preferred representatives." Thornburg v. Gingles, 478 U.S. 30, 47 (1986). It has been very effective in eliminating generational claims of voting discrimination. Litigation according to Section 2 of the act is time-consuming and expensive. Until Congress restores Section 4 of the VRA, Section 2 remains the best tool to combat laws that discriminate against minority voters.

46. Legal Defense Fund, *The Cost (in Time, Money, and Burden) of Section 2 of the Voting Rights Act Litigation*, NAACP (Sept. 2, 2017), www.naacpldf.org.

47. Crayton interview.

48. *Id.*

49. Leah Aden et al., *Warning Signs: The Potential Impact of* Shelby County v. Holder *on the 2016 General Election*, LEADERSHIP CONFERENCE EDUCATION FUND (June 2016).

50. Legal Defense Fund, *Democracy Diminished: State and Local Threats to Voting Post Shelby County, Alabama v. Holder*, NAACP (Sept. 2018), www.naacpldf.org.

51. Michael Wines, *Critics See Efforts by Counties and Towns to Purge Minority Voters from Rolls*, N.Y. TIMES, July 31, 2016.

52. *The Story of Moral Mondays, the North Carolina NAACP and Building the Forward Together Movement*, N.C. NAACP (Jan. 2014).

53. *Id.*

54. Sari Horwitz, *Texas Voter-ID Law Is Blocked*, WASH. POST, Aug. 30, 2012, www.washingtonpost.com.

55. Crawford v. Marion County Election Board, 553 U.S. 181 (2008).

56. *Id.*

57. *Greensboro Students Protest NC Voter Legislation, North Carolina AT&T Bennett College*, YOUTUBE (Sept. 4, 2017), www.youtube.com.

58. Aaron Blake, *North Carolina Governor Signs Extensive Voter ID Law*, WASH. POST, Aug. 12, 2013.

59. Dan Hopkins, *What We Know about Voter ID Laws*, FIVETHIRTYEIGHT (Aug. 21, 2018), https://fivethirtyeight.com.

60. Ari Berman, *A New Strategy for Voting Rights*, NATION, July 22–29, 2013.

61. In 2014, Congressman James Sensenbrenner and 177 cosponsors introduced the Voting Rights Amendment Act. H.R. 3899: Voting Rights Amendment Act of 2014, www.congress.gov. Congress continues to introduce remedial legislation. The current iteration of the Voting Rights Amendment Act is contained in H.R. 1799: Voting Rights Amendment Act of 2019, www.congress.gov.

62. H.R. 3899: Voting Rights Amendment Act of 2014.

63. H.R. 1799: Voting Rights Amendment Act of 2019 (introduced Mar. 14, 2019).

64. *See id.*

65. See Berman, *supra* note 60.

66. Crayton interview.

67. Derrick Johnson, speech at NAACP National 109th Convention, San Antonio, TX (July 30, 2018).

68. Purpose and need statements are vital components of the Environmental Impact Statement. *See, e.g.*, 28 C.F.R. § 51.27 (2008).

69. US CONST. art. I, § 4. "The times, places and manner of holding elections for Senators and Representatives, shall be prescribed in each State by the Legislature thereof; but the Congress may at any time by law make or alter such regulations, except as to the places of choosing Senators."

70. Ex Parte Siebold, 100 U.S. 371, 384 (1879).

71. Smiley v. Holm, 285 U.S. 355, 366 (1932).

72. 40 C.F.R. § 1502.13 (2008).

73. Dr. Martin Luther King Jr., *Sermon at Temple Israel of Hollywood* (Feb. 25, 1965).

CHAPTER 3. VOTER IDENTIFICATION

Epigraph: Ailsa Chang, *In Rural N.C., New Voter ID Law Awakens Some Old Fears*, NATIONAL PUBLIC RADIO (Aug. 16, 2013), www.npr.org.

1. *Id.* ("Currie says she's endured plenty of racism in her rural corner of the South. Like the time she was hired to clean a high school, and white students splashed cans of urine on her when she walked home from work. The new voting law in North Carolina means Currie will now have to vote absentee. But she says that's not really voting. You need to show up in person to vote with dignity.")

2. Election Reform Information Project, *Voter ID Laws*, PEW CENTER ON THE STATES (2008), www.pewcenteronthestates.org.

3. Carter-Baker Commission on Federal Election Reform, *Status of the Recommendations, September 2005–June 2007*, US ELECTION ASSISTANCE COMMISSION 3 (2007), www.eac.gov.

4. Help America Vote Act of 2002 (HAVA), Pub. L. No. 107-252, 116 Stat. 1668 (codified at 42 U.S.C. §§ 15301–545 (2006).

5. *See id.* (clarifying HAVA requirements).

6. Tracy Curry, *Where Is Your State on the Voting Map of Shame?*, MSNBC.COM (Oct. 13, 2012).

7. Voter ID laws progressed from requesting documentation to requiring documentation in order to vote.

8. *Voter ID History*, NATIONAL COUNCIL OF STATE LEGISLATORS (May 31, 2017), www.ncsl.org.

9. Wendy Underhill, *Voter Identification Requirements*, NATIONAL COUNCIL OF STATE LEGISLATORS (Jan. 17, 2019), www.ncsl.org.

10. ERIC FONER, A SHORT HISTORY OF RECONSTRUCTION: 1863–1877, at 183 (1988).

11. J. MORGAN KOUSSER, THE SHAPING OF SOUTHERN POLITICS: SUFFRAGE RESTRICTION AND THE ESTABLISHMENT OF THE ONE-PARTY SOUTH, 1880–1910, at 66 (1974).

12. FREDERIC OGDEN, THE POLL TAX IN THE SOUTH 13–14 (1958) ("The events in [South Carolina] suggest that a significant factor in the suffrage reform movement was not so much white supremacy as such but the supremacy of a particular group of whites.").
13. Article 5.02 of the Texas Election Code, V.A.T.S. See also Willis v. Duncan, 294 S.W.2d 914, 915 (Tex. Civ. App. 1956), aff'd, 157 Tex. 316, 302 S.W.2d 627 (1957).
14. Willis, 302 S.W. at 000.
15. Karen Shanton and Wendy Underhill, Cost of Voter Identification, NATIONAL CONFERENCE OF STATE LEGISLATURE (June 2014), www.ncsl.org.
16. See, e.g., Sheryll D. Cashin, Democracy, Race, and Multiculturalism in the Twenty-First Century: Will the Voting Rights Act Ever Be Obsolete?, 22 WASH. U. J.L. & POL'Y 71, 83 (2006) ("As mechanisms like poll taxes became constitutional requirements, white solidarity often had the effect of disenfranchising poor whites as well. Indeed, Jim Crow segregation laws were a form of appeasement for poor whites. If they could not share fully in voting suffrage or the spoils of an economic caste system, then the racial caste system of Jim Crow would accord them the psychological balm of legally sanctioned racial superiority.")
17. Justin Levitt, A Comprehensive Investigation of Voter Impersonation Finds 31 Credible Incidents out of One Billion Ballots Cast, WASH. POST, Aug. 4, 2014, www.washingtonpost.com; see also Justin Levitt, The Truth about Voter Fraud, BRENNAN CENTER FOR JUSTICE, www.brennancenter.org (last visited Feb. 17, 2019).
18. Frank v. Walker, 773 F.3d 783 (7th Cir. 2014).
19. In this table, included in Judge Posner's dissent, he shows the balance of power and the overwhelming Republican legislative leanings in states that imposed preventive ID:

Table 2

States with Strict Photo ID Laws—Political Makeup When the Laws Were Adopted
Arkansas: Democratic governor, but both the House and Senate were under Republican control.
Georgia: Republican governor, Republican control of both the House and Senate.
Indiana: Republican governor, Republican control of both the House and Senate.
Kansas: Republican governor, Republican control of both the House and Senate.
Mississippi: Adopted by the voters through a ballot initiative. Republicans, who already controlled the governorship and the state Senate, won a majority of seats in the House in that same election.
Tennessee: Republican governor, Republican control of both the House and Senate.
Texas: Republican governor, Republican control of both the House and Senate.
Virginia: Republican governor, Republican control of both the House and Senate.
Wisconsin: Republican governor, Republican control of both the House and Senate.

See id.
20. Id. at 790–91.
21. Keesha Gaskins and Sundeep Iyer, The Challenge of Obtaining Voter Identification, BRENNAN CENTER FOR JUSTICE (July 18, 2012), www.brennancenter.org.

22. Aasif Mandvi's interview of Don Yelton, THE DAILY SHOW WITH JON STEWART (Oct. 23, 2013), www.cc.com.

23. N. Carolina State Conference of NAACP v. McCrory, 831 F.3d 204, 229 (4th Cir. 2016), *cert. denied sub nom.*, North Carolina v. N. Carolina State Conference of NAACP, 137 S. Ct. 1399, 198 L. Ed. 2d 220 (2017) (citing Yelton testimony, transcript of public hearing of the North Carolina General Assembly, House Elections Committee (Apr. 10, 2013), at 51.).

24. *Id.* at 229.

25. One Wisconsin Inst., Inc. v. Thomsen, 198 F. Supp. 3d 896, 901 (W.D. Wis. 2016).

26. *Frank*, 17 F. Supp. 3d at 857–60 (citations and footnotes omitted).

27. Signed by Bettye Jones on Apr. 20, 2012.

28. Jennifer L. Patin, *The Voting Rights Act at 50: The Texas Voter ID Story*, LAWYERS' COMMITTEE FOR CIVIL RIGHTS UNDER LAW (Aug. 6, 2015), www.lawyerscommittee.org.

29. *Id.*

30. *Id.*

31. Judith Davidoff, *Madison Voters Turned Away at Polls for Lacking Photo ID*, ISTHMUS (Feb. 22, 2012, 10:53 AM), www.thedailypage.com.

32. Elizabeth Gholar, oral videotaped deposition, Veasey v. Perry, 2:13-CV-00193 (S.D. Tex. 2014).

33. Trial transcript, *id.*

34. *Crawford*, 472 F.3d at 953–54.

35. *Id.* at 954.

36. *Frank*, 17 F. Supp. 3d at 847.

37. *Id.* at 788.

38. *Id.* at 791.

39. Veasey v. Perry, 135 S. Ct. 9, Nos. 14A393, 14A402, 14A404 (2014).

40. Angelica Rolong, *Access Denied: Why the Supreme Court's Decision in* Shelby County v. Holder *May Disenfranchise Texas Minority Voters*, 46 TEX. TECH L. REV. 519 (2014).

41. Interview with Nicole Austin-Hillery, Sept. 1, 2015.

42. Mark P. Jones et al., *The Texas Voter ID Law and the 2016 Election: A Study of Harris County and Congressional District 23*, UNIVERSITY OF HOUSTON HOBBY SCHOOL OF PUBLIC AFFAIRS (Apr. 2017), http://uh.edu.

43. Trip Gabriel and Manny Fernandez, *Voter ID Laws Scrutinized for Impact on Midterms*, N.Y. TIMES, Nov. 18, 2014, www.nytimes.com.

44. See TEXAS SECRETARY OF STATE, TURNOUT AND VOTER REGISTRATION FIGURES (1970–CURRENT), www.sos.state.tx.us.

45. Austin-Hillery interview.

46. *Purcell v. Gonzalez*, 549 U.S. 1, 4, 127 S. Ct. 5, 166 L.Ed.2d 1 (2006) (per curiam) (before enjoining election issues, federal courts must "weigh, in addition to the

harms attendant upon issuance or nonissuance of an injunction, considerations specific to election cases.").

47. Veasey v. Perry, 2:13-CV-00193 (S.D. Tex. 2014).

48. Adam Liptak, *Supreme Court Allows Texas to Use Strict Voter ID Law in Coming Election*, N.Y. TIMES, Oct. 18, 2014, www.nytimes.com.

49. *See id.*

50. Miles Parks, *Fact Check: Trump Repeats Voter Fraud Claim about California*, NPR (Apr. 5, 2018), www.npr.org; see also Tina Nguyen, *White House Defends Trump Voter Fraud Lie, Offers No Evidence*, VANITY FAIR (Jan. 24, 2017), www.vanityfair.com.

51. See, e.g., Sharad Goel, Marc Meredith, Michael Morse, David Rothschild, and Houshmand Shirani-Mehr, *One Person, One Vote: Estimating the Prevalence of Double Voting in U.S. Presidential Elections*, Jan. 13, 2017 (scholars from Harvard, Stanford, University of Pennsylvania, Yale, and Microsoft Research found insignificant existence, 0.002 percent, of double voting); Justin Levitt, *A Comprehensive Investigation of Voter Impersonation Finds 31 Credible Incidents out of One Billion Ballots Cast*, WASHINGTON POST, Aug. 6, 2014; Justin Levitt, *The Truth about Voter Fraud*, BRENNAN CENTER FOR JUSTICE, 2007.

52. Lorraine C. Minnite, *The Politics of Voter Fraud*, PROJECT VOTE (Mar. 5, 2007).

53. Trip Gabriel and Manny Fernandez, *Voter ID Laws Scrutinized for Impact on Midterms*, N.Y. TIMES, Nov. 18, 2014, www.nytimes.com.

54. Lorraine C. Minnite, PhD, Expert Report, North Carolina State Conference of the NAACP v. McCrory, et al., Exhibit B, Case No.: 1:13-cv-00658-TDS-JEP (M.D.N.C. Dec. 4, 2015), https://moritzlaw.osu.edu; see also North Carolina State Conference of NAACP v. McCrory, 831 F.3d 204, 235–36 (4th Cir. 2016) ("The State has failed to identify even a single individual who has ever been charged with committing in-person voter fraud in North Carolina.").

55. Corbin Carson and Natasha Kahn, *Comprehensive Database of U.S. Voter Fraud Uncovers No Evidence That Photo ID Is Needed*, NEWS21 (Aug. 12, 2012), https://votingrights.news21.com.

CHAPTER 4. VOTER DECEPTION

Epigraph: In *Something's Gotta Give*, Harry (Jack Nicholson) tells a suspicious Erica (Diane Keaton) that he has always told her "some version of the truth."

1. Steve Burns, *Georgia Mayor Creates Firestorm with Election Day Post*, ATLANTA J.-CONSTITUTION, Nov. 8, 2016, www.ajc.com.

2. Olivia Dimmer, *Some College Students Are Being Met with Voter Suppression Tactics*, USA TODAY, Nov. 8, 2016, http://college.usatoday.com.

3. Abby Phillip & Mike DeBonis, *Without Evidence, Trump Tells Lawmakers 3 Million to 5 Million Illegal Ballots Cost Him the Popular Vote*, WASH. POST, Jan. 23, 2017, www.washintonpost.com; *see also* Sam Chamberlain, *Trump Tells*

Congressional Leaders 3–5 Million "Illegals" Cost Him Popular Vote, FOX NEWS, Jan. 24, 2017, www.foxnews.com.

4. *Merriam-Webster Online*, "deception," accessed 2018, www.merriam-webster.com.

5. The prevalence of deceptive practices and misinformation in the political arena has raised the profile of several websites dedicated to providing accurate information. *See, e.g.*, FactCheck.org, www.factcheck.org (last visited Oct. 7, 2009); PolitiFact.com, www.politifact.com (last visited Oct. 7, 2009); Snopes.com; www.snopes.com.

6. Sheryll D. Cashin, *Democracy, Race, and Multiculturalism in the Twenty-First Century: Will the Voting Rights Act Ever Be Obsolete?*, 22 WASH. U. J.L. & POL'Y 71, 79–84 (2006).

7. ERIC FONER, A SHORT HISTORY OF RECONSTRUCTION: 1863–1877, at 189 (1988).

8. *Id.*

9. CHARLES LANE, THE DAY FREEDOM DIED: THE COLFAX MASSACRE, THE SUPREME COURT AND THE BETRAYAL OF RECONSTRUCTION (2008).

10. *Id.* at 216–17.

11. Danny Lewis, *The 1873 Colfax Massacre Crippled the Reconstruction Era*, SMITHSONIAN.COM: SMARTNEWS (Apr. 13, 2016), www.smithsonianmag.com; *see also* LEEANNA KEITH, THE COLFAX MASSACRE: THE UNTOLD STORY OF BLACK POWER, WHITE TERROR, AND THE END OF RECONSTRUCTION xii (2009).

12. LANE, *supra* note 9, at 216.

13. Sheryll D. Cashin, *Democracy, Race, and Multiculturalism in the Twenty-First Century: Will the Voting Rights Act Ever Be Obsolete?*, 22 WASH. U. J.L. & POLICY 71, 83 (2006).

14. Meyer v. Grant, 486 U.S. 414, 421–22, 428 (1988) (holding that a prohibition against paying petition circulators violated the First Amendment).

15. Mitchell v. Comm'n on Adult Entm't Establishments of Del., 10 F.3d 123, 132 (3d Cir. 1993) (citation omitted).

16. Mills v. Alabama, 384 U.S. 214, 218, 220 (1966) (holding that the Alabama Corrupt Practices Act, which provided criminal penalties for publication of newspaper editorials on Election Day urging people to vote a certain way on specific issues, violated the constitutional protection of free speech and press).

17. Garrison v. Louisiana, 379 U.S. 64, 74–75 (1964) (holding that the statute is unconstitutional as punishing false statements against public officials (1) if made with ill will without regard to whether they were made with knowledge of their falsity or in reckless disregard of whether they are true or false or (2) if not made in reasonable belief of their truth).

18. US CONST. amend. I (providing that "Congress shall make no law respecting an establishment of religion, or prohibiting the free exercise thereof; or abridging the freedom of speech, or of the press, or the right of the people peaceably to

assemble, and to petition the Government for a redress of grievances"). The Fourteenth Amendment to the US Constitution makes the First Amendment applicable to the states. See N.Y. Times Co. v. Sullivan, 376 U.S. 254, 277 (1964).

19. *See, e.g.*, Buckley v. Valeo, 424 U.S. 1, 14–15 (1976).
20. *See, e.g.*, Citizens United v. FEC, 558 U.S. 310 (2010).
21. Monitor Patriot Co. v. Roy, 401 U.S. 265, 272 (1971) (finding that the First Amendment "has its fullest and most urgent application precisely to the conduct of campaigns for political office").
22. United States v. Grace, 461 U.S. 171, 177, 183 (1983) (quoting Perry Educ. Ass'n v. Perry Local Educator's Ass'n, 460 U.S. 37, 45 (1983)) (holding that the statute denying "'display' of any flag, banner, or device designed or adapted to bring public notice to a party, organization, or movement" in or on the grounds of the Supreme Court Building was unconstitutional because it could not be justified as a reasonable place provision).
23. Richmond Newspapers, Inc. v. Virginia, 448 U.S. 555, 578 (1980) (indicating that "[p]eople assemble in public places not only to speak or to take action, but also to listen, observe, and learn; indeed, they may 'assembl[e] for any lawful purpose'") (quoting Hague v. CIO, 307 U.S. 496, 519 (1939)). *See, e.g.*, Texas v. Johnson, 491 U.S. 397, 404 (1989) (citing Spence v. Washington, 418 U.S. 405, 409–10 (1974)) (upholding attaching peace flag to sign); W. Va. State Bd. of Educ. v. Barnette, 319 U.S. 624, 632, 636 (1943) (finding that refusing to salute the flag is constitutionally protected); Stromberg v. California, 283 U.S. 359, 368–70 (1931) (finding that displaying a red flag is constitutionally protected).
24. United States v. Bell, 414 F.3d 474, 479–80 (2005) ("The threshold inquiry is whether the commercial speech involves unlawful activity or is misleading.")
25. Burson v. Freeman, 504 U.S. 191, 206, 211 (1992). In *Burson*, the Court recognized that the exercise of free speech rights conflicts with the fundamental right to cast a ballot in an election free from intimidation and fraud. *Id.* at 211. Given the conflict between these two rights, the Court held that "requiring solicitors to stand 100 feet from the entrances to polling places does not constitute an unconstitutional compromise." *Id.*
26. United States v. O'Brien, 391 U.S. 367, 375 (1968). The Court held that "[a] law prohibiting destruction of Selective Service certificates no more abridges free speech on its face than a motor vehicle law prohibiting the destruction of drivers' licenses, or a tax law prohibiting the destruction of books and records." *Id.*
27. Garrison v. Louisiana, 379 U.S. 64, 75 (1964).
28. *Id.*
29. *See, e.g.*, Matthew Fraser & Soumitra Dutta, *Obama and Facebook Effect: His Masterful Use of Web Tools Helped Him Win the Presidency*, MEDIAWEEK, Nov. 24, 2008, at 10, *available at* 2008 WLNR 25922891; Joe Garofoli, *Obama Eyes New Role for Internet*, S.F. CHRON., Nov. 24, 2008, at A1; Laura Olsen, *Obama Team Capitalizes on Link to Youth*, CHI. TRIB., Nov. 26, 2008, at 7C.

30. *See, e.g.*, Ben Conery, *Electronic Scams Attempt to Keep New Voters at Home*, WASH. TIMES, Nov. 5, 2008, at B02 (discussing voter suppression tactics in which the perpetrators utilized text messages and Facebook and detailing Facebook messages that said election schedules had changed or that various parties were supposed to vote on different days). Conery's article also discusses problems at Drexel University, where students were told via fliers that they "would be arrested at the polls if they had unpaid parking tickets." *Id.* Overall, however, according to the article, incidents of voter suppression were far less prominent and on a much-lesser scale than in past elections. *Id.; see also* COMMON CAUSE, THE LAWYERS COMMITTEE FOR CIVIL RIGHTS UNDER LAW, AND THE CENTURY FOUNDATION, DECEPTIVE PRACTICES 2.0: LEGAL AND POLICY RESPONSES (2008); Dan Morain, *Some Obama Links Will Mislead*, L.A. TIMES, Aug. 30, 2008, at A18; JoyAnn Reid, *Bogus Emails Raise Anxiety over Voter ID Law*, S. FLA. TIMES, Oct. 3, 2008, at A1.

31. The use of computers and other electronic mechanisms in the distribution of political information has created yet another difficulty in thwarting these activities. Federal and state laws are ill equipped for internet-based deception.

32. John Wagner, *Top Ehrlich Aide, Consultant Indicted in Md. Robocalls Case*, WASH. POST, June 16, 2011, www.washingtonpost.com.

33. Peter Hermman, *Schurick Will Not Serve Jail Time in Robocalls Case*, BALT. SUN, Feb. 16, 2012, http://articles.baltimoresun.com.

34. *Lawyers' Committee Testifies before Maryland Senate on Deceptive Practices*, LAWYERS' COMMITTEE FOR CIVIL RIGHTS UNDER LAW (Feb. 16, 2012), www.lawyerscommittee.org.

35. Josh Eidelson, *Nasty Robo-calls in Wisconsin?*, SALON, June 5, 2012, www.salon.com.

36. *Id.*

37. *Bates College Students Say Election Fliers on Campus Are Voting Scare Tactics*, WGME (Nov. 6, 2016), http://wgme.com.

38. *Id.*

39. *See, e.g.*, S. Rep. No. 1, 76th Cong., 1st Sess. 12, 25, 39 (1939); 84 CONG. REC. 9604 (1939). The Hatch Act, which addresses voter intimidation, is codified at 18 U.S.C. § 594 (2006) and states in part, "it shall be unlawful for any person to intimidate, threaten or coerce, or to attempt to intimidate, threaten or coerce, any other person for the purpose of interfering with the right of such other person to vote or to vote as he may choose, or of causing such other person to vote for, or not to vote for, any candidate for the office of President, Vice President, Presidential elector, Member of the Senate, Member of the House of Representatives . . . at any election held solely or in part for the purpose of electing such candidate, shall be fined under this title or imprisoned not more than one year, or both." *Id.*

    See, e.g., United States v. Beaty, 288 F.2d 653, 655–56 (6th Cir. 1961) (involving eviction of black sharecroppers and finding relief against economic coercion); United States v. Wood, 295 F.2d 772, 781 (5th Cir. 1961) (granting relief against state prosecution of a black person engaged in voter registration work); United States v. Clark, 249 F. Supp. 720, 828 (S.D. Ala. 1965) (granting relief against baseless arrests and unjustified prosecutions). Others may have been thwarted by the inability to prove purposeful discrimination. *See, e.g.,* United States v. Bd. of Educ. of Greene County, Miss., 332 F.2d 40, 46 (5th Cir. 1964) (affirming a decision involving a school board's refusal to rehire a black teacher who took part in voter registration activities); United States v. Edwards, 333 F.2d 575, 57879 (5th Cir. 1964) (affirming a trial court's decision involving a physical attack on blacks who sought to register to vote).

40. Section 11(b) of the VRA reads as follows: "No person, whether acting under color of law or otherwise, shall intimidate, threaten, or coerce, or attempt to intimidate, threaten, or coerce any other person for voting or attempting to vote, or intimidate, threaten, or coerce, or attempt to intimidate, threaten, or coerce any person for urging or aiding any person to vote or attempt to vote, or intimidate."

41. H.R. 4463, 109th Cong. (2005); H.R. 5815, 112th Cong. (2012); H.R. 6607, 115th Cong. (2018).

42. H.R. 4463 § 2(b)(1)(A); H.R. 5815 § 2(b)(1)(b), 112th Cong. (2012).

43. H.R. 6607, 115th Cong. (2018): "(i) knows such information to be materially false; and (ii) has the intent to impede or prevent another person from exercising the right to vote in an election."

44. *Id.*

45. S. 1975, 109th Cong. (2005). This bill defined a deceptive practice this way:
(A) It shall be unlawful for any person to knowingly deceive another person regarding
  (i) the time, place, or manner of an election described in subparagraph (B), or the qualifications for or restrictions on voter eligibility for any such election, with the intent to prevent such person from exercising the right to vote in such election;
  (ii) the political party affiliation of any candidate running in any election described in subparagraph (B);
  (iii) the sponsor, endorser, or originator of any electronic, written, or telephonic communication, or any other public communication . . . that promotes, supports, attacks, or opposes a clearly identified candidate in any election described in subparagraph (B).

46. *Id.*

47. The definition should provide the following principles:
  1. Dissemination of false information:
    - The explanation must be broad enough to capture not only traditional print and oral communications but also telephonic (i.e., robocalls) and electronic (i.e., email, spyware, social media) communications.
  2. False information:

- Information communicated must contain a false statement of fact or an omission of a fact resulting in a false statement.
- The false statement must regard the time, place, or manner of voting or the voter's qualifications or eligibility to vote.
- This definition does not include lying about a candidate's qualification for the position, as that would probably face First Amendment scrutiny.
- Err on the side of caution when using the word "statement," as communication may not actually include a statement but instead might be a picture or drawing that could be misleading (e.g., a thumbs-up with an elephant next to the candidate's picture).

3. Intent to prevent a voter from voting:
   - Information must be shared with the specific intent to prevent or deter another person from voting.

48. 42 U.S.C. § 1971(b) reads as follows:

No person, whether acting under color of law or otherwise, shall intimidate, threaten, coerce, or attempt to intimidate, threaten, or coerce any other person for the purpose of interfering with the right of such other person to vote or to vote as he may choose, or of causing such other person to vote for, or not to vote for, any candidate for the office of President, Vice President, presidential elector, Member of the Senate, or Member of the House of Representatives, Delegates or Commissioners from the Territories or possessions, at any general, special, or primary election held solely or in part for the purpose of selecting or electing any such candidate.

Section 1971(c) authorizes the attorney general to bring civil actions for "preventive relief" against violations of Section 1971(b).

49. Additional information on voter intimidation and deception can be found in my law review article: Gilda R. Daniels, *Voter Deception*, 43 IND. L. REV. 343 (2010), http://ssrn.com.

50. 42 U.S.C. § 1973gg-10(1), renumbered as 52 U.S.C.A. § 20511, provides,

A person, including an election official, who in any election for Federal office—

(1) knowingly and willfully intimidates, threatens, or coerces, or attempts to intimidate, threaten, or coerce, any person for—

(A) registering to vote, or voting, or attempting to register or vote;

(B) urging or aiding any person to register to vote, to vote, or to attempt to register or vote; or

(C) exercising any right under this subchapter; or

(2) knowingly and willfully deprives, defrauds, or attempts to deprive or defraud the residents of a State of a fair and impartially conducted election process, by—

(A) the procurement or submission of voter registration applications that are known by the person to be materially false, fictitious, or fraudulent under the laws of the State in which the election is held; or

(B) the procurement, casting, or tabulation of ballots that are known by the person to be materially false, fictitious, or fraudulent under the laws of the State in which the election is held,

shall be fined under title 18, United States Code (which fines shall be paid into the general fund of the Treasury, miscellaneous receipts (pursuant to section 3302 of title 31, United States Code), notwithstanding any other law), or imprisoned not more than 5 years, or both.

51. Press Release, Sen. Barack Obama, Obama Bill Would Make Election Fraud, Voter Intimidation Illegal (June 7, 2007), http://sweetness-light.com. The unsuccessful Obama bill, cosponsored by New York Senator Charles Schumer, linked deceptive practices and intimidation, defining "deceptive practices" as "involv[ing] the dissemination of false information intended to prevent voters from casting their ballots, intimidate the electorate, and undermine the integrity of the electoral process." Deceptive Practices and Voter Intimidation Prevention Act of 2007, S. 453, 110th Cong. § 2 (2007).

52. The Public Integrity Section (PIN) of the Department of Justice defines voter suppression as follows:

Voter suppression schemes are designed to ensure the election of a favored candidate by blocking or impeding voters believed to oppose that candidate from getting to the polls to cast their ballots. Examples include providing false information to the public—or a particular segment of the society— regarding the qualifications to vote, the consequences of voting in connection with citizenship status, the dates or criteria for absentee voting, the date of an election, the hours for voting, or the correct voting precinct. Another voter suppression scheme attempted recently with partial success, involved impeding access to voting by jamming the telephone lines of entities offering rides to the polls to prevent voters from requesting needed transportation.

RICHARD C. PILGER, FEDERAL PROSECUTION OF ELECTION OFFENSE 61 (U.S. Dep't of Just., Crim. Division, Pub. Integrity Sect., 8th ed., 2017), available at www.justice.gov.

53. *Id.*

54. Daniels, *supra* note 49, at 376.

55. *See, e.g.*, Ala. Code § 17-17-33 (1975) (effective Jan. 1, 2007) (barring intimidation and threats for the election of "any candidate for state or local office or any other proposition at any election"). The statute also qualifies intimidation as a class A misdemeanor. *Id.*

56. Christopher Famighetti, Douglas Keith, and Myrna Pérez, *Noncitizen Voting: The Missing Millions*, BRENNAN CENTER FOR JUSTICE (May 5, 2017), www. brennancenter.org.

57. *Id.*

58. *Id.*

59. Molly Ball, *Donald Trump and the Politics of Fear*, ATLANTIC, Sept. 2, 2016, www.theatlantic.com; Jeremy W. Peters, *In a Divided Era, One Thing Seems to Unite: Political Anger*, N.Y. TIMES, Aug. 17, 2018, www.nytimes.com.

60. Federal statutes define intimidation as those actions that involve threats and interfere with a voter's right to exercise the franchise. *See* 42 U.S.C. § 1971(b) (2006).

61. Deferred Action for Childhood Arrivals (DACA) is the product of a 2012 executive order that allows persons who entered the United States as children to defer a removal action for a specified period of time. *See, e.g.,* Department of Homeland Security, *Deferred Action for Childhood Arrivals* (June 2019), www. ice.gov.

62. Famighetti, Keith, and Pérez, *supra* note 56.

63. Corey Hutchins, *Voters Keep Un-registering in Colorado: Most of Them Are Democrats*, COLORADO INDEPENDENT, July 17, 2017, www.coloradoindepen-dent.com.

64. *Id.*

65. "Denver's McReynolds, an unaffiliated voter, said she believes it 'disingenuous' to label the in-state reaction as a political stunt, adding, 'voters have told us directly their withdrawals are due to privacy concerns.'" *Id.*

66. Asa Royal, *Florida Voters Cancel Their Own Registration: Is Trump's Fraud Commission the Cause?*, TAMPA BAY TIMES, July 31, 2017, www.tampabay.com.

67. *Id.*

68. *Id.*

69. Vanita Gupta, *The Voter Purges Are Coming*, N.Y. TIMES, July 19, 2017, www. nytimes.com. Ms. Gupta called some members of the commission the "voter suppression dream team." ("To enact his plan, President Trump has assembled the voter suppression dream team of Kris Kobach, Ken Blackwell, Hans von Spakovsky and J. Christian Adams, who have all made wildly inflated claims about voter fraud.")

70. Amber F. McReynolds, *Trump's Voter Commission Is Frightening Away Voters*, DENVER POST, July 10, 2017, www.denverpost.com.

71. *Id.* "I have concerns that my individually-identifiable information would be misused for illegitimate purposes. I sincerely hope that the Denver Elections Division does not support, or respond to, any such requests involving private information in the future." "I am sending this email to state my objection to providing any private information to the commission, should the Denver Elections Division (or the Colorado Secretary of State) be pressured in the future to provide such information." "I am officially requesting that you DO NOT release my name to the federal government, in terms of my act of voting, or my voting record, or any information at all. Voting should remain a citizen's private duty, and there is no need to do this." "I'm afraid to withdraw my voter registration

because some law or rule may change in the interim that won't allow me to register again."

72. Kris Kobach, *It Appears That Out-of-State Voters Changed the Outcome of the New Hampshire US Senate Race*, BREITBART, Sept. 7, 2017, www.breitbart.com.

73. *See, e.g.*, Secretary of State, New Hampshire, *How to Register to Vote*, http://sos. nh.gov (Students must be "18 years of age or older on election day; a United States citizen, and domiciled in the town or ward where the person seeks to vote."). In 2018, the state of New Hampshire changed its requirements for voter registration to require proof of age, residency, and citizenship. *Id.*

74. *See, e.g.*, Michelle Ye Hee Lee, Fact Checker: Kris Kobach's Claim That There Is Now "Proof" of Voter Fraud in New Hampshire, WASH. POST, September 25, 2017, www.washingtonpost.com.

75. Department of Justice, *Fact Sheet on Justice Department's Enforcement Efforts Following* Shelby County *Decision*, www.justice.gov.

76. Press Release, US House Committee on the Judiciary, Chairman Jerrold Nadler, Chairman Nadler Opening Statement for Hearing on H.R. 1, "For the People Act of 2019" (Jan. 29, 2019), https://judiciary.house.gov ("It does not help that President Trump has encouraged conspiracy theories about massive voter fraud as a justification for voter identification laws and other voter suppression tactics. . . . The President seized on tentative and unverified information from Texas election officials about potential non-citizens who were registered to vote. He sent a wildly misleading tweet about the report, calling voter fraud rampant, and demanding voter ID laws. I hope our witnesses today will help dispel the dangerous myth of widespread voter fraud.")

77. *Id.*

78. Felicia Sonmez, *McConnell Says Bill That Would Make Election Day a Federal Holiday Is a Power Grab by Democrats*, WASH. POST, Jan. 30, 2019, www. washingtonpost.com.

79. Simon Shuster, *German Election 2017: The Fact-Checkers Fighting Fake News*, TIME, Aug. 9, 2019, http://time.com.

80. *Id.*

81. Jocelyn Benson, *Voter Fraud or Voter Defrauded? Highlighting an Inconsistent Consideration of Election Fraud*, 44 HARV. C.R.-C.L. L. REV. 1, 20–24 (2009).

82. Hunt Allcott & Matthew Gentzkow, *Social Media and Fake News in the 2016 Election*, 31 J. ECON. PERSP. 211, 212 (2017), https://web.stanford.edu (containing troubling statistics on fake news): "1) 62 percent of US adults get news on social media; 2) the most popular fake news stories were more widely shared on Facebook than the most popular mainstream news stories; 3) many people who see fake news stories report that they believe them; and 4) the most discussed fake news stories tended to favor Donald Trump over Hillary Clinton. Putting these facts together, some commentators have suggested that Donald Trump

would not have been elected president were it not for the influence of fake news" (citations omitted).

CHAPTER 5. VOTER PURGES

Epigraph: Nina Totenberg, *Supreme Court Upholds Controversial Ohio Voter Purge Law*, NPR (June 11, 2018), www.npr.org.

1. Rev. Joseph Lowery, former president of the Southern Christian Leadership Council, responding to a proposed list of voters that would be purged. He recognized the common names of people in his community, such as Johnson and Smith. He also said, "I think [the Republicans] would use anything they can find. Their desperation is rising." Greg Palast, *Jim Crow Returns: Millions of Minority Voters Threatened by Electoral Purge*, ALJAZEERA AMERICA (Oct. 29, 2014), http://projects.aljazeera.com.

2. *See* Xi Wang, *Black Suffrage and the Redefinition of American Freedom, 1860–70*, 17 CARDOZO L. REV. 2153 (1996).

3. *See id.* at 2168–74.

4. *See generally* James W. Fox Jr., *Imitations of Citizenship: Repressions and Expressions of Equal Citizenship in the Era of Jim Crow*, 50 HOW. L.J. 113, 156–58 (2006).

5. John Lewis & Archie E. Allen, *Black Voter Registration Efforts in the South*, 48 NOTRE DAME L. REV. 105, 107 (1972) (citing BLACK PROTEST: HISTORY, DOCUMENTS, AND ANALYSES, 111 (Joanne Grant ed., 1970)).

6. 42 U.S.C. § 1973gg–gg-10. See the text of the law at www.justice.gov.

7. 52 U.S.C.A. § 20501 (West).

8. 42 U.S.C. § 1973gg-6.

9. The NVRA also provides additional safeguards under which registered voters would be able to vote notwithstanding a change in address in certain circumstances. For example, voters who move within a district or a precinct will retain the right to vote even if they have not reregistered at their new address.

10. Condon v. Reno, 913 F. Supp. 946 (D.S.C. 1995).

11. ACLU/DEMOS, *Purged! How a Patchwork of Flawed and Inconsistent Voting Systems Could Deprive Millions of Americans of the Right to Vote* (Oct. 2004), www.demos.org.

12. Critics of voter purges suggest that instead of carrying out the primary function of the NVRA—increasing voter registration and participation—the Department of Justice's Voting Section is concentrating its NVRA enforcement priority on pressuring jurisdictions to trim the voter rolls. Contrary to the NVRA's mandate to make voting more accessible and to increase voter participation, recently the Department of Justice threatened to sue ten states in an attempt to force them to purge voter rolls before the 2008 presidential election. *See What Congress Should Do*, N.Y. TIMES, Oct. 24, 2004, www.nytimes.com; Steven Rosenfeld, *Bush*

Government to Poor Voters: We Don't Want You to Vote, ALTER NET (July 17, 2007), www.alternet.org.

13. "[T]he right of citizens of the United States to vote is a fundamental right." 52 U.S.C. § 20501(a)(1).

14. *See* 39 U.S.C.A. § 3629; 52 U.S.C.A. §§ 20501–511.

15. *See* S. Rep. No. 103-6, at 17 (1993).

16. *See id.* at 18.

17. *The Impact of the National Voter Registration Act of 1993 on the Administration of Federal Elections*, FEDERAL ELECTION COMMISSION (June 1997), www.fec. gov.

18. 531 U.S. 98 (2000).

19. Help America Vote Act of 2002, 42 U.S.C. ch. 146, § 15301 *et seq.* (providing robust federal investments into local voting infrastructure to facilitate access to the franchise and setting basic standards for election administration).

20. *See, e.g.*, Condon v. Reno, 913 F. Supp. 946, 949 (D.S.C. 1995).

21. *See* Richard L. Hasen, *The 2016 Voting Wars: From Bad to Worse*, 26 WM. & MARY BILL RTS. J. 629, 630 (2018) (Figure 6.2: "Election Challenge" Cases per Year: 1996–2016).

22. I served as amici in Brief of Amici Curiae for Eric C. Holder et al., Husted v. A. Philip Randolph Institute (filed Sept. 22, 2017) (arguing that for almost three decades through Republican and Democratic administrations, the Department of Justice had maintained the position that the NVRA prohibited removal for not voting); *Husted v. A. Philip Randolph Institute*, SCOTUSBLOG (Oct. 2017), www. scotusblog.com.

23. Brief for the United States as Amicus Curiae Supporting Petitioner at 10, John Husted v. A. Phillip Randolph Institute et al., No. 16-980 (U.S. Aug. 7, 2017).

24. Brief of Amici Curiae for Eric C. Holder et al.

25. Gilda R. Daniels, *Husted v. A. Philip Randolph Institute: To Vote, or Not to Vote: That Is the Question*; AMERICAN CONSTITUTION SOCIETY, SUPREME COURT REVIEW 2017–2018, at 61 (2nd ed., Nov. 28, 2018), www.acslaw.org.

26. Nina Totenberg, *Supreme Court Upholds Controversial Ohio Voter Purge Law*, NPR (June 11, 2018), www.npr.org.

27. Ohio has a sordid history in the area of voting rights. It has attempted to employ a number of disenfranchising methods throughout the years. *See, e.g.*, Stewart v. Blackwell, 356 F. Supp. 2d 791 (N.D. Ohio 2004). Ne. Ohio Coal. for the Homeless v. Husted, 837 F.3d 612 (6th Cir. 2016), *cert. denied*, 137 S. Ct. 2265, 198 L. Ed. 2d 699 (2017); *see also* James Dao, Fessenden Ford & Tom Zeller Jr., *Voting Problems in Ohio Spur Call for Overhaul*, N.Y. TIMES, Dec. 2004, www.nytimes.com.

28. Husted v. A. Philip Randolph Inst., 138 S. Ct. 1833, 1865 (2018) (Sotomayor, J., dissenting).

29. *See id.* at 1856 (Breyer, J., dissenting).

30. *Id.* at 1856.

31. *See* Brief for League of Women Voters et al. as Amici Curiae, Husted v. A. Philip Randolph Institute (filed Sept. 22, 2017), at 16 and n. 12 (citing Ohio Secretary of State, 2014 Official Election Results).

32. 570 U.S. 529 (2013) (finding Section 4 of the Voting Rights Act of 1965 unconstitutional, effectively stripping federal protections found in Section 5 of the act using a states'-rights rationale). *See generally* Gilda R. Daniels, *Unfinished Business: Protecting Voting Rights in the Twenty-First Century*, 81 GEO. WASH. L. REV. 1928 (2013).

33. Jonathan Brater, Kevin Morris, Myrna Pérez & Christopher Deluzio, *Purges: A Growing Threat to the Right to Vote*, BRENNAN CENTER FOR JUSTICE (July 20, 2018), www.brennancenter.org.

34. *Id.*

35. *Id.*

36. Jacqueline Thomsen, *Study: States with Racial Discrimination History Purge Voter Rolls More Aggressively*, THE HILL (July 20, 2018), www.thehill.com.

37. *Id.*

38. GREG PALAST, THE BEST DEMOCRACY MONEY CAN BUY 44–47 (2002).

39. Myrna Pérez, *Voter Purges*, BRENNAN CENTER FOR JUSTICE 3 (2008), www.brennancenter.org.

40. Ford Fessenden, *Florida List for Purges of Voters Proves Flawed*, N.Y. TIMES, July 10, 2004, www.nytimes.com.

41. *Id.*

42. AP, *Florida Scraps Flawed Felon Voting List*, USA TODAY, July 10, 2004, www.usatoday.com.

43. Pérez, *supra* note 39, at 33.

44. Marsha Shuler, *Registrar Drops More than 21,000 from Voters Rolls*, THE ADVOCATE, Aug. 17, 2007, at A10.

45. Joe Gyan Jr., *Study: N.O. Population Older, Less Poor, City Remains Majority Minority*, THE ADVOCATE, Sept. 13, 2007, at A1 (reporting that New Orleans's black population dropped from 67 percent before Hurricane Katrina to 58 percent a year later).

46. Pérez, *supra* note 39, at Appendix 1, 1–5.

47. *Id.* at Appendix 2, 6–10.

48. Abbie Boudreau & Scott Bronstein, *Some Voters "Purged" from Voter Rolls*, CNN (Oct. 2008), www.cnn.com.

49. *Id.*

50. Brater et al. *supra* note 33.

51. Ian Urbina, *States' Purges of Voter Rolls Appear Illegal*, N.Y. TIMES, Oct. 8, 2008, www.nytimes.com.

52. Removals within ninety days are only permitted when voters die, notify the authorities that they have moved out of state, or have been declared unfit to vote.

53. Frank Emmert et al., *Trouble Counting Votes? Comparing Voting Mechanisms in the United States and Other Selected Countries*, 41 CREIGHTON L. REV. 3, 30–34 (2007).

54. David Schultz, *Less than Fundamental: The Myth of Voter Fraud and the Coming of the Second Great Disenfranchisement*, 34 WM. MITCHELL L. REV. 483, 487–92 (2008).

55. Emmert et al., *supra* note 53, at 3.

56. Palast, *supra* note 1.

57. *Open Voter Purge List*, VERIFIED VOTING FOUNDATION (June 12, 2004), www.verifiedvotingfoundation.org.

58. Fessenden, *supra* note 40. State officials admitted that the list was racially discriminatory: "After The New York Times examined the data, state officials acknowledged that the method for matching lists of felons to those of voters automatically exempted all felons who identified themselves as Hispanic," thus accounting for the significant disparities in the number of blacks and Hispanics on the felon list. Ford Fessenden, *Campaign 2004: Civil Rights Board Wants Inquiry on Florida Voter-Purge List*, N.Y. TIMES, July 16, 2004; Robert Yoon, *CNN Asks Florida Court for Ineligible Voters List: County Boards Reviewing List for Accuracy*, CNN (May 28, 2004), www.cnn.com.

59. Partisan concerns are an issue in voter ID and voter purge legislation. It is, however, very difficult to ignore that in the Florida voter purge, it has been Republican officials endorsing the use of flawed purge lists that have overwhelmingly targeted African American and Democratic voters. *See* Fessenden, *supra* note 40.

60. *America Scrubs Millions from the Voter Rolls: Is It Fair?*, THE CENTER FOR PUBLIC INTEGRITY (Aug. 22, 2016, updated Apr. 12, 2017), www.publicintegrity.org.

61. *Id.*

62. *Id.*

63. Joe Helle, *Joe Helle: I Was Purged from the Voter Rolls*, LET AMERICA VOTE (Sept. 21, 2017), www.facebook.com.

64. *Questions & Answers: Interstate Crosscheck Program ("Crosscheck") & Electronic Registration Information Center ("ERIC")*, ADVANCEMENT PROJECT (Aug. 12, 2015), https://advancementproject.org.

65. *Id.* (quoting *ERIC: Technology and Security Overview* (Mar. 3, 2015), www.ericstates.org).

66. *See, e.g.*, Sharad Goel et al., One person, One Vote: Estimating the Prevalence of Double Voting in U.S. Presidential Elections (Jan. 17, 2019) (unpublished manuscript).

67. Palast, *supra* note 1.

68. *Id.*

69. *Id.*

70. 42 U.S.C. § 1973 (2006). Section 2 of the VRA prohibits voting practices and procedures that discriminate on the basis of race or color. Traditionally, Section 2 cases have involved challenges to at-large methods of election. However, Section 2's nationwide prohibition against racial discrimination in voting applies to any voting standard, practice, or procedure, including redistricting plans.

71. Joshua Douglas, *The Right to Vote under State Constitutions*, 67 VAND. L. REV. 89 (2014).

72. Under the Real ID Act, jurisdictions are required to provide cross-communication between states and exchange information regarding driver's license renewals and other pertinent information.

73. John Lewis & Archie E. Allen, *Black Voter Registration Efforts in the South*, 48 NOTRE DAME L. REV. 105, 128 (1972).

74. Australians who fail to vote receive a $20 fine for a first offense and $50 fine for a subsequent offense. *See Failure to Vote*, WESTERN AUSTRALIAN ELECTION COMMISSION (Dec. 2018), www.elections.wa.gov.au.

75. *See, e.g.*, Steve Barber et al., *The Purging of Empowerment: Voter Purge Laws and the Voting Rights Act*, 23 HARV. C.R.-C.L. L. REV. 483 (1988).

76. Jocelyn Benson, *Voter Fraud or Voter Defrauded? Highlighting an Inconsistent Consideration of Election Fraud*, 44 HARV. C.R.-C.L. L. REV. 1 (2009).

77. Lewis & Allen, *supra* note 73, at 105 (quoting testimony of John Lewis, Hearings before the Civil Rights Oversight Subcommittee (Number 4) of the House Committee on the Judiciary, ser. 8, at 244–45 (1971)).

78. Husted v. A. Philip Randolph Inst., 138 S. Ct. 1833, 1838 (2018) (citing Pew Center on the States, Election Initiatives Issue Brief (Feb. 2012)).

79. *Id.* at 1865.

80. Gail Ablow, *Voter Fraud, Explained*, MOYERS (June 24, 2016), https://billmoyers.com.

81. 52 U.S.C.A. § 20501 (West).

CHAPTER 6. FELON DISENFRANCHISEMENT

Epigraph: Trop v. Dulles, 356 U.S. 86, 92, 78 S. Ct. 590, 593, 2 L. Ed. 2d 630 (1958) (finding that the plaintiff had not lost his nationality because of a conviction in a military court).

1. US CONST. art. I, § 9: "The Migration or Importation of such Persons as any of the States now existing shall think proper to admit, shall not be prohibited by the Congress to the Year one thousand eight hundred and eight, but a Tax or duty may be imposed on such Importation, not exceeding ten dollars for each Person."

2. US CONST. art. I, § 2: "No Person held to Service or Labour in one State, under the Laws thereof, escaping into another, shall, in Consequence of any Law or Regulation therein, be discharged from such Service or Labour, but shall be delivered up on Claim of the Party to whom such Service or Labour may be due."

3. 1 THE RECORDS OF THE FEDERAL CONVENTION OF 1787, at 486–87 (rev. ed., Max Farrand ed., 1966).

4. US CONST. art. I, § 2.

5. DAVID WALDSTREICHER, SLAVERY'S CONSTITUTION: FROM REVOLUTION TO RATIFICATION (2007); HANES WALTON JR. & ROBERT C. SMITH, AMERICAN POLITICS AND THE AFRICAN AMERICAN QUEST FOR UNIVERSAL FREEDOM (2006).

6. Lincoln's response to Horace Greeley, *To Abraham Lincoln, President of the United States*, N.Y. TRIB., Aug. 20, 1862, *in* CIVIL RIGHTS AND AFRICAN AMERICANS 192–94 (Albert P. Blaustein & Robert L. Zangrando ed., 1991).

7. US CONST. amend XIV, § 2.

8. 1865 FLA. HOUSE J. 39–41.

9. 1866 FLA. HOUSE J. 77.

10. *See also* Andrew L. Shapiro, *Challenging Criminal Disenfranchisement under the Voting Rights Act: A New Strategy*, 103 YALE L.J. 537, 540 (1993) ("[B]etween 1890 and 1910, many Southern states tailored their criminal disenfranchisement laws, along with other preexisting voting qualifications, to increase the effect of these laws on black citizens.").

11. *Id.* at 541.

12. *Id.* at 541 n.30.

13. *Id. See Statement of Carter Glass*, REPORT OF THE PROCEEDINGS AND DEBATE OF THE CONSTITUTIONAL CONVENTION, STATE OF VIRGINIA 3076 (1906); *see also Summary of the Governor's Restoration of Rights Order Dated April 22, 2016*, OFFICE OF GOVERNOR TERRY MCAULIFFE (2016), https://commonwealth.virginia.gov.

14. *See* Matt Ford, *The Racist Roots of Virginia's Felon Disenfranchisement*, ATLANTIC, Apr. 27, 2016, www.theatlantic.com.

15. Pantea Javidan, *Legal Post-Racialism as an Instrument of Racial Compromise in Shelby County v. Holder*, 17 BERKELEY J. AFR.-AM. L. & POL'Y 127, 136 (2015) (citing Michael J. Klarman, Brown, *Racial Change, and the Civil Rights Movement*, 80 VA. L. REV. 7 (1994); IAN HANEY LÓPEZ, DOG WHISTLE POLITICS: HOW CODED RACIAL APPEALS HAVE REINVENTED RACISM & WRECKED THE MIDDLE CLASS (2014)).

16. Jean Chung, *Felony Disenfranchisement: A Primer*, SENTENCING PROJECT (July 17, 2018), www.sentencingproject.org.

17. Code Miss. R. 1-10.

18. *Id.*

19. Barack Obama, Remarks by the President at the NAACP Conference, Philadelphia, PA, July 14, 2015.

20. *Clemency Shift Upholds Rule of Law*, ST. PETERSBURG TIMES, Mar. 16, 2011.

21. List of felon disenfranchisement case law on ProCon: http://felonvoting.procon.org.

22. 418 U.S. 24, 56 (1974).

23. Johnson v. Bush, 405 F.3d 1214, 1228 (11th Cir. 2005).

24. Owens v. Barnes, 711 F.2d 25, 27 (3d Cir. 1983).

25. 471 U.S. 222 (1985).

26. Hunter v. Underwood, 471 U.S. 222, 223 (1985).

27. 623 F.3d (9th Cir. 2010).

28. Democracy Restoration Act of 2015, H.R. 1459, 114th Cong. (2015–16), www. congress.gov.

29. *See* Ford, *supra* note 14.

30. Vann R. Newkirk II, *How Letting Felons Vote Is Changing Virginia*, ATLANTIC, Jan. 8, 2018, www.theatlantic.com.

31. Interview with Sabrina Kahn, Sept. 2018.

32. Richie Canady Declaration, ¶¶ 7–11, Brief of New Virginia Majority and Advancement Project, Tram Nguyen, Jon Liss, and Judith A. Browne Dianis, as Amici Curiae in Support of Respondents in Howell v. McAuliffe, 788 S.E. 2d 706 (Va. 2016).

33. *Testimonials*, SECRETARY OF THE COMMONWEALTH: RESTORATION OF RIGHTS (rights restored Oct. 14, 2016), www.restore.virginia.gov.

34. FLA. CONST. art. VI, § 4.

35. Hand v. Scott, 285 F. Supp. 3d 1289, 1292 (N.D. Fla. 2018).

36. Steven Bosquet, *Florida's Felon Disenfranchisement System under Intense National Glare*, TAMPA BAY TIMES, Sept. 11, 2018, www.tampabay.com.

37. Andrew Pantazi, *Felony Convictions Won't Stop Jacksonville's Newest Voters*, FLA. TIMES-UNION, Jan. 8, 2019, www.jacksonville.com.

38. LA. CONST. art. I, § 10(A), which reads in full, "Every citizen of the state, upon reaching eighteen years of age, shall have the right to register and vote, except that this right may be suspended while a person is interdicted and judicially declared mentally incompetent or is under an order of imprisonment for conviction of a felony."

39. LA. REV. STAT. ANN. 18:2(8), 18:102(A)(1).

40. Voice of Ex-Offender v. State, 2017-1141 (La. App. 1 Cir. Apr. 13, 2018), 249 So. 3d 857, 863, *reh'g denied* (Apr. 27, 2018), *reh'g denied* (May 9, 2018), *writ denied*, 2018-0945 (La. Oct. 29, 2018), 255 So. 3d 575 ("In La. Const. art. 1, sec. 10(A), the meaning of "under an order of imprisonment" is certain. A convicted felon serving their term of probation or parole is clearly under an order of imprisonment. This is the only interpretation consistent with the purpose of the law. The fact that a convicted felon is not in prison is irrelevant. Convicted felons on parole and/or probation are still in a "custodial" setting under an order of imprisonment, as they are still serving a portion of a criminal sentence.").

41. Norris Henderson, Founder and Executive Director of VOTE. *Norris Henderson*, VOICE OF THE EXPERIENCED, www.vote-nola.org.

42. Complaint, Voice of the Ex-Offender et al. v. State of Louisiana, No. 2017-CA-1141 (La. Ct. App. May 9, 2018).
43. Elena Holodny, *Millions of American Adults Are Not Allowed to Vote*, BUSINESS INSIDER (Jan. 3, 2018), www.businessinsider.com.
44. Jeff Manza and Christopher Uggen, LOCKED OUT (2006, Oxford University Press).
45. *Voters and Voting Registration Parole, 2018* COLO. LEGIS. SERV. Ch. 261 (S.B. 18-150) (West).
46. *Id.*
47. *Id.* The legislation provides, "(3)(a) Notwithstanding section 1-2-103(4), a person who is otherwise qualified to register and is on parole may preregister and update his or her preregistered information in the manner prescribed by the secretary of state. (b) When the secretary of state receives notification under section 17-2-102(14)(d) that an individual who is preregistered under subsection (3)(a) of this section has been released from parole, the individual shall be automatically registered to vote. (c) The registration requirements of section 1-2-201 apply to a person preregistering to vote under this subsection." *Id.*
48. Adam Pampuro, *Colorado Bill Aims to Register 10,000 Parolees to Vote*, COURTHOUSE NEWS SERVICE, Apr. 26, 2018.
49. Sandra E. Garcia, *Texas Woman Sentenced to 5 Years in Prison for Voter Fraud Loses Bid for New Trial*, N.Y. TIMES, June 13, 2018, www.nytimes.com. Farah Stockman, *They Served Their Time, Now They Are Fighting for Other Ex-Felons to Vote*, N.Y. TIMES, May 11, 2018.
50. Farah Stockman, *They Served Their Time. Now They're Fighting for Other Ex-Felons to Vote.*, N.Y. Times, May 11, 2018, www.nytimes.com.

CHAPTER 7. CHANGING DEMOGRAPHICS

1. Losmin Jimenez serves as the project director for the Immigrant Justice Project at Advancement Project, national office.
2. Interview with Losmin Jimenez, June 2019 (certificate issued by the University of the State of New York, the State Education Department, is in Attorney Jimenez's possession).
3. Interview with Judith Browne-Dianis, Executive Director, Advancement Project (national office), Aug. 20, 2018.
4. Marisa Franco, *Marisa Franco of Mijente and Why This Immigration Debate Is Too Simplistic*, LATINO REBELS (July 15, 2018), www.latinorebels.com.
5. *Hispanic Americans: Census Facts*, INFOPLEASE, www.infoplease.com.
6. *See e.g.*, Sudeep Reddy, *Hispanics Fuel Growth in Decade*, WALL STREET J., Mar. 25, 2011, www.wsj.com.
7. *Hispanic Americans, supra* note 5.
8. William Frey, *The U.S. Will Become "Minority White" in 2045, Census Projects*, BROOKINGS INSTIT.: THE AVENUE (Mar 14, 2018), www.brookings.edu.

9. *Id.*

10. *See* Elise Foley, *Alabama Immigration Law Might Change after Governor's Review*, HUFFINGTON POST (Dec. 9, 2011), www.huffingtonpost.com.

11. ROBERT GRIFFIN, WILLIAM H. FREY, RUY TEIXEIRA, BROOKINGS INSTIT., STATES OF CHANGE—DEMOGRAPHIC CHANGE, REPRESENTATION GAPS, AND CHALLENGES TO DEMOCRACY, 1980–2060, at 7 (Feb. 2017), www.brookings.edu.

12. *Id.* at 8.

13. *Id.*

14. *Id.*

15. *Id.* at 11.

16. *Id.* at 12.

17. THE PEW CTR. ON THE STATES, INACCURATE, COSTLY, AND INEFFICIENT: EVIDENCE THAT AMERICA'S VOTER REGISTRATION SYSTEM NEEDS AN UPGRADE 2 (2014), www.pewtrusts.org.

18. Browne-Dianis interview.

19. Franco, *supra* note 4.

20. US CONST. art. II, § 3.

21. Ed Pilkington, *Obama Lifts Shadow of Deportation for Thousands of Young People*, GUARDIAN, June 15, 2012, www.theguardian.com.

22. Jeffrey S. Passell and Mark Hugo Lopez, *Up to 1.7 Million Unauthorized Immigrant Youth May Benefit from New Deportation Rules*, PEW RESEARCH CENTER HISPANIC TRENDS (Aug. 14, 2012), www.pewhispanic.org.

23. Kate Reilly, *Here's What President Trump Has Said about DACA in the Past*, TIME, Sept. 5, 2017, www.time.com.

24. United States Citizenship and Immigration Services, *Temporary Protected Status*, www.uscis.gov.

25. D'Vera Cohn, *Many Immigrants with Temporary Protected Status Face Uncertain Future*, PEW RESEARCH CENTER (Feb. 21, 2019).

26. Eli Watkins & Abby Phillip, *Trump Decries Immigrants from "Shithole" Countries" Coming the US*, CNN (Jan. 12, 2018), www.cnn.com. *See also* Philip Bump, *Most Americans Considered Trump's "Shithole" Comments Racist*, WASH. POST, Jan. 17, 2018, www.washingtonpost.com.

27. 42 C.F.R. § 435.407:
Types of acceptable documentary evidence of citizenship.
(a) Stand-alone evidence of citizenship. The following must be accepted as sufficient documentary evidence of citizenship:
(1) A U.S. passport, including a U.S. Passport Card issued by the Department of State, without regard to any expiration date as long as such passport or Card was issued without limitation.
(2) A Certificate of Naturalization.
(3) A Certificate of U.S. Citizenship.

(4) A valid State-issued driver's license if the State issuing the license requires proof of U.S. citizenship, or obtains and verifies a SSN from the applicant who is a citizen before issuing such license.

(5)

(i) Documentary evidence issued by a Federally recognized Indian Tribe identified in the FEDERAL REGISTER by the Bureau of Indian Affairs within the U.S. Department of the Interior.

28. Complaint, Fish v. Kobach, Case No. 2:16-cv-02105 (D. Kan. filed Feb. 18, 2016), at ¶ 10.

29. *Id.* at ¶ 11.

30. Paragraphs 14 and 15, Complaint, League of Women Voters of the United States, League of Women Voters of Alabama, League of Women Voters of Georgia, League of Women Voters of Kansas, Georgia State Conference of the NAACP, Georgia Coalition for the People's Agenda, Marvin Brown, Joann Brown and Project Vote, Plaintiffs, v. Brian D. Newby, in his capacity as the Acting Executive Director & Chief Operating Officer of The United States Election Assistance Commission; and The United States Election Assistance Commission, Defendants, 2016 WL 616592 (D.D.C.), Fish v. Kobach.

31. *See* Justin Levitt, *The Truth about Voter Fraud*, BRENNAN CENTER FOR JUSTICE, www.brennancenter.org (last visited Feb. 17, 2019); LORRAINE C. MINNITE, THE MYTH OF VOTER FRAUD (2010).

32. Press Release, US Dep't of Commerce, U.S. Department of Commerce Announces Reinstatement of Citizenship Question to the 2020 Decennial Census (Mar. 26, 2018).

33. 136 S. Ct. 1120 (2016).

34. *Id.* at 1132.

35. State of New York et al. v. Department of Commerce, et al., ___ S.D.N.Y. ___ (2018).

36. Hansi Lo Wang, *Documents Shed Light on Decision to Add Census Citizenship Question*, MORNING EDITION (June 10 2018), www.npr.org.

37. Michael Wines, *Why Was a Citizenships Question Put on the Census? "Bad Faith," a Judge Suggests*, N.Y. TIMES, July 10, 2018, www.nytimes.com.

38. Dara Lind, *The Citizenship Question on the 2020 Census, Explained*, VOX (Mar. 28, 2018), www.vox.com ("The not-so-subtle implication, critics say, is that that it's part of a broader project by Attorney General Jeff Sessions and company to take America back to the pre-civil rights era.").

39. Shirin Jaafarri, *The US Is Using an Expanded Fingerprint Database to Review the Citizenship of Thousands of Americans*, PRI'S THE WORLD (July 10, 2018), www. pri.org.

40. *Id.*

41. *Register to Vote*, CITY OF TAKOMA PARK, MARYLAND, https://takom-aparkmd.gov. *See also* Julie Lasky, *Takoma Park, MD: A Diverse Washington D.C. Suburb*, N.Y. TIMES, Nov. 25, 2016, www.nytimes.com.

42. *Voting by Nonresidents*, NATIONAL CONFERENCE OF STATE LEGISLATURES (June 20, 2018), www.ncsl.org.
43. *Id.*

CHAPTER 8. THIS TOO SHALL PASS

Epigraph: MALCOLM X SPEAKS: SELECTED SPEECHES AND STATEMENTS 198 (George Breitman ed., 1990).

1. Derrick Johnson, speech at NAACP 109th national convention, San Antonio, TX (July 30, 2018).
2. Pamela Karlan, *Lessons Learned: Voting Rights and the Bush Administration*, 4 DUKE J. CONST. L. & PUB. POL'Y 17 (2009).
3. Crayton interview.
4. Johnson, *supra* note 1.
5. Gilda R. Daniels, *Voting Realism*, 104 KY. L.J. 583 (2017).
6. *Id.*
7. Frederick Douglass, *West India Emancipation*, August 3, 1857.
8. Justice Ruth Bader Ginsburg, excerpt from Transcript of Oral Argument at 52, Crawford v. Marion Co., Nos. 07-21, 07-25 (Jan. 9, 2008).
9. US CONST. amend. XV, § 1 (prohibiting race discrimination in voting).
10. US CONST. amend. XIX (prohibiting discrimination based on sex).
11. US CONST. amend. XXVI (prohibiting the denial of the right to vote to citizens over eighteen).
12. US CONST. amend XXIV (prohibiting poll taxes).
13. Martin Newhouse, *Voting Rights and Voting Wrongs: An Interview with Lani Guinier*, MASS HUMANITIES (Spring 2007), http://masshumanities.org.
14. *See, generally,* Advancement Project, *In Pursuit of an Affirmative Right to Vote: Strategic Report* (July 2008), http://nationalrighttovote.org.
15. Bush v. Gore, 531 U.S. 98, 104 (2000) (per curiam).
16. Heather K. Gerken, *The Right to Vote: Is the Amendment Game Worth the Candle?*, 23 WM. & MARY BILL RTS. J. 11 (2014); see also Keith Ellison et al., *Room for Debate: Should Voting Be a Constitutional Right?*, N.Y. TIMES (Nov. 3, 2014), www.nytimes.com; Scott Lemieux, *The Big Problem with the Constitutional Right to Vote Amendment*, THE WEEK (Nov. 14, 2014), www.theweek.com.
17. Daniels, *supra* note 5.
18. *See, e.g.,* Jonathan Soros & Mark Schmitt, *The Missing Right: The Constitutional Right to Vote*, 28 DEMOCRACY (Spring 2013), http://democracyjournal.org.
19. Interview with Nicole Austin-Hillery, Sept. 1, 2015.
20. *Id.*
21. *Id.*
22. Gilda R. Daniels, *Husted v. A. Philip Randolph Institute: To Vote, or Not to Vote: That Is the Question*, AMERICAN CONSTITUTION SOCIETY SUPREME COURT REVIEW 2017–2018.

23. Johnson, *supra* note 1.
24. *Id.*
25. *Democracy Day*, BERNIE SANDERS WEBSITE, www.sanders.senate.gov.
26. Osita Nwanevu, *Maybe Making Election Day a National Holiday Wouldn't Really Work*, SLATE (Nov. 3, 2016), www.slate.com.
27. *See id.* In 2014, registered voters from households making more than $150,000 a year were the most likely to say they were too busy to head to the polls—more than 35 percent of them claimed so, while none of the income brackets less than $40,000 had more than 25 percent of respondents report they were too busy. Unsurprisingly, lower-income nonvoters are more likely than wealthier nonvoters to cite illness and disability or trouble getting to the polls as problems. Wealthier nonvoters, less impeded by these kinds of challenges, say they have mostly their schedules to blame. Given this, an Election Day holiday would remove a significant barrier to participation for relatively well-to-do potential voters while doing little to make voting easier for a significant number of less privileged ones. *See also* Suzanne Lucas, *No, Election Day Should Not Be Made a Federal Holiday*, INC. (Oct. 24, 2016). www.inc.com; Janet Nguyen, *Why Election Day Isn't a Federal Holiday*, MARKETPLACE (Nov. 2, 2016), www.marketplace.org.
28. Austin-Hillery interview.
29. Richard Fry, *Younger Generations Make Up a Majority of the Electorate, but May Not Be a Majority of Voters This November*, PEW RESEARCH CENTER (June 14, 2018), www.pewresearch.org.
30. Kelly Born, *Increasing Voter Turnout: What, If Anything, Can Be Done?*, STANFORD SOCIAL INNOVATION REV., Apr. 25, 2016, https://ssir.org.
31. JOHN HOPE FRANKLIN & ALFRED A. MOSS JR., FROM SLAVERY TO FREEDOM: A HISTORY OF AFRICAN AMERICANS 285 (8th ed. 2000).
32. Dr. Martin Luther King Jr., Remaining Awake through a Great Revolution: A Knock at Midnight, speech delivered at the National Cathedral, Washington, DC (Mar. 31, 1968), CONG. REC., Apr. 9, 1968, https://kinginstitute.stanford.edu.

CONCLUSION

1. Sam Cooke, "A Change Is Gonna Come" (RCA Records, 1964).

INDEX

Abbott, Greg, 84

absentee voting, 64, 79, 80, 226n1

Acharya, Avidit, 10

activism: Black Lives Matter, 26, 197; felon voting rights, 157–65; hate awakening and hope fueling, 209–11; of Michaux, 37, 38–39, 53, 62, 221–22; in voter ID laws fight, 90–93. *See also* civil rights movement

Adams, J. Christian, 236n69

Advancement Project, 159–60, 165, 199

African Americans: absentee voting for, 64, 79, 226n1; elected officials, history of and present-day, 15, 28–30, 40, 217n22, 219n58, 221–22, 222nn8–9; incarceration statistics for, 167; in-person voting views of, 64, 226n1; Johnson, L., on rights for, 26–27; Louisiana post-Katrina demographics for, 240n45; underrepresentation of, 176; voting rights history for, 14–18, 20–21, 23–27, 34, 40, 41–42, 62–63, 143, 150–51; after VRA, experience for, 27–30, 37, 63–64, 125, 143, 219n57; Wilmington Riot deaths of, 38; women right to vote and, 21

African American voter registration: in Alabama historically, 21–22, 28, *124*, 219n57; early 1960s, 23–25; in late 1800s, 15, 19, 218n32; rates from 1920s to 1950s, 20–22; in southern states historically, 15, 21–22, 28, 37, 123–24, *124*, 218n32, 219n57; after VRA, 27–28, 37, 219n57; white voter rates compared with, 123–24, *124*, 177, 218n32

African American voter suppression/disenfranchisement: Alabama 1950s, 22, 23–25, 218n41; ballot rejection and, 31; "Black Codes" role in, 16, 40–41; Constitutional Conventions agenda of, 68, 152, 217n24; Constitution role in, 5, 36, 148–50, 153, 170,

171, 242nn1–2; election reform role in, 2–5, 11, 31–32; felon disenfranchisement impact on, 5–6, 133–34, 136, 153–54, 159, 161, 165–67, 170, 171, 241n58, 243n10; Georgia tactics of, 50; historical methods and context for, 4, 6, 9, 10–25, 38–39, 40–42, 68–69, 98, 124, 148–52, 172, 209, 217n24; Jim Crow laws in, 18–20, 40–41, 68–69, 124; literacy tests in, 17, 19, 22, 63; Louisiana history of, 13–15, 18, 19, 23; MLK on, 9, 10–11, 13, 102, 215n2; North Carolina history of, 38–39, 98; poll taxes role in, 17, 19, 68–69; redistricting in, 23–25, 218n41; secret ballots in, 17; *Shelby County, Alabama v. Holder* impact on, 50; violent methods of, 16–18, 20–21, 23, 26–27, 38, 41, 96–100, 123–25; voter deception targeting, 5, 103–4; voter ID laws in, 11–14, 34, 55, 66, 71–79, 88; voter intimidation in, 21–22, 96–100; voter roll purges in, 20, 115, 123–25, 133–37, 241nn58–59; white supremacists tactics of, 98–99, 146, 151–52

Alabama: African American voter registration historically in, 21–22, 28, *124*, 219n57; African American voter suppression in 1950s, 22, 23–25, 218n41; Bloody Sunday march and impacts in, 4, 26–27, 32, 34, 41–42, 209; civil rights movement in, 21–22, 24; districting/redistricting in, discriminatory, 23–25, 218n41; felon disenfranchisement in, 156; incarceration rates for people of color in, 167; literacy tests in 1950s, 22; Montgomery Bus Boycott in, 22; noncriminal disenfranchisement historically in, 152; voter registration rates from 1992 to 2016, 127, *127*; voter roll purges historically in, *124*. See also *Shelby County, Alabama v. Holder*

ABOUT THE AUTHOR

Gilda R. Daniels is Associate Professor at the University of Baltimore School of Law. Previously, Professor Daniels served as a Deputy Chief in the United States Department of Justice, Civil Rights Division, Voting Section, under both the George W. Bush and Bill Clinton administrations. She serves as Director of Litigation for the Advancement Project, a national civil rights organization. She is a national speaker and consultant on civil rights and voting issues. She is a proud graduate of Grambling State University and New York University School of Law. She lives in Maryland with her loving husband and two wonderful children.